Unashamed

OF THE

Gospel

VOLUME 1

Unashamed
OF THE
Gospel

An Expository Devotional on the
Book of Romans

CHAPTERS 1-8

JOSHUA WEST

AMBASSADOR INTERNATIONAL
GREENVILLE, SOUTH CAROLINA & BELFAST, NORTHERN IRELAND
www.ambassador-international.com

UNASHAMED OF THE GOSPEL

AN EXPOSITORY DEVOTIONAL ON THE BOOK OF ROMANS, VOLUME 1

©2025 by Joshua West
All rights reserved

ISBN: 978-1-64960-734-8, hardcover
ISBN: 978-1-64960-735-5, paperback
eISBN: 978-1-64960-771-3

Cover Design by Karen Slayne
Interior Typesetting by Dentelle Design
Edited by Katie Cruice Smith
Joshua's sermons that inspired this book were transcribed by Julie Klose

Unless otherwise indicated, all Scriptural quotations are taken from the HOLY BIBLE, ENGLISH STANDARD VERSION, ESV. Copyright © 2008 by Crossway, a publishing ministry of Good News Publishers. All rights reserved.

Scripture marked NASB taken from the (NASB®) New American Standard Bible®, Copyright © 1960, 1971, 1977, 1995, 2020 by The Lockman Foundation. Used by permission. All rights reserved. lockman.org.

Ambassador International titles may be purchased in bulk for education, business, fundraising, or sales promotional use. For information, please email sales@emeraldhouse.com.

AMBASSADOR INTERNATIONAL
Emerald House
411 University Ridge, Suite B14
Greenville, SC 29601
United States
www.ambassador-international.com

AMBASSADOR BOOKS
The Mount
2 Woodstock Link
Belfast, BT6 8DD
Northern Ireland, United Kingdom
www.ambassadormedia.co.uk

The colophon is a trademark of Ambassador, a Christian publishing company.

DEDICATION

TO SAM AND ANGELA: YOU have never treated me merely as the man who married your daughter. You have always received me as a son. You both stood with me when I was weak and I failed and always celebrated and cheered the loudest as I succeed. I love and admire you both more than words could ever express. Thank you for your friendship and for modeling what it looks like to serve Jesus and others.

To my son Jameson: I have many hopes for you in this life! That you are happy and healthy, that you gain character in your failures and stay humble in your successes, that God would grant you a wife as good as your mother, and that you would work hard to be a man worthy of her. I hope your home is filled with peace, joy, love, Scripture, music, and children. But more than anything, I pray that you are a man who truly knows God and walks with Him all the days of your life, that you might "[live] in the house of the Lord forever" (Psalm 23:6).

To my wife Kiara: You have made our home a refuge from the storm; a shield from the arrows; a sanctuary where we live, love, worship God, and teach our children to do the same. You are the love of my life, my dearest and most valued treasure, and my most trusted friend and ally. The years I walked in life before I knew you are a faint whisper drowned out by the beautiful sound of your voice. The depths of your eyes and the sound of your voice will always be my home; and no matter where I am in the world, I am always on my way back to you.

TABLE OF CONTENTS

PREFACE

WE ARE ABOUT TO EMBARK on a lofty journey through Paul's epistle to the Romans. Perhaps no book in the entire New Testament is more theologically rich. Every line is thought out and detailed, and I look forward to walking with you along this "Roman Road" as we seek to know God from His Word and be conformed to the image of Christ.

Romans has a very personal meaning in my life. It was this book of the Bible that I was reading in a jail cell in Dallas, Texas, when my life was changed forever. For the first time, the Scripture came alive; and I realized these were not mere words but the very words of God. Paul's letter exposed the depth of sin in me; and honestly, it scared me. In the first chapters of Romans, I began to fear the Lord and realized the words on these pages were more than just an ancient text.

Through the witness of a fellow inmate and through the study of Romans, I became convinced of the truth of the gospel and the power of Scripture. This letter has so much depth that it is beneficial for saints who have walked with God for many years but also simple enough to draw a lost sinner to Christ. My hope, as lofty as it might be, is that this book would do the same—that the Word of God will come alive for you and grip you in a way that changes your life, as it did mine. If the Word of God doesn't change your life, then you are not reading it as it was meant to be read. My prayer is that the Spirit of God will help you decipher Scripture and that your hearts will soften to the knowledge of God's truth.

This, like all books written by human hands, is imperfect. But in this book, I hope to do what all excellent Christian books should do: draw the reader closer to God and help you grow in knowledge and understanding of the Scripture so that you might be conformed to the image of Christ. I pray that the Spirit of God uses this writing in that way. As you read this expository devotional, I pray that ultimately, Christ will be exalted and worshiped.

INTRODUCTION TO ROMANS
JUSTIFICATION BY GRACE THROUGH FAITH

MARTIN LUTHER SAID THAT THE epistle to the Romans can be summed up in one powerful line of Scripture: "'The righteous shall live by faith'" (Rom. 1:17). This is the encompassing structure of the entire book. Romans teaches about righteousness and faith and how these two words are intertwined in Christian life. It answers the question: what does it mean to be righteous, and how do we walk by faith?

Faith is not about wanting something or believing in something that we really want to happen. Biblical faith is knowing that we are justified before God based on what Christ did for us on the cross and that God keeps the promises He has made in His Word. Paul writes extensively about this as he draws from the Old Testament and explains that Jesus is not only the long-awaited Jewish Messiah but also the Savior of the entire world. When Paul says, "'The righteous shall live by faith,'" he quotes the prophet Habakkuk in the Old Testament. It says, "Behold, his soul is puffed up; it is not upright within him, but the righteous shall live by his faith" (Hab. 2:4). The prophet was contrasting the priests in Israel who were puffed up at that time. They acted as if they were righteous outwardly but were not right with God in their hearts. To be righteous means to have a right standing with God. In the first several chapters of Romans, Paul explains in great detail why none of us are righteous and no one can be right with God apart from Christ. The central doctrine of Romans is justification by grace, through faith. Everything else in Romans revolves around this truth.

Paul's letter also explains what it means to be justified and sanctified. These words have two distinct meanings. Justification occurs immediately upon one becoming a regenerate believer. In regeneration we are given the gift of faith and we confess with our mouth what we have come to believe in our heart. However, not every person who confesses saving faith with their mouth is a Christian but only those who genuinely believe in their heart, confess with their mouth, and bear witness with their lives to the fact that they are justified before God based on what Christ did—His life, death, and resurrection. If you are truly a Christian, at that moment, you are justified.

Sanctification is the lifelong process of being conformed to the image of Christ. Sometimes, there is a question when people are struggling in sin who claim to be Christians: is this a long U-turn on the road of sanctification, or is this evidence that maybe you are not justified before God? A righteous person—a regenerated life—will be transformed by the power of the Spirit working and living in them, but they will not be perfect. This might seem confusing to new believers or people outside the faith. But if the Spirit Christ has regenerated you, He is sanctifying you; and ultimately, He will perfect you in death. This is why we must strive to apply the Bible to our lives rightly.

When I first became a Christian, people looked at me because of where I came from and probably questioned whether or not I was a Christian. I was rough around the edges and wrong about many things. But my heart had been transformed. I believed in God, and He was changing my life. Slowly, over weeks, months, and years, my life transformation became apparent to others. But we must acknowledge that we can deceive ourselves as we travel on the long road of sanctification. This was me. I had to answer the question: was I rightly applying God's Word to my life?

Paul wants the book of Romans to do that for the reader. As a preacher, I teach Scripture to help others apply it to their lives. But first and foremost, I must apply God's Word to my life. Preaching comes second. Paul references this in 1 Corinthians:

> Do you not know that in a race all the runners run, but only one receives the prize? So run that you may obtain it. Every athlete exercises self-control in all things. They do it to receive a perishable wreath, but we an imperishable. So I do not run aimlessly; I do not box as one beating the air. But I discipline my body and keep it under control, lest after preaching to others I myself should be disqualified (1 Cor. 9:24-27).

In other words, we must run our own race, ensuring that our lives align with God because that is what is most important. We must use God's Word to shine the light of truth in the dark places of our lives.

THE PURPOSE AND STRUCTURE OF PAUL'S LETTER

There are many reasons why Paul wrote to the Romans. Rome was the home of the Roman Empire, and Paul was called to be an apostle to the Gentiles. The church in Rome probably began with a mix of Jewish and Gentile proselytes or converts—Gentile people who had been converted to Judaism and believed in the one true God. On the day of Pentecost, when the Holy Spirit came and thousands of people were converted, it was likely that this mix of Jews and Gentiles were present. A large group was in Jerusalem at that time for the feast and celebration of the Passover, and the day of Pentecost followed fifty days later.

Scripture references this time when Peter stood on the steps of the temple proclaiming the gospel. It says, "And there were added that day about three thousand souls" (Acts 2:41). Most church historians believe this is where the people who started the church in Rome came from. Paul wanted to preach the gospel to the Romans to help strengthen the body of believers already there.

Paul is also writing to this church to help raise financial support for needy Christians who are under persecution in some areas of Israel. It was typical for Paul to add missionary fundraising sections in his letters. There were many wealthy people and affluent churches in Rome. Paul appeals to them to help those in need in the poorer churches.

By this time, extreme Rome Persecution had broken out among the Christians and Jews in Israel, and many scattered to various places. Most of the apostles who were still living in Israel, Jerusalem, and the regions of Judea were dispersed and in hiding. God's sovereignty allowed this persecution because He had told the disciples to take the gospel to the ends of the earth, but they did not go. So, a little fire under the pot set everybody moving out. Ultimately, we know from church history that these apostles would eventually die for the sake of the gospel in different places all over the world. Some died in Ethiopia and Asia Minor, which is modern-day Turkey. Some of the apostles died in Israel, like James the Just, who was put to the sword.

The structure of Paul's letter is very similar to the history of the Jews and follows the pattern of Jewish or Old Testament writing. It is a pattern of slavery, exile, and rescue. God blesses his people; they disobey Him. They fall into slavery and exile, and God rescues them. This pattern repeats itself over and over again. Looking back at Jewish history, it seems like they just could not get it right. But the truth of Scripture reveals this pattern repeats itself throughout humanity until the Perfect arrives. A permanent rescue was needed not just for the Jews but for everyone. The difference is the Jews understood this to some extent. It was evident to them because they knew God, but everyone else was simply lost and lawless.

Paul's message highlights God's faithfulness and His covenant with Israel. But it also shows that all humanity is in slavery and exile because of sin. Paul uses this traditional Jewish writing style to explain that it is not just the Jews. It is not just a worldly prison or exile. No, we all are slaves to sin. The Old Covenant and law could not defeat death or bring eternal life, nor was it intended to. Through Christ, who in His earthly lineage descended from David and in His spiritual nature was the only true and eternal Son of God, we gain life and forgiveness of our sins. Because of Christ's life, death, and resurrection, both Jews and Gentiles can be free from the slavery of sin and death. They can have eternal life as part of a new race of people united in Christ through the gospel.

The Jews are God's chosen people, who were set apart for His glory. It was out of the Jewish people that God gave the oracles, the patriarchs, and the scriptures. It is also from the Jews God sent the Savior into the world. Everyone who is not a Jew is considered a Gentile. There are other places in Scripture where Gentile is translated as Greek, but it always refers to the world outside or those who were not Jewish. Paul makes this distinction so that no one misunderstands. He is writing to a Gentile audience; but eventually, he clarifies that this group comprises many nationalities. Paul writes that he is going to the barbarian, to the Gentile, and he starts naming different groups of people so that everyone understands that this gospel is not merely for the Jew but for the world.

ROMANS ROAD

There is a phrase in Christianity known as "the Romans Road to Salvation." It is a sound approach to explaining the need, purpose, and power of the gospel. It explains the complete and true gospel of Jesus Christ. Romans can be divided into two parts: chapters one through eleven deal with what Christ has done in the gospel, and chapters twelve through sixteen tell us what we must do as Christians because of the gospel.

In Romans 3:23, Paul writes, "For all have sinned and fall short of the glory of God." When we understand this verse, we realize our desperate need for the precious gift of the gospel. This is difficult to understand in American culture because we are raised to focus on self-help, self-love and self-esteem.

We are told that the answer is inside of us. Perhaps life has messed you up a little. You might have some trauma, but you are going to be okay. After all, deep down you are a good person. However, Paul writes, you are not okay because "*all* have sinned and fall short of the glory of God."

Paul was writing to a culture of people where this verse would have been difficult for some to accept. Many were Jews who thought it was possible to live righteously enough to be right with God. When Paul writes the word *all*, he is saying this is not just for the Gentiles but also for the Jews as well. He confirms this by referring back to the Old Testament. "As it is written: 'None is righteous, no, not one'" (Rom. 3:10).

In our modern-day world, this can be applied to the seeker-sensitive and attractional church models. These church growth philosophies and systems typically start with the presupposition that people are mostly good and that they are seeking God but have been unable to find Him because the church is too harsh or judgmental, and the gospel of Jesus Christ and his inerrant Scriptures are not enough. Most of them will not come out and plainly say this, but their methods and actions prove that this is what they believe. But Paul demolishes this flawed presupposition as he exposes the error their approach reminding us that the Scripture teaches that no one is looking for God—no, not one!

Some might say, "But I have been looking for God my whole life." However, Jesus says that is a lie because those who ask will receive. "Ask, and it will be given to you; seek, and you will find; knock, and it will be opened to you'" (Matt. 7:7). If we seek God, we will find Him. If we are honest, we are not seeking God; we only seek what He can provide, and we want those things without surrendering to His Lordship. Yes, we want peace, purpose, significance, and happiness. However, we do not want them at the expense of surrendering the throne of our hearts and control of our lives.

> "None is righteous, no, not one; no one understands; no one
> seeks for God. All have turned aside; together they have become

worthless; no one does good, not even one." "Their throat is an open grave; they use their tongues to deceive." "The venom of asps is under their lips." "Their mouth is full of curses and bitterness." "Their feet are swift to shed blood; in their paths are ruin and misery, and the way of peace they have not known." "There is no fear of God before their eyes" (Rom. 3:10-18).

That last line explains why we do not seek God. Because we have venomous mouths, we seek wicked schemes and have murder in our hearts. Perhaps you think I have never killed anyone, but have you looked at someone with anger? Jesus said you are a murderer at heart (Matt. 5:21-22). Have you glanced at someone of the opposite sex too long who is not your spouse? The Bible says you are an adulterer (Matt. 5:28). No fornicators, no homosexuals, no one who has sex outside of marriage—none of us who have vile, wicked minds will inherit the kingdom of Heaven (1 Cor. 6:9-10). This is grim and dark, and it is supposed to be. All of Paul's writing in Romans and all the convicting words of the New Testament are meant to point us toward one exclusive path. There is only one way life and salvation, and it is found in Christ alone.

One reason humanity continues in its sin and depravity is because there is no fear of God. Proverbs 9:10 says, "The fear of the Lord is the beginning of wisdom, and the knowledge of the Holy One is insight." If you do not fear God, it is because you do not know God. If you have never looked at your life and realized you cannot measure up to God and deserve damnation, then you are not a Christian. To surrender your life to God, you must see God for Who He truly is. God is holy. God is perfect. God is entirely self-sufficient. We have to see God in a way that makes us realize that our best work or intentions regarding salvation are like a pile of garbage. "We have all become like one who is unclean, and all our righteous deeds are like a polluted garment" (Isa. 64:6).

Romans 6:23 says, "For the wages of sin is death, but the free gift of God is eternal life in Christ Jesus our Lord." The wages of sin bring death; but when you become a regenerated follower of Christ, you become connected to the vine, as described in John 15:5. This is a description of how, as Christians, being connected to Christ brings eternal life. How is this accomplished in our lives? Through the promised plan of salvation that God set in motion from eternity past.

- "But God shows his love for us in that while we were still sinners, Christ died for us" (Rom. 5:8).
- "Because, if you confess with your mouth that Jesus is Lord and believe in your heart that God raised him from the dead, you will be saved" (Rom. 10:9).
- For "everyone who calls on the name of the Lord will be saved" (Rom. 10:13).

Yet there is work to be done to discuss what it truly means to be a follower of Christ. Millions of people who have confessed the name of Jesus under compulsion or in a momentary burst of emotion have not truly been reborn in Christ. Many preachers emphasize the confession of the mouth as the means of salvation. "If I can just get them to say the magic words: please repeat after me, 'Jesus, I'm a sinner, forgive me of my sins and come into my heart.' Now you are a Christian." No! The most important part is whether you believe by faith in your heart, and the evidence will be your life after that confession of faith.

God is sovereign, and He will judge everyone. Those who are not in Him will be thrown into an unquenchable fire for the sake of His justice and denying the blood sacrifice of His Son. A person who comprehends this at the heart level will live differently. But understand this cannot happen apart from God. You cannot do this in your own power. The evidence that you are a Christian regenerated with a new nature will be in good works or deeds because it shows that you have been changed, but this is because there is a new nature inside of you. You will know that better than anyone else based on the thoughts and desires you have in your life. This typically manifests in being awakened to the reality that you are more of a sinner than you originally thought. When sinful thoughts and lust take over your mind, you feel the weight of this because you are now truly aware of your sin.

Previously, you might have understood the consequences of sin—and not just the personal consequences of your own sin but also how others suffer because of your sin. But then, we begin to see the result of salvation; this is an awakening to just how bad off we actually are. As Romans 5:1 says, "Therefore, since we have been justified by faith, we have peace with God through our Lord Jesus Christ" (Rom. 5:1). And Romans 8:1 tells us, "There is therefore now no condemnation for those who are in Christ Jesus."

Romans 8:38-39 reveals the ultimate surety of our salvation: "For I am sure that neither death nor life, nor angels nor rulers, nor things present nor things to come, nor powers, nor height nor depth, nor anything else in all creation, will be able to separate us from the love of God in Christ Jesus our Lord."

GOD'S SOVEREIGNTY

Hebrews connects Jesus to the Old Testament more than any other book in the New Testament. But the book of Romans reconciles the Old Testament *with* the New Testament. It reconciles the things left undone, left incomplete in the Old Testament to the person and work of Christ. Every answer we need for this is found in Romans. That is what is so beautiful about this letter. There is not one theological premise left undone from the Old Testament that is not rectified and reconciled in the book of Romans. How? Through Jesus. It demonstrates in great detail how humanity is reconciled to God through the gospel of Jesus Christ. God has always kept his covenant promises, and the gospel is the ultimate example of this truth.

God kept his covenant with Moses. God kept his covenant with Israel. He was faithful even when they were faithless. This is what makes the gospel so beautiful in its truth. The Old Covenant was never meant to save anyone, nor could it. Its purpose was to showcase the perfection of God, the imperfection of man, and to prepare the way for Christ to come and reconcile all things to Himself. Another difference is that the New Covenant of Christ promises that no one who truly is saved through the atoning work of Christ will ever be separated from His love, and nothing will be able to snatch us from His hand (John 10:28). This is our surety as Christians—God is sovereign in salvation.

Much of the book of Romans is about God's sovereignty in salvation and God's sovereignty in all things. It is about God from eternity past putting the plan of salvation into action to save a people unto Himself to "'worship him in spirit and in truth'" forever (John 4:24). However, this is often problematic for many people because of wickedness and evil in the world. The question arises: how could God allow evil? Why does God allow this or that to happen? But the very reason we question God and think we know better is because we are wicked. As humans we do not like any inconvenience, suffering, or pain. And we will go to great lengths to create a god who will promise us a life without these things, or we will invent philosophies they say we can discard Him altogether.

Yet the Bible says, "Count it all joy, my brothers, when you meet trials of various kinds" (James 1:2). Having faith in God is about trusting God with everything. It is human nature to want a simple and easy answer to our problems. But being a Christian is about coming to a place where you do not need an explanation because we love and trust the Lord. Our obedience doesn't save us, but our obedience is evidence that we truly do believe in Jesus. Jesus said, "'If you love me, you will keep my commandments'" (John 14:15). This is not about perfection but genuineness. Are you a real Christian? Is the Spirit of God living in you and transforming you? You are not a Christian because you repeated a prayer one time. Paul says the way you will know you are saved is that your life will bear fruit, and you will desire to live in obedience to Christ.

The book of Acts shares Paul's conversion testimony. Paul was persecuting the church because he thought he knew Who God was. He truly believed that persecuting Christians was the right thing to do. He was sincere; but unfortunately, he was sincerely wrong. He was building his life on sinking sand as he lived a false religious life. What happened? One day, Paul met Jesus on the road to Damascus. Suddenly, this cataclysmic shift took place in his life. He went from being the noble and zealous Pharisee respected by his peers and society to abandoning that life altogether because he came to know the truth. He became a devout follower of Christ, a missionary, and began serving the very people he once persecuted. Ultimately, we know from church history that he died a martyr's death for his obedience to the gospel.

If we look at the book of Romans as merely something to be studied and analyzed, we are missing the main point. We should labor in studying this book and analyzing its truths; but remember that the preparation is only so that we can apply, internalize, live-out, and proclaim its message. But it is important to study and dissect this book. We have to rightly divide God's word of truth to apply it rightly (2 Tim. 2:15). What is that message? Romans 1:16-17 proclaims it: "For I am not ashamed of the gospel, for it is the power of God for salvation to everyone who believes, to the Jew first and also to the Greek. For in it the righteousness of God is revealed from faith for faith, as it is written, 'The righteous shall live by faith.'"

We live *not* by sight anymore but by faith. You are now being directed by something external (the Bible) and something internal (the Holy Spirit) that God has placed inside you. Faith comes by hearing the Word of the Lord, and faith itself is a gift of God—just like salvation and just like sanctification. Salvation is of the Lord, and we are called to believe and live by faith as we proclaim the good news of God's gospel.

1

SET APART FOR THE GOSPEL OF GOD

ROMANS 1:1-7

Paul, a servant of Christ Jesus, called to be an apostle, set apart for the gospel of God, which he promised beforehand through his prophets in the holy Scriptures, concerning his Son, who was descended from David according to the flesh and was declared to be the Son of God in power according to the Spirit of holiness by his resurrection from the dead, Jesus Christ our Lord, through whom we have received grace and apostleship to bring about the obedience of faith for the sake of his name among all the nations, including you who are called to belong to Jesus Christ, To all those in Rome who are loved by God and called to be saints: Grace to you and peace from God our Father and the Lord Jesus Christ.

WHEN THE APOSTLE PAUL WROTE his letter to the church in Rome, he had not yet had the opportunity to visit there. He would eventually journey there, and his letter reveals how he longed to be with them since they were living for Christ in the heart of the Roman Empire. However, God sovereignly allowed Paul's delayed visit to Rome for our benefit.

Since Paul did not preach the gospel in person to those in Rome as he did in Corinth, Ephesus, and other regions he traveled to, he gives a detailed explanation of the gospel in this letter. The letter is filled with detailed and legal language as he explains the gospel in the greatest detail we find anywhere in the entire New Testament. Paul explains Jewish history and takes great pains to show how the Gentiles are also grafted in as God's people. Paul emphasizes and reiterates the gospel line by line much more than his other letters. So, the book of Romans gives the most straightforward description and explanation of the gospel, which benefits us greatly.

BELONGING TO GOD

"Paul, a servant of Christ Jesus, called to be an apostle set apart for the gospel of God" (v.1).

The New American Standard Bible (NASB) uses the word *bondservant*, meaning a lifelong servant who will never be free from servitude. A bondservant would sometimes complete their duty as a servant, paying off their debt. However, because their master was good to them and the living conditions were good, they realized staying in service to the master would afford them a much better life than they could provide for themselves. They bond themselves to the servitude of this man forever. This might be difficult to understand in our culture, where independence is the ultimate crux of everything. We cannot imagine being a slave or servant to anyone. But Paul makes it clear that we are either slaves to sin or we are slaves to righteousness. There is no middle ground. So, the NASB says, "a bondservant of Christ," which can also translate as the word *slave*.

Why does Paul open his letter by saying "a servant" or "bondservant" of Christ Jesus? He is not as interested in introducing the reader to who he is as much as he is in letting them know *Whose* he is. Who does he belong to? He is a servant. He is a slave of Christ—called not by his own compulsion but by the sovereignty and providence of God. God saved him and called him to be a slave to Christ, and Christ gave him apostleship. Paul was called and said through the sovereignty of God, by the grace of God, and for the glory of God. But we see this bear fruit in Paul's obedience. This is why it is so important that we do not quickly skip past the term "slave" or "bondservant." Paul was saved by grace but he responded with obedience. A slave is bought at a price and belongs to the purchaser. Paul wants to ensure that the reader understands right from the beginning that he belongs to Christ.

Paul, like all humanity, rightfully belongs to God. God created humanity by the power of His words—in the very image of God—and solely for His glory. But we have become estranged because of sin. Paul doubly belongs to God because not only was he made in the image of God; but now he also has been purchased through the blood of Christ, which is true of all "who [call] on the name of the Lord" (Rom. 10:13). Sin had separated him from God, although he rightfully belonged to Him. Paul acknowledged that the life of sin we lead is against the God to Whom we belong.

We are not our own. We did not create ourselves. We did not make the world we live in. The food we eat is a gift from God. The air we breathe is being loaned to us by God. The blood coursing through our veins, causing our hearts to beat, is a gift from God. We belong to God, but sin has estranged us and disconnected us from Him. Paul not only said that he is no longer a slave to sin, but he declared that he now belongs to God forever. He is a bondservant; nothing can change that and separate him from God. As Christians, we are bondservants to Christ for our benefit and for His glory.

This is illustrated in the story of the prophet Hosea, who married a prostitute. He is married to her, but she runs back to her old ways. In a tremendous act of love, Hosea pays the price for her to return. He could have had her stoned in the city square. She was his wife, and she was unfaithful and sold herself to other men. But instead, in a type of Messianic act, he redeems her. Hosea bought back the wife that already belonged to him, despite her sin of infidelity.

This is the same picture Paul is painting. He is a bondservant of Christ who is called to be an apostle—set apart by the gospel of Christ. If you are a Christian, you have also been set apart by and for the gospel.

> For I would have you know, brothers, that the gospel that was preached by me is not man's gospel. For I did not receive it from any man, nor was I taught it, but I received it through a revelation of Jesus Christ. For you have heard of my former life in Judaism, how I persecuted the church of God violently and tried to destroy it. And I was advancing in Judaism beyond many of my own age among my people, so extremely zealous was I for the traditions of my fathers. But when he who had set me apart before I was born, and who called me by his grace, was pleased to reveal his Son to me, in order that I might preach him among the Gentiles, I did not immediately consult with anyone (Gal. 1:11-16).

When was Paul set apart? At birth, before anything else. In our human understanding, this might seem confusing. What about the life Paul lived before he surrendered to Christ, where he persecuted and mistreated the church and had Christians killed? Why did God let him become a Pharisee and persecute Christians, participating in the imprisonments and the deaths of many Christians? To demonstrate God's mercy and patience and show God's glory. God used the most unlikely candidate and raised him up to be an apostle called to the Gentiles. Paul says, "But I received mercy for this reason, that in me, as the foremost, Jesus Christ might display his perfect patience as an example to those who were to believe in him for eternal life" (1 Tim. 1:16).

Being a Christian is about living as a slave to Christ and being set apart for the gospel. It is not about our hopes and dreams. It is not about having our best life now. It is about abandoning control of our lives for Christ's proclamation, glory, and service. "And we know that for those who love God all things work together for good, for those who are called according to his purpose" (Rom. 8:28). Somehow, through God's providence and by His sovereign hand, the persecution Paul inflicted on the church worked together for good. In my life, the fact that I sold drugs and did drugs and pursued wicked things, somehow, God is now working that together for His good. He knew who I was before I left that grievous life of sin; and still, He called me and saved me. This has produced humility in my life because God owes me nothing but damnation. But instead, He is using me; and He has given me good things, none of which I deserve.

THE PROMISED GOSPEL

"Which he promised beforehand through his prophets in the holy Scriptures, concerning his Son, who was descended from David according to the flesh and was declared to be the Son of God in power according to the Spirit of holiness by his resurrection from the dead, Jesus Christ our Lord" (vv. 2-4).

The gospel of God was always the plan. God wasn't surprised by the fall of man. The gospel wasn't a revision or a plan B. The entire Old Testament is about Jesus. This is the completion and fulfillment of God's covenant that the prophets gave to fulfill the Davidic covenant. A promised King from the lineage of David would sit on his throne forever. He is the Son of God according to the spirit of holiness. What does holiness mean? The word *holy* means "to be set apart." In the case of God, it means completely set apart. He is entirely different; He is "other." God is not like us in any shape, form, or fashion. Set apartness—holiness. When God calls for us to be holy, this doesn't mean we are like God but are set apart for God's holy purposes.

Further, in Romans, Paul clarifies that Jesus is not only the Jewish Messiah of which the prophets foretold; but He is also the Savior of the entire world, and this includes the Gentiles. This is the blessing of Abraham. I have repeatedly heard men in my Christian life say that the blessing of Abraham was like tapping into this financial system of prosperity. "Be blessed like Abraham." But here is what the blessing of Abraham is: "Know then that it is those of faith who are the sons of Abraham. And the Scripture, foreseeing that God would justify the Gentiles by faith" (Gal. 3:7-8a). What did God do? It says He "preached the gospel beforehand to Abraham, saying, 'In you shall

all the nations be blessed.' So then, those who are of faith are blessed along with Abraham, the man of faith" (Gal. 3:8b-9).

The gospel of Jesus Christ is the blessing of Abraham. What came out of Abraham? The Savior of the world. Do not listen to anyone who tries to tell you the blessing of Abraham is about monetary things. The book of Hebrews makes it clear that it is not about this world. Abraham lived in tents. Noah built an ark. And like them, we are living and "looking forward to a city that has foundations, whose designer and builder is God" (Heb. 11:10). Here is what the gospel has afforded us: the grace and love of God in salvation.

THE OBEDIENCE OF FAITH

"Through whom we have received grace and apostleship to bring about the obedience of faith for the sake of his name among all the nations, including you who are called to belong to Jesus Christ" (vv. 5-6).

There are a couple of things to understand from verse six. First, the only people who are saved will be according to the gospel of God. If we do not belong to Christ, if we are not slaves to Christ, if His ownership is not over our life, if we are not in Him and He in us, then we are not saved. No one but God truly knows who is saved or where a person is in the process of sanctification. However, we better rightly apply this to our life, accepting that He is God and Lord. There is not some golden ticket, only His precious blood. We were bought. The Bible says you are purchased with the precious blood of Jesus Christ: "Knowing that you were ransomed from the futile ways inherited from your forefathers, not with perishable things such as silver or gold, but with the precious blood of Christ, like that of a lamb without blemish or spot" (1 Peter 1:18-19).

If someone does not like this language, it is because they do not know Jesus. I am so grateful God bought me with His Son's precious blood. The precious blood of Christ bought us so that we might belong to Him.

Second, Paul addresses God's sovereign calling. Paul said he "received . . . apostleship to bring about the obedience of faith for the sake of his name among all the nations" (v. 5). It is important to note that he is not writing to everyone here but only to those who will belong to Christ. From the beginning, God knows who belongs to Him. God is using your life and working it together to send you down a gospel road as He draws you to Himself. He is doing this before you become a Christian.

As Paul was killing Christians, God knew he would be one of His greatest apostles. Paul did not know, but God knew. God is sovereign in salvation. God knows who are His because, like Paul, throughout our life, he is continually working "all things together for good" (Rom. 8:28). He is opening and closing doors to get us where we need to be. Sometimes, that is going to be painful and difficult because we "are called according to his purpose" (Rom. 8:28), which is to make His name known and proclaim His glorious gospel.

SET APART FOR CHRIST

"To all those in Rome who are loved by God and called to be saints: Grace to you and peace from God our Father and the Lord Jesus Christ" (v. 7).

Lastly, Paul is writing this letter to those called to be saints like him. He is writing to Christians. He uses the phrase "grace to you," but he is not referring to common grace. This is Paul's introduction in many of his epistles. He writes, "Grace to you and peace from God our Father and the Lord Jesus Christ" in his letters to the Ephesians and the church in Corinth. This is not merely a standard greeting with empty and meaningless words. Paul is emphasizing grace—saving grace. Christians experience faith and peace in Christ because they belong to God. This is a letter to Christians; and in the context of this verse, Paul is speaking of God's saving grace. We know this is true because it says, "To all those in Rome who are loved by God and called to be saints."

In Philippians 1:6, Paul writes, "And I am sure of this, that he who began a good work in you will bring it to completion at the day of Jesus Christ." Jesus is "the founder and perfecter of our faith" (Heb. 12:2). Abraham was set apart to be the father of faith, just as Paul was set apart to be the apostle to the Gentiles. By faith, when you "[call] on the name of the Lord [to] be saved" (Rom. 10:13), you are responding to the sovereign work of the Lord in salvation. Everything in the Bible supports the gospel. To attempt to make the gospel, the Bible, or Christianity about anything other than Jesus is blasphemy! Jesus did not come so you could be rich. Jesus did not come so we could be happy and healthy in this life. He did not come to make all our fleshly dreams come true. "Jesus came . . . to save sinners," of whom Paul says he is chief (1 Tim. 1:15). The book of Romans lays this out in great detail, but it is also explained in Paul's letter to Timothy:

> I thank him who has given me strength, Christ Jesus our Lord, because he judged me faithful, appointing me to his service, though formerly I was a blasphemer, persecutor, and insolent opponent. But I received mercy because I had acted ignorantly in unbelief, and the grace of our Lord overflowed for me with the faith and love that are in Christ Jesus. The saying is trustworthy and deserving of full acceptance, that Christ Jesus came into the world to save sinners, of whom I am the foremost. But I received mercy for this reason, that in me, as the foremost, Jesus Christ might display his perfect patience as an example to those who were to believe in him for eternal life. To the King of the ages, immortal, invisible, the only God, be honor and glory forever and ever. Amen (1 Tim. 1:12-17).

What does he say in verse fourteen? "The grace of our Lord overflowed for me with the faith and love that are in Christ Jesus." The blasphemer, the Christian persecutor, and the opponent of the faith received mercy because in his unbelief, he didn't know God, meaning that he was not a Christian.

Remember that Jesus came to save sinners, and Paul says he is one of those. However, because the grace of God overflowed for him, now the grace of God overflows *in* him. If the grace of God does not overflow in your life, it may be because the grace of God has not overflowed *for* you. Paul is not doing this out of compulsion or because it will make him happy, comfortable, or rich. In fact, he would eventually die for this faith. He is doing it because he is "not ashamed of the gospel, for it is the power of God for salvation to everyone who believes, to the Jew first and to the Greek. For in it the righteousness of God is revealed from faith for faith, as it is written, 'The righteous shall live by faith'" (Rom. 1:16-17).

Paul is overflowing with grace because he is genuinely in Christ, and Christ is truly in Him. Hebrews 11:6 says that "without faith it is impossible to please him, for whoever would draw near to God must believe that he exists and that he rewards those who seek him." "'The righteous shall live by his faith'" (Hab. 2:4); and when Paul writes about faith, he means saving faith. It is about knowing that we stand justified before God based solely on Christ's finished work on the cross and that God will keep His promises in His Word. We are part of the blessing of Abraham if we are connected to this lifesaving and lifegiving branch—the vine of which Jesus says, "You are grafted into Me" (Rom. 11:11-31).

God is sovereign in the gospel; and salvation is of the Lord, not of man. In verse one, Paul refers to the gospel as the "gospel of God." This is an intentional word choice. He could have called it the gospel of Christ, which would have been true. It is the gospel of Christ. But throughout the book of Romans, he will demonstrate the Trinitarian work of God in the gospel—God the Father who implemented the gospel, Jesus Christ to accomplish the gospel, and the Spirit of God who lives and moves and has His being in us (Acts 17:28), by which "we cry 'Abba Father!' (Rom. 8:15). We get to call God our Father! The God that once seemed far away, who was unreachable and unobtainable to sinful man, we now get to call our Father. Abba—what a personal name and what a beautiful truth!

If you truly are living a life of faith, which means you have been saved through the overflow of God's grace and mercy, you will proclaim the gospel of Jesus Christ because it saved you and because you believe it is the only means by which men are saved. If you believe in Heaven and Hell and have been saved by grace and you can freely give it to other people, why wouldn't you? Why is it not overflowing out of you? It could be that you are still living like the Lord of your own life. Being a Christian is about being saved and transformed by God; and because of the grace you have been given, you want to see others saved and transformed. This is the gospel of God, which Paul was set apart for, which I am set apart for, and which you are set apart for if, in fact, you truly have been saved.

2

UNASHAMED OF THE GOSPEL

ROMANS 1:8-17

First, I thank my God through Jesus Christ for all of you, because your faith is proclaimed in all the world. For God is my witness, whom I serve with my spirit in the gospel of his Son, that without ceasing I mention you always in my prayers, asking that somehow by God's will I may now at last succeed in coming to you. For I long to see you, that I may impart to you some spiritual gift to strengthen you—that is, that we may be mutually encouraged by each other's faith, both yours and mine. I do not want you to be unaware, brothers, that I have often intended to come to you (but thus far have been prevented), in order that I may reap some harvest among you as well as among the rest of the Gentiles. I am under obligation both to Greeks and to barbarians, both to the wise and to the foolish. So I am eager to preach the gospel to you also who are in Rome. For I am not ashamed of the gospel, for it is the power of God for salvation to everyone who believes, to the Jew first and also to the Greek. For in it the righteousness of God is revealed from faith for faith, as it is written, "The righteous shall live by faith."

WHEN THE CHURCH IN ROME received this deeply profound letter from the apostle Paul, they might have wondered why this well-known apostle was interested in them. Obviously, they knew who Paul was, but they had never spent time with him and did not know him personally.

Why was he so concerned with them? Paul addresses this question and wants the church to know his letter is not just a formality. He is deeply concerned for them and loves them.

What bonds Paul with the Roman church is deeper than any human bond. A genuine Christian is bound to faith in Christ and the body of Christ at a deeper level than he is in any fraternal or paternal relationship. Jesus said, "'If anyone comes to me and does not hate his own father and mother and wife and children and brothers and sisters, yes, and even his own life, he cannot be my disciple" (Luke 14:26). These might seem like harsh words; and to the world, this might look like hate. But Jesus is not saying hate your wife, husband, or your kids. He is saying our allegiance to Christ must be greater than anything else, even our own family.

This is further illustrated when Jesus was preaching to a crowd in a room where His mother and brothers were waiting outside. His family sent word through the people that they were looking for Him. Jesus asked the crowd, "'Who are my mother and my brothers?'" (Mark 3:33). Then Jesus looked at His followers sitting around him and said, "'Here are my mother and my brothers! For whoever does the will of God, he is my brother and sister and mother'" (Mark 3:34-35). This explains what it means to be *in Christ*, a truly transformed life forgiven of sin permeates our existence.

These Christian were in the cradle of the Roman Empire, which was a great concentration of pagan wickedness and depravity. The Romans were also notorious for their cruelty to anyone who would dare come against them. They were experts who were well equipped in all methods of torture and murder. To them it was a science and an art. They liked to make examples of anyone who threatened them or appeared to stand against them. We see this in Scripture as they put Jesus on the cross as if He was some type of insurgent or revolutionary. They were quick to put anyone on a cross or to lash them with thirty-nine stripes on their back, taking them to the brink of death. Roman history recorded people being beaten within an inch of their lives, nursed back to health, and then beaten severely again. The Romans were skilled experts in torture, punishment, and execution. Because of this, the apostle Paul knew that the Christians in Rome might be tempted not to proclaim the gospel boldly. So, he writes this letter to encourage them not to be ashamed of the person, the power, and the cross by which they obtained eternal life.

We can all relate to these Roman Christians. We may not be facing death or torture, but all of us could be bolder in our proclamation of the gospel. We might be apprehensive about being a bold witness to a family member, a coworker, or a person who might mock us. Perhaps some of us are not ashamed of the gospel but merely tired, knowing that a conversation will cost time and deplete our emotions. We need to pray for holy boldness!

Paul is not writing a rebuke to these believers but instead giving them words of encouragement. He demonstrates that he is not ashamed of the gospel, and he is calling for those to whom he is writing to also be unashamed of the person and the means by which eternal life is gained. That person is Jesus Christ, and the means is the cross.

The true Christian must come to terms with his death in this life. A good proclaimer of the gospel is a person who has put to death his life path, plans, hopes, and dreams. Someone who is not looking to be praised or respected by the world. There are many Christians who abandon their integrity because they want to be accepted by the culture or academia. They separate themselves from those who believe in a six-day creation or those who believe that the entire Bible is true. But for those who believe in Christ, nothing in this world is worth trading our integrity. Those who mock or disrespect our beliefs are the very ones who need us to stand bold in our faith. Every atheist needs a person to courageously and faithfully proclaim the gospel to them, even unto death.

In Luke 9:23-26, Jesus said:

> "If anyone would come after me, let him deny himself and take up
> his cross daily and follow me. For whoever would save his life will
> lose it, but whoever loses his life for my sake will save it. For what
> does it profit a man if he gains the whole world and loses or forfeits
> himself? For whoever is *ashamed of me and of my words*, of him will
> the Son of Man be ashamed when he comes in his glory and the
> glory of the Father and of the holy angels" (emphasis added).

These words spoken by Jesus are not a scare tactic but a litmus test to apply to our lives. Are we ashamed of Christ or any of the inerrant God-breathed inspired words of the Bible? The totality of Scripture is the witness of the apostles and prophets. It is the story of the God we serve and His plan to save a people unto Himself through Christ's death on the cross. The Bible is the very words of God. It is all hinged together, and it is all or nothing!

If we are ashamed of Christ, His words, and His gospel, He is ashamed of us. This means He is not advocating before the Father for us. He is not our atonement. He is not the lawyer pleading our case—redeeming us from sin. Ashamed means we will not inherit eternal life. This is why Paul declares he is unashamed of the gospel (v. 16). He knows the gospel is his salvation and salvation for all who believe. This includes Jews and non-Jews. There might have been some people in Rome who thought the God of the Jews came to save the Jews and that one of the Greco-Roman gods might save the Greeks. However, Paul clarifies that if our God truly is God, He is the only means by which men are saved.

Paul said, "For to me to live is Christ, and to die is gain" (Phil. 1:21). This life motto defined him. Christians who understand this will boldly proclaim the gospel no matter the cost. If we have truly been saved, how could we not? If we were scheduled for destruction and eternal judgment, yet Someone gave His life to intervene and save us into eternal life, would we not accept it?

A PERSONAL GOD

"First, I thank my God through Jesus Christ for all of you,
because your faith is proclaimed in all the world" (v. 8).

This verse distinguishes Paul as a Christian and differentiates him from the religion of the Jews and Gentiles. No Gentile would have referred to a monotheistic or solitary God. They would not have said a personalized phrase like *my* God. Neither would most Jews. Even though the Old Testament uses this language, most Jews did not refer to God in an intimate way. The apostle Paul writes very personally about Jesus, and this is where we derive the phrase "personal Savior" from. Jesus, John, Paul, and Peter speak of those who are saved in Christ as having a direct relationship and access to God because of the gospel and through the Spirit.

God is not sitting up in Heaven with a clipboard checking boxes of works, deeds, and performances of His children. That describes the god of the Jehovah's Witnesses, the Mormons, the Muslims, and the god of almost every other false religious system. But here is the truth about the one true God: no good deeds could ever be enough for us to be right in His sight because He is holy. Unlike those other false gods, the one true God took on flesh and came to us. He is a personal God Who sent His Son, Jesus Christ; and after Christ ascended to Heaven, He sent His Spirit to be our Helper, to lead us into all truth and conform us to the image of Christ.

In the Old Testament, God desired a personal relationship with His people; but this was a prophetic utterance pointing to a future time. We see this manifested in the person of Jesus, the God Who took on flesh. In most cultures, their gods were not personal because that would have undermined their power and deity.

"Now therefore thus says the Lord, the God of Israel, concerning this city of which you say, 'It is given into the hand of the king of Babylon by sword, by famine, and by pestilence': Behold, I will gather them from all the countries to which I drove them in my anger and my wrath and in great indignation. I will bring them back to this place, and I will make them dwell in safety. And they shall be my people, and I will be their God. I will give them one heart and one way, that they may fear me forever, for their own good and the good of their children after them. I will make with them an everlasting covenant, that I will not turn away from doing good to them. And I will put the fear of me in their hearts, that they may not turn from me. I will rejoice in doing them good, and I will plant them in this land in faithfulness, with all my heart and all my soul (Jer. 32:36-41).

This passage in Jeremiah is about the Jews being brought back to Israel after their time of exile, but it is also a prophetic utterance of the salvific work of Christ the Savior. This passage is not merely about the Jews returning to the Promised Land under the Old Covenant. It is prophetically saying that God will make a permanent covenant with both Jews and Gentiles who repent and believe in Christ. How do we know this? In the book of John, the Jews said to Jesus, "'We are offspring of Abraham and have never been enslaved to anyone. How is it that you say, *You will become free*'?" (John 8:33).

Jesus responded to them:

"Truly, truly, I say to you, everyone who practices sin is a slave to sin. The slave does not remain in the house forever; the son remains forever. So if the Son sets you free, you will be free indeed. I know that you are offspring of Abraham; yet you seek to kill me because my word finds no place in you. I speak of what I have seen with my Father, and you do what you have heard from your father" (Jer. 8:34-38).

Jesus is describing a people who will truly belong to and serve God, worshiping Him "'in spirit and in truth'" (John 4:24), people in the Old Testament who looked to a future Messiah. But since the New Testament, those who live by faith look back on the life, death, and resurrection of Christ as we worship a living Messiah, Who is currently ruling and reigning, seated at the right hand of the Father.

FAMOUS FOR THEIR FAITH

Paul wants the Roman Christians to know that they are united with him in a way that supersedes every other human bond. Through the gospel, his God is also their God. Paul is thankful for them because they are his brothers and sisters in Christ, and their faith is proclaimed throughout the world. Their faith is known because they are living in one of the most opposed places to the gospel—a dark, oppressive, tyrannical place. But light shines the brightest in the darkest night. Truth shines bright in places of persecution. One struck match in pitch black darkness can draw all our eyes to the flickering light. Paul is saying they are famous for their faith in these conditions of darkness and persecution because "the light shines in the darkness, and the darkness has not overcome it" (John 1:5).

Biblical faith is not really wanting something or really believing something you hope will happen will come true. Biblical faith is knowing we stand justified before God based on what Christ did on the cross and the fact that God will keep the promises He has made in His Word. Our faith is not rooted in something but in *Someone*—a living God Who showed His love for us by laying down His life "while we were still sinners" (Rom. 5:8). Paul is not saying that if they have this faith, they will survive or the church will grow but that those who belong to Him are recipients of the promises of God. It is like looking through a glass dimly, knowing that one day we will see Him face to face.

THE GOSPEL BOND

"For God is my witness, whom I serve with my spirit in the gospel of his Son, that without ceasing I mention you always in my prayers, asking that somehow by God's will I may now at last succeed in coming to you" (vv. 9-10).

Paul is purposefully united with them and wants to encourage them in the faith. He wants them to know that he thinks about them, loves them, and is praying for them. Paul understands all too well that the persecution they are experiencing is heavy and deep, but that they are connected by the same unbreakable bond of the gospel.

On some level, I can understand what Paul is writing about. I have a group of friends in India and Pakistan that I have supported and have had a close relationship with for many years. I love them, and we have become very good friends. One pastor friend in Pakistan has been taking the gospel to remote places, heavily dominated by Islam. He has been beaten, and his building has been burned down. This pastor's life reminds me how comfortable my life is in America by comparison and how many brothers and sisters worldwide serve God faithfully in the most difficult of circumstances.

In 2020, I planned to visit a group of pastor friends in India. I would speak to them via Zoom twice a month and was looking forward to finally meeting them face to face. We were very excited about the chance to encourage each other mutually in the faith. I was brokenhearted when my trip was canceled due to the COVID-19 pandemic. I sent them a long message explaining the situation. Because of the bond that unites us, I grieved over being unable to travel there. It is not about the music we listen to, our clothes, our culture, or our family upbringing; our bond is the gospel of Jesus Christ, which means more than anything else.

SPIRITUAL GIFTS

"For I long to see you, that I may impart to you some spiritual gift to strengthen you" (v. 11).

In this verse, Paul is not referring to the spiritual gifts he describes in 1 Corinthians. The Scripture says the Spirit imparts those gifts according to His will. He is also not talking about sharing the gospel with them because he is writing to Christians in Rome. Instead, he is communicating something that he imparted to many other churches. The spiritual gift Paul is speaking about here to strengthen them is mutual encouragement. It is teaching, preaching, and using Paul's abilities and talents as an apostle to help, just as he did to the church in Ephesus.

Paul adds to his reason for visiting: "that is, that we may be mutually encouraged by each other's faith, both yours and mine" (v. 12). As an apostle, Paul did not think he was above being edified by the people he preached to. That is not the model of Christ's church. A true pastor or minister is not highly anointed, sitting on a far-removed platform where he looks down on the flock as if they are inferior. No, a pastor is a member of the body of Christ, using his gift and calling to edify the church, as he is also edified by the giftings and callings of others in the body. All gifts and all the parts of the body are essential.

We need preachers, but we also need men standing in workplaces telling people that God loves them and died for them. Practice is important and the pep rally is great, but we need people in the game. Who cares about the plan, the plays, team spirit if nobody is playing on the field? Preaching is an important part of the church but not the only part, and Paul understood this.

Christianity is about "iron sharpen[ing] iron" (Prov. 27:17). It is about believers encouraging one another. Yes, spiritual leaders need encouragement and correction, too, because they are also growing in the faith. God has given pastors a specific set of standards that, if not met, might make a person unqualified to preach. This is why Paul cautions those young in the faith and warns them that spiritual teachers will be judged more severely. Pastors are not above the words preached in Scripture—they are even more accountable to them.

DO NOT BE UNAWARE

"I do not want you to be unaware, brothers, that I have often intended to come to you (but thus far have been prevented), in order that I may reap some harvest among you as well as among the rest of the Gentiles" (v. 13).

Paul frequently uses the phrase "I do not want you to be unaware" in his letters. He uses this phrase to draw attention when he wants to make an important point. In Romans 11:25, he writes, "Lest you be wise in your own sight, I do not want you to be unaware of this mystery, brothers: a partial hardening has come upon Israel, until the fullness of the Gentiles has come in." He is explaining to the Jews that they should not be unaware that God did not just come to bring salvation to them but also for a harvest of the Gentiles. The phrase is used to convey something serious. Paul uses it in verse thirteen to communicate to the Christians in Rome his deep desire to meet with them and encourage them in the faith. Like every ministry endeavor, it is partially to encourage the church and partially evangelistic. The church should preach sound doctrine to the saints but should also be evangelistic and gospel centric.

Paul wants them to know that he deeply desires to encourage them in the faith and also to be encouraged by them. However, he is an apostle to the Gentiles, and this God-given title is evangelistic in and of itself. His purpose is to come and reap a harvest amongst the Gentiles. So, he plans to preach on the streets of Rome: visiting synagogues, witnessing in front of pagan idols, talking to philosophers about the wisdom and philosophy of the day, and sharing the good news about Jesus of Nazareth.

BOLD AND UNASHAMED

"I am under obligation both to Greeks and to barbarians, both to the wise and to the foolish. So I am eager to preach the gospel to you also who are in Rome" (vv. 14-15).

This verse is a significant juxtaposition. The Greeks of that day were considered to be society's top echelon of intellect and philosophical understanding. They wore nice robes and waxed philosophically on street corners. On the opposite end of the spectrum were the barbarians, and other less civilized people who roamed the desert and lived in caves. Paul is saying he is equally obligated to preach to both groups of people.

John MacArthur said, "Paul's external obligation to minister did not preclude his internal desire to fulfill that obligation."[1] In other words, Paul was willing and eager to preach the gospel to the people in Rome. If our eyes are open to the fact that people will perish apart from the saving truth of God's gospel, we, too, will be eager. God has put us in this world to be salt and light. This means living lives of missionary sacrifice and being devoted to the call of the King.

The word *doulos* is used often in Scripture. It means "slave." We are willing slaves of Christ. We do it out of joy because the Master is good. Martyn Lloyd-Jones said in his commentary on Romans, "Paul was very eager and also determined to preach in Rome, just as he was in Jerusalem, despite the fact in both cases great danger awaited him."[2]

In the book of Acts, Paul says, "And now, behold, I am going to Jerusalem, constrained by the Spirit, not knowing what will happen to me there, except that the Holy Spirit testifies to me in every city that imprisonment and afflictions await me" (Acts 20:22-23). Paul knows he will probably be ridiculed, beaten, or imprisoned in Jerusalem. However, he continues, "But I do not account my life of any value nor as precious to myself, if only I may finish my course and the ministry that I received from the Lord Jesus, to testify to the gospel of the grace of God" (v. 24).

Like Paul, to be effective in ministry, we must conclude that what we have been entrusted with is more valuable than our lives. This is not a sign of mature Christianity; this is a basic 101 of the Christian faith. It is an understanding that our lives are not more valuable than the call to Christ and that temporal life is not more valuable than eternal life. Treating this temporal life as more valuable proves we are unaware of our eternal life. Regarding the popular criticism, "Don't be so heavenly minded that you are no earthly good," John Piper responds, "The only people that are of any earthly good in this life are those who are so radically heavenly-minded that they are free of this world."[3]

FROM FAITH FOR FAITH

"For I am not ashamed of the gospel, for it is the power of God for salvation to everyone who believes, to the Jew first and also to the Greek. For in it the righteousness of God is revealed from faith for faith, as it is written, 'The righteous shall live by faith'" (vv. 16-17).

Paul was imprisoned in Philippi, chased out of Thessalonica, smuggled out of Damascus and Berea, laughed at in Athens, considered a fool in Corinth, declared a blasphemer and a lawbreaker in Jerusalem, and stoned and left for dead in Lystra. The religious leaders of Jerusalem tried to intimidate him. The prominent pagans of Rome and Greece tried to hinder his commitment to God. But Paul did not waver because he had met the risen Christ. He believed in God with all of his heart. He abandoned his place in this life, claiming, "Indeed, I count everything as loss because of the surpassing worth of knowing Christ Jesus my Lord. For his sake I have suffered the loss of all things and count them as rubbish, in order that I may gain Christ" (Phil. 3:8).

If we see Christ as the King and Treasure of the ages, like a treasure hidden in the field, we will gladly abandon everything else for the sake of

Christ. Christ is worth living for because He is worth dying for! He gave His life to give us life. However, as faithful followers of Jesus and unashamed ambassadors of the gospel, there is some bad news. We will face adversity inside and outside of church. The atheistic world will mock, scoff, and minimize you; but so, will the falsely religious. The lukewarm and lawless who simply want to go with the flow as well as the legalistic who believe that salvation by grace alone, through faith alone, in Christ alone is scandalous. Those who want a Ted Talk, therapeutic, self-help kind of Christianity will despise you. The falsely religion of the Pharisee as well as the pagan world will minimize and persecute you.

Paul dealt with the religious people of his day, and he dealt with the pagan scoffers. Popular religion will call you a zealot or a fanatic as they offer a more culturally acceptable version of Christianity, which is what most megachurch, seeker-friendly, flesh-centered "churches" are offering in place of the true gospel. The apostle Paul also cautions that the intelligentsia and the wisdom of the secular world will also reject us:

> Where is the one who is wise? Where is the scribe? Where is the debater of this age? Has not God made foolish the wisdom of the world? For since, in the wisdom of God, the world did not know God through wisdom, it pleased God through the folly of what we preach to save those who believe. For Jews demand signs and Greeks seek wisdom, but we preach Christ crucified, a stumbling block to Jews and folly to Gentiles, but to those who are called, both Jews and Greeks, Christ the power of God and the wisdom of God. For the foolishness of God is wiser than men, and the weakness of God is stronger than men (I Cor. 1:20-25).

If we have truly been saved through the gospel, how could we ever be ashamed of that gospel? The gospel is the power of Christianity. The word "power" is translated from the Greek word *dunamis* or *dynamis*, which is the root of the English words "dynamite" and "dynamic." The power of God in the gospel, is how people are saved from their sins. It is explosive and transforming; and it comes from God, not men.

When the church at Corinth was arguing over who baptized them and spiritual gifts, Paul responded, "For Christ did not send me to baptize but to preach the gospel, and not with words of eloquent wisdom, lest the cross of Christ be emptied of its power. For the word of the cross is folly to those who are perishing, but to us who are being saved it is the power of God" (1 Cor. 1:17-18). The word of the cross is folly to false converts who insist that the gospel is some prayer they recited that didn't seem to have any real impact on their lives, a prayer that gives kingdom blessings and pronounces one saved but asks nothing of the person reciting that prayer. That is not Christianity. If you disagree, find the Bible verse that says to repeat a magic prayer and ask Jesus in your heart.

A more valid description of the gospel comes from one of my favorite preachers, Paul Washer. He explained it as God holding off His wrath with one hand while reaching out to us with the other, inviting us in. But one day, both hands will drop. This is a picture of God saving us from His wrath, which we deserve. This is the gospel. If we reject God and His Son, Whom He sent to die for us, what is left for us? The book of Hebrews says nothing but a "fearful expectation of judgment, and a fury of fire that will consume the adversaries" (Heb. 10:27). It is the righteous wrath and condemnation of God for those who reject God's mercy and grace, but it is His "power for salvation" for those of us who are being saved (Rom. 1:16). This is why we should meditate on and think about the cross often. Thinking about the sin God saved us from is healthy because it draws us toward His grace.

Paul wants to make sure that both Jewish and Gentile readers of this epistle understand that although the Scripture and the gospel were given through the Jews and is rightly first for the Jews, it is not a gospel only to the Jews. It is a gospel for the whole world. He writes in 1 Timothy, "For there is one God, and there is one mediator between God and men, the man

Christ Jesus" (1 Tim. 2:5). There are no various gods for different countries and cultures.

People might say, "What right do you have to say that your God is the true God? People often say "be more loving, accepting, or tolerant of other people's religious views." This would be agreeable if what we believe were not true. However, if what we believe is true, then the most hateful thing we could do is let someone languish in their false religion. Those in Christ know that Jesus is "'the way, and the truth, and the life. No one comes to the Father except through [Him]" (John 14:6).

On Mars Hill, Paul declared to the academic elite of the day, who were the philosophers and debaters of Athens, Greece, "'The times of ignorance God overlooked, but now he commands all people everywhere to repent, because he has fixed a day on which he will judge the world in righteousness by a man whom he has appointed; and of this he has given assurance to all by raising him from the dead'" (Acts 17:30-31).

Jesus is God in the flesh; we have proof because He was raised from the dead. Mohammed was not raised from the dead, nor was Buddha or Krishna. There are no witness accounts of these gods coming back from the dead. Yes, we have to believe in the resurrection of Christ by faith, but the Spirit empowers us to believe; and if we truly seek, we will find the truth.

Primarily this means that God is able to save sinners who deserve judgment while keeping the perfection of His justice intact. God is holy and righteous; so because of this, God could not simply ignore our sins. For God to be just, a sufficient payment had to be made. And through the shedding of Jesus's innocent blood, the price was paid; we were saved; and God's righteous perfection remains intact. So, God's righteousness is revealed in the work of the gospel.

What is Paul saying that "the righteousness of a God is revealed from faith for faith?"? In Greek, this phrase means that faith will spread or grow from sharing one individual's faith with another. This means that this faith will grow and become greater—not that we will do greater works but this will grow from faith for faith—as it spreads because there is only *one* faith in *one* Savior. There is only one gospel that has the power to save. As people are converted and make disciples, it grows—from faith to faith as the righteous live by faith.

This parallels the statement "to everyone who believes" (v. 16). To put it another way, Paul is not ashamed of the gospel because it is in the gospel that we experience the saving power of God. It saved him, and it also saves all who believe. It also reveals the righteousness of God, the righteousness of those who believe from person to person or from individual faith to individual faith. Paul quotes Habakkuk 2:4: "The righteous shall live by his faith."

Habakkuk had to have the "father of faith" in mind when he said this. In the Old Testament, this was about following Yahweh God, the God of Abraham, Isaac, and Jacob. This is not only in the Old Testament God but also in the same God we follow, who called Abraham to be the father of faith.

"Now faith is the assurance of things hoped for, the conviction of things not seen. For by it the people of old received their commendation. By faith we understand that the universe was created by the word of God, so that what is seen was not made out of things that are visible" (Heb. 11:1-3). This verse in Hebrew means we believe the creation account that God spoke the world into existence. The same word of power that spoke the world to existence is the same power that called Abraham to be the father of many nations, that led the Israelites out of Egypt by Moses, and that raised Jesus from the dead.

Hebrews chapter eleven is often referred to as the faith chapter.

> By faith Abel offered to God a more acceptable sacrifice than Cain, through which he was commended as righteous, God commending him by accepting his gifts. And through his faith, though he died, he still speaks. By faith Enoch was taken up so that he should not see death, and he was not found, because God had taken him. Now before he was taken he was commended

as having pleased God. And without faith it is impossible to please him, for whoever would draw near to God must believe that he exists and that he rewards those who seek him. By faith Noah, being warned by God concerning events as yet unseen, in reverent fear constructed an ark for the saving of his household. By this he condemned the world and became an heir of the righteousness that comes by faith.

By faith Abraham obeyed when he was called to go out to a place that he was to receive as an inheritance. And he went out, not knowing where he was going. By faith he went to live in the land of promise, as in a foreign land, living in tents with Isaac and Jacob, heirs with him of the same promise. For he was looking forward to the city that has foundations, whose designer and builder is God. By faith Sarah herself received power to conceive, even when she was past the age, since she considered him faithful who had promised. Therefore from one man, and him as good as dead, were born descendants as many as the stars of heaven and as many as the innumerable grains of sand by the seashore (Heb. 11:4-12).

All these people listed in Hebrews died in faith, not receiving the promises. If it is only about this life, then these people missed out. But it is not about this life! They died not receiving the things promised but, having seen them and greeted them from afar, having acknowledged that they were strangers and exiles on the earth. This is not just referring to a time before Jesus because the apostle Peter used the same language, saying that we live like strangers and exiles on this earth. We desire a better country that is heavenly; and God is not ashamed to be called our God, for he is preparing for us a city. If we are ashamed of God, he will be ashamed of us. If we live by faith in Christ, God is not ashamed to be called our God. Paul is linking these Roman Christians to the same thread of saving faith that goes back to the beginning of time. He calls these Roman Christians to be bold and unashamed about the gospel because "it is the power of God for salvation"—salvation for them and salvation for us if we believe.

Examine your life and your faith with this statement: "For I am not ashamed of the gospel, for it is the power of God for salvation to everyone who believes, to the Jew first the Jew and also to the Greek. For in it the righteousness of God is revealed to us from faith for faith, as it is written, 'The righteous shall live by faith'" (Rom. 1:16-17). The righteous will live according to the faith by which they are being saved. How could we ever be ashamed of the Savior Who saves us? How could we be ashamed of the words of Scripture by which that salvation was revealed? How could we be ashamed of the cross by which He accomplished that salvation?

Many places in my life "fall short of the glory of God" (Rom. 3:23). Although I am justified because of Christ's finished work on the cross, I am still being sanctified and conformed to the image of Christ. I, like all Christians, am a work in progress. But I "am not ashamed of the gospel" of Jesus Christ because "it is the power of God for salvation to everyone who believes." Jesus said if you are ashamed of His words in front of men, he will be ashamed of you before the Father (Luke 9:26). True meditation and contemplation on the reality of the cross, how it has saved us, and what it promises for our future will burn away any fear you have of the men who will one day be made a footstool that will be put beneath the feet of Jesus (Psalm 110:1).

3
THE WRATH AND JUDGMENT OF GOD

ROMANS 1:18–32

For the wrath of God is revealed from heaven against all ungodliness and unrighteousness of men, who by their unrighteousness suppress the truth. For what can be known about God is plain to them, because God has shown it to them. For his invisible attributes, namely, his eternal power and divine nature, have been clearly perceived, ever since the creation of the world, in the things that have been made. So they are without excuse. For although they knew God, they did not honor him as God or give thanks to him, but they became futile in their thinking, and their foolish hearts were darkened. Claiming to be wise, they became fools, and exchanged the glory of the immortal God for images resembling mortal man and birds and animals and creeping things.

Therefore God gave them up in the lusts of their hearts to impurity, to the dishonoring of their bodies among themselves, because they exchanged the truth about God for a lie and worshiped and served the creature rather than the Creator, who is blessed forever! Amen.

For this reason God gave them up to dishonorable passions. For their women exchanged natural relations for those that are contrary to nature; and the men likewise gave up natural relations with women and were consumed with passion for one another, men committing shameless acts with men and receiving in themselves the due penalty for their error.

And since they did not see fit to acknowledge God, God gave them up to a debased mind to do what ought not to be done. They were filled with all manner of unrighteousness, evil, covetousness, malice. They are full of envy, murder, strife, deceit,

maliciousness. They are gossips, slanderers, haters of God, insolent, haughty, boastful,

inventors of evil, disobedient to parents, foolish, faithless, heartless, ruthless. Though

they know God's righteous decree that those who practice such things deserve to die,

they not only do them but give approval to those who practice them.

THE TONE OF THIS CHAPTER is different from the last two. The title might clue you into why. The conclusion of Romans 1 shifts its tone and focuses to the righteous wrath and judgment of God that made the gospel necessary. In verse seventeen of chapter one, it tells us that in the gospel the righteousness of God is revealed. On one hand, by Christ's death on the cross, God is saving those who repent and put their trust in Christ by faith while keeping the perfection of His justice intact. On the other hand, His righteousness is revealed in pouring out His wrath and judgment on those who do not repent and put their trust in Christ, giving them what they deserve. God will be glorified in both things.

Previously, Paul laid out the centrality of the gospel in the Christian faith, as he unashamedly proclaims it as the only hope of humanity and the only means by which men might be made right with God. He draws a clear line in the sand as he quotes Habakkuk 2:4: "But the righteous shall live by his faith." Romans 1:16-17 is the launching pad into the continuing verses in the chapter.

THE TRUE GOSPEL

God's wrath and judgment are not popular topics; and because of that, they are one of the reasons why the cross of Christ is offensive to the world. Rarely do we hear this topic preached, although it is clearly taught in the New Testament. Nearly one-fourth of Jesus' teachings discuss the world's end and the wrath and judgment of God. Yet it is hardly ever taught in most churches today, which reveals that the complete and true gospel is a rarely preached message. We cannot preach the gospel without preaching about God's wrath, the final judgment, or the sin of men.

Martyn Lloyd-Jones wrote on this section of scripture in Romans:

> There is no evangelistic message in the whole of the Bible that *starts* with the love of God. It must *include* the love of God, but first, we must establish who God is and how we have offended His Holiness, and then call for men to repent as we share with them this great love of God, a God of whose wrath they are now being saved from. This is the message of all the prophets of the Old Testament, John the Baptist in the New Testament, and the beloved Savior Himself. Like Peter, on the day of Pentecost, we must preach repentance from sin, which drives the hearer to either reject God or to respond as so many did to Peter's preaching by asking the question: "What then must we do to be saved?"[4] (emphasis added).

That was the response on the day of Pentecost. People like to talk about the miraculous nature of Pentecost or how thousands were drawn to God that day. It is a great topic to discuss, but we also need to talk about what Peter actually preached: a message of repentance from sin. It was bold in spirit and power, so men were left asking questions. Some remarked, "Get out of here, drunks. Why are you babbling?" They thought they were drunk because they were under the power of the Spirit. However, like Peter's message, the true gospel draws a line in the sand. Are you ashamed of the gospel? Is it "the power of God for salvation" (Rom. 1:16) in your life?

There is no greater tragedy than calling yourself a church but not preaching the fullness of the gospel and the whole council of God. This is not a side note, a secondary issue, or a fringe doctrine. It is the centerpiece of Christianity. Throughout the history of the Bible, you will not find a prophet, an apostle, or an evangelist who simply said, "Hey, God loves you. Goodbye!" That is not the message they preached when they encountered people. Their message was, "Repent of your sin and put your faith in Christ to save you from the wrath that is coming." There is no forgiveness of sin without the shedding of blood. The blood of Jesus is so very precious—precious enough to save us fully and completely.

John Piper once said, "The blood of Jesus is not precious because it saves us,[sic] it saves us because it is precious." The Jews should have understood the price of sin. Because of man's sin, there was a consistent need for sacrifice; and because of this, the temple was a bloody place. There was blood all over the temple floor because of their sin, and we have to understand this, too. The gospel cost something. It was a great sacrifice, and we must be aware of our sins to see salvation as a beautiful gift. "Indeed, under the law almost everything is purified with blood, and without the shedding of blood there is no forgiveness of sins" (Heb. 9:22).

CONSEQUENTIAL WRATH

There are many expressions of God's wrath in the Bible and our fallen world. Eternal wrath in judgment awaits those who do not surrender to the lordship of Christ in this life. We know that the wrath of God will be poured out at the end of the age in the second coming of Christ. However, we also see expressions of God's wrath and judgment in natural disasters. We often think God has no control over these calamities, but the Bible reveals something different. God allows things to happen to people who turn their backs on Him. There are specific judgments on nations, cultures, and people who suppress the knowledge of God for the sake of their sins.

Paul wrote this letter for the Christians living in Rome, but these verses are also a snapshot of the world we live in. He speaks of consequential wrath, which we see in nations, people groups, and individuals. We must recognize the harvest that sin produces in our lives and the lives of those around us. Even if we have not turned our backs on God, we still suffer the repercussions of sin. Surrendering to the call to follow Jesus does not mean that we will not suffer consequences for the sinful lives we led before Christ, as well as the sins we commit as Christians.

All people bear physical, spiritual, and emotional scars due to their sins. All problems in this life result from sin coming into the world. The problem with living in a fallen world is that sometimes, we do not just pay the consequences for our sins; we pay the consequences for the sins of others. Perhaps others have paid the consequences of your sin and my sin. The Bible says that what we sow, we will reap; and God will not be mocked (Gal. 6:7). This is what makes the mercy and grace of God wonderful and beautiful. In the gospel, God extends mercy to us, which means he doesn't give us what we deserve, which is eternal judgment and condemnation. But He also gives us amazing grace, which means He gives us something that we don't deserve: life, Divine fellowship, and a place in the eternal family of God.

In Romans, we see the wrath of God displayed as He abandons a nation or a culture because they have abandoned Him. Even those not saved benefit from the structure of nations submitted to or based on the law of God. The closer a culture is to following God's law, the more blessed that culture will be. If you lived in Israel when they were following God and you came in as a foreigner, you would have benefited from the fact that they were a nation that served and feared the Lord. However, there is a point in history when God turned His back on Israel. Proverbs explains what happens when God rejects a society of people:

> Wisdom cries aloud in the street, in the markets she raises her voice; at the head of the noisy streets she cries out; at the entrance of the city gates she speaks: "How long, O simple ones, will you love being simple? How long will scoffers delight in their scoffing and fools hate knowledge? If you turn at my reproof, behold, I will pour out my spirit to you; I will make my words known to you. Because I have called and you refused

to listen, have stretched out my hand and no one has heeded, because you have ignored all my counsel and would have none of my reproof, I also will laugh at your calamity; I will mock when terror strikes you, when terror strikes you like a storm and your calamity comes like a whirlwind, when distress and anguish come upon you. Then they will call upon me, but I will not answer; they will seek me diligently but will not find me. Because they hated knowledge and did not choose the fear of the LORD, would have none of my counsel and despised all my reproof, therefore they shall eat the fruit of their way, and have their fill of their own devices. For the simple are killed by their turning away, and the complacency of fools destroys them; but whoever listens to me will dwell secure and will be at ease, without dread of disaster" (Prov. 1:20-33).

A HARDENED HEART

First and foremost, this is a message to be heeded on an individual level. This does not mean God will change the nation based on you, but you can guarantee that God will hear your cries if you do not harden your heart. Hebrews says, "'Today, if you hear his voice, do not harden your hearts as you did in the rebellion, on the day of testing in the wilderness'" (Heb. 3:7-8). Individually, we can always turn to God and find forgiveness for our sins. We are not judged eternally based on the nation we were born into or the people group we are a part of. We stand before God based on our own lives and whether or not we are being saved by the gospel of Jesus Christ.

But the Bible teaches that nations and societies that are made up of people will also suffer or benefit based on their posture toward the one true God. When God destroyed Sodom and Gomorrah with fire, Abraham pleaded with him beforehand. In Genesis 18:22-33, he said, "What if there are fifty righteous people in Sodom?" God said, "I will save the city for them." Then

Abraham said, "What about forty-five?" And God said, "I will save the city for them." But as Abraham made the same request again and again with smaller and smaller numbers of people, he realized that God already knew there were no other righteous people in Sodom. God sent two angels to save Lot and his family from the city before He destroyed it, except for Lot's wife because although the angels commanded them not to look back as they were fleeing, she did and was turned into a pillar of salt.

In the book of Matthew, think about the severity of what Jesus says regarding the Pharisees:

> And he called the people to him and said to them, "Hear and understand: it is not what goes into the mouth that defiles a person, but what comes out of the mouth; this defiles a person." Then the disciples came and said to him, "Do you know that the Pharisees were offended when they heard this saying?" He answered, "Every plant that my heavenly Father has not planted will be rooted up. Let them alone; they are blind guides. And if the blind lead the blind, both will fall into a pit" (Matt. 15:10-14).

Notice the phrase, "'Let them alone.'" In other words, their fate is sealed. Jesus knew they were not going to respond to Him. They turned their backs on God, and He turned His back on them. Now, individually, there were some Pharisees who acknowledged the risen Christ and followed and believed in Him. Praise God for that; but ultimately, that corrupt religious system would not endure. Jesus looked at the temple, which was supposed to be a temple for the worship of God, that they turned into a den of robbers. He said, "'There will not be left here one stone upon another that will not be thrown down'" (Matt. 24:2b). This is God's righteous wrath and judgment.

Paul is writing a warning to the church in Rome, but it is not just for them; it is for all people of all times. Today, we have a front-row seat as we watch the judgment of God unfold in America as He has turned his back on us. Romans tells us what it looks like when God turns His back on a society. Does this mean there is no chance of recovery? I do not know because I am not God, but He has turned his back on us and is revealing what unrestrained wickedness looks like. Judgment is not just fire and doom and gloom. It is God taking His hand of grace off of a people and letting them run wild with their sinful desires. He has turned His back to let us revel in our unrestrained wickedness and idolatry.

God will also let us revel in the consequences of our wickedness.

> For the wrath of God is revealed from heaven against all ungodliness and unrighteousness of men, who by their unrighteousness suppress the truth. For what can be known about God is plain to them, because God has shown it to them. For his invisible attributes, namely, his eternal power and divine nature, have been clearly perceived, ever since the creation of the world, in the things that have been made. So they are without excuse (Rom. 1:18-20).

God has given us the gospel; and for those who respond to it, it is the power of God unto salvation. For those who reject it, it will cause their hardening process of the heart. It will not only damn the soul, but it will also pour gasoline on the fire of sin and wicked desires. Some have tasted that in life as they waver between two opinions. At some point, you rejected help and hope; and your heart hardened to the point where you turned your back and ran deep into the darkness. Gasoline was poured on the fire of your sin as you found yourself becoming more depraved and more degenerate and not caring one bit about it. Thank God that His grace extends deep enough and far enough to reach us.

Everyone is made in the image of God. Creation bears witness to that, and this is the truth of God that we are denying. We ignore it because we love sin and suppress the truth about God so that we can feel free to revel in our sins. We want sexual freedom. We want personal freedom.

What we want is unrestrained access to our wicked hearts' desires. This is why the wrath of God is being poured out on our nation because we have given ourselves over to the worship of everything but God. Some may ask, "What about the people who do not know God?" This Scripture refutes that question because, deep down, the *imago Dei* (image of God) is imprinted on our hearts. Something in our hearts and minds tells us that God is true because the Bible says it is true, and all creation bears witness to this.

When I witness to people, I do not try to convince them that there is a God. What I do is I take God's word for it, and I present the gospel to them. My hands are clean and clear because I have much more faith in God than in my ability to persuade someone analytically.

It says in Jeremiah, "The heart is deceitful above all things and desperately sick; who can understand it?" (Jer. 17:9). Deep down, our hearts know there is a God. We know there is a right and a wrong, and God deserves our worship. Yet we suppress the truth about God because we want freedom from Him so we can have the freedom to sin. When someone says they want freedom, it does not mean they want to live according to God's law of liberty. No, they want freedom *from* God. He may remove His hand of common grace in this person's life so that they might turn their heart to Him. But eventually and ultimately, if you continue to reject God, He will give you the desire of your heart; and you will be free from God for all eternity. Then, you will realize the grace that enveloped you in this life: the grace of air flowing in and out of your lungs, the grace that caused the ground to produce food, that kept blood circulating through your veins so your heart continued to beat, the common grace extended to all by the sovereign Lord of the universe. But mostly, it was the grace of God in the gospel that you trampled to hold on to the illusion that you were free and the lord of your own life.

REJECTING THE LIGHT

"For although they knew God, they did not honor him as God or give thanks to him, but they became futile in their thinking, and their foolish hearts were darkened. Claiming to be wise, they became fools, and exchanged the glory of the immortal God for images resembling mortal man and birds and animals and creeping things" (vv. 21-23).

Paul is writing to the people in his day, but this is true of all humanity in all times. He says, "Look to the God who created all things, the God who created the birds and the animals, the God who created nature, the God who created you. Why do you not worship Him? Why, instead, do you worship His creation? Why do you worship yourself?"

Our world is full of all sorts of immorality and deceit. One popular deception is the worship of nature and the idea that there is power in "Mother Nature." Extreme environmentalists believe that the world will end if they do not take control of things. God has given us this earth, and we should be good stewards of it; but God is in control of it, not man, not the weather or some vague spirituality we try to attribute to it. We worship all sorts of things: ourselves, sensuality, entertainment, sports. We worship the wicked desires of our hearts. We exchange the glory of the immortal God for lesser things. Yet everything we benefit from in this life comes from His hand. God gave us life, and He sustains the universe. We are not doing Him a favor when we worship Him; we owe Him praise, worship, and obedience. However, we suppress the truth about God because we do not want to give Him what rightfully belongs to Him.

When we reject the true source of knowledge, we become futile in our thinking. We turn off the light of the knowledge of God and His truth so that our sins will not be exposed. Jesus said, "For everyone who does wicked things hates the light and does not come to the light, lest his works should be exposed" (John 3:20). We want the benefit of light, but we do not want the Source of light—the Lord to Whom we must bow down before. When we resist the Light of the world, the only Source of life and light, we become futile in our thinking. The Bible says, "Your word is a lamp to my feet and a light to my path" (Psalm 119:105). According to John 1:1, Jesus is the Word, the Word made flesh and revealed in the written Scriptures.

We see just how futile and deceived our culture has become when highly educated academics and our world's so-called "thought leaders" are debating whether or not a man can give birth to a baby. Adults commit child abuse by propagating the destructive lie that boys can become girls, and girls can become boys, and that gender is merely an oppressive social construct rather than empirical and biological truth. They praise everything the Bible says is depraved and abominable, and basic logic has become a relic of the past.

When God created the world, He established a natural order. It is written, "And God saw everything that he had made, and behold, it was very good" (Gen. 1:31). When we say what God said is good, why is it not good enough? It is because we are depraved and debased in our minds. We want self-gratification as the standard of what is good more than anything else, and we ignore reality to have it. Some do it with addiction, some with sexual immorality, and some with arguing the basic logic of two genders, male and female. But we suppress the truth for the sake of gratifying our flesh at any cost.

The Bible says there are consequences to sin:

> But understand this, that in the last days there will come times of difficulty. For people will be lovers of self, lovers of money, proud, arrogant, abusive, disobedient to their parents, ungrateful, unholy, heartless, unappeasable, slanderous, without self-control, brutal, not loving good, treacherous, reckless, swollen with conceit, lovers of pleasure rather than lovers of God, having the appearance of godliness, but denying its power. Avoid such people (2 Tim. 3:1-5).

In Romans 1, Paul explains how God responds when we refuse to acknowledge and worship Him according to His Word.

> Therefore God gave them up in the lusts of their hearts to impurity, to the dishonoring of their bodies among themselves, because they exchanged the truth about God for a lie and worshiped and served the creature rather than the Creator, who is blessed forever! Amen. For this reason God gave them up to dishonorable passions. For their women exchanged natural relations for those that are contrary to nature; and the men likewise gave up natural relations with women and were consumed with passion for one another, men committing shameless acts with men and receiving in themselves the due penalty for their error (vv. 24-27).

Paul uses the word "therefore" to reflect his previous statements. The central statement of these verses is from verse 18a: "For the wrath of God is revealed from heaven against all ungodliness and unrighteousness of men." The wrath of God was revealed because they suppressed God's truth for the sake of sin. The wrath of God was revealed because they neither honored nor worshipped God. They worshipped themselves and the things God created.

In our culture, evolution means we are merely a product of an accident of nature. It is the survival of the fittest. There is no soul, no consequences. Our culture says there is no right or wrong in creation or nature. John MacArthur said, "The first indication in a society of the wrath of abandonment is sexual immorality. When a society becomes pornographic, when the general character of a society can be seen to be immoral, this wrath is in effect."[5] In other words, sexual immorality does not bring the judgment of God. Sexual immorality *is* the judgment of God. The sexual revolution of our culture is God's judgment upon us.

We decided we did not need God in the late 1800s and the early 1900s. By the 1960s, the sexual revolution exploded. It has contributed to millions of unwanted pregnancies and the legalization of abortion. We have abandoned our consciences when we murder babies in the womb because they are "inconvenient." Our society legalizes the killing of babies so we can engage in our sexual sins. It has intensified to the point where states are trying to pass legislation to murder babies up until and even after birth.

The progression of the sexual revolution over the last sixty years is staggering. What started as "free love," apart from what was viewed as the oppressive bounds of martial fidelity, has given way to every kind of perverted sexual act and lifestyle. It is also the causation of the wicked desire to murder unwanted babies produced from these godless acts. First, it did not matter whether someone was married or how many sexual partners they had. Now, it has advanced to a debate about whether we can allow children to take puberty blockers or mutilate their genitalia. What is it going to take for our culture to wake up? The only thing that will lighten their eyes to the truth is the Word of God. God's truth must pierce their hearts. We desperately need men with backbones to proclaim these truths from the pulpits of our churches. Not only does God command them to, but it is also unloving not to for this generation. We must not abandon proclaiming the truth of God's Word!

Sexual immorality is the body following the unrestrained desires of the wicked heart.

This is everything our society is about. Our culture is so pornographic we barely realize it anymore. God has taken His hands off of our nation to some extent and has let us revel in our sins and the consequences of those sins. John says, "Do not love the world or the things in the world. If anyone loves the world, the love of the Father is not in him. For all that is in the world—the desires of the flesh and the desires of the eyes and pride of life—is not from the Father but is from the world. And the world is passing away along with its desires, but whoever does the will of God abides forever" (1 John 2:15-17).

THE CREATED ORDER

For this reason God gave them up to dishonorable passions. For their women exchanged

natural relations for those that are contrary to nature; and the men likewise gave up

natural relations with women and were consumed with passion for one another, men

committing shameless acts with men and receiving in themselves the due penalty for

their error (vv. 26-27).

Most people who claim to know and fear the Lord are too cowardly to speak out about these things because they do not want to be called bigots or be accused of being unloving. You may be attracted to someone of the same sex, but God disapproves of this. It is neither good nor right. Yet if you have no established understanding of God's authority, who gets to decide what is right and wrong?

Our society says love is love; do not judge me. But sin is sin; and if we follow God, we must live in obedience to His created order. Rejecting God's created order brings harsh consequences. It is like rejecting the manufactured order of a vehicle you drive. You put the tires on backward, and the engine is upside down. The car is not running and cannot run properly because there is a right and created order that was intended by the manufacturer. We were created by God in His created order, for His purposes; and He, as the Creator, decides that order. The world hates God; and because of this, they hate God's created order. When God created man and woman, He said it was good; but the sexual revolution began and said it was not good. So we began to chase our own desires, and even many who do not engage in these abominations still bow down in acceptance of them.

A DEBASED MIND

And since they did not see fit to acknowledge God, God gave them up to a

debased mind to do what ought not to be done. They were filled with all manner of

unrighteousness, evil, covetousness, malice. They are full of envy, murder, strife, deceit, maliciousness. They are gossips, slanderers, haters of God, insolent, haughty, boastful, inventors of evil, disobedient to parents, foolish, faithless, heartless, ruthless (vv. 28-31).

A debased mind is so warped, dark, and wicked that we destroy ourselves because of our minds. We are destroying our families and society at the same time. We do not have to look back at the sexual revolution to find the poison that defiles us; all we need do is look at our pasts. Following your heart will destroy your life. But if you follow God, there is life, liberty, and salvation.

A debased mind is aimed at destroying itself and everything around it for the sake of momentary pleasure. This is what's destroying our children and society. Our minds are so debased and depraved that we are not only murderous, sexually immoral, and self-destructive; we also fight for the right to do these things. We celebrate these judgments as freedoms and attack anyone who would dare get in the way. This is our culture today, and our world's supposed brightest minds are at the forefront of this way of thinking. Those who celebrate the things God calls detestable do so because they hate God, so they invent new ways to be wicked. They are haughty and boastful in their sin. With their pride, they bring a double portion of judgment and destruction on themselves.

Pointing out this wickedness is not a message of hate but rather a message of love. We must call sinners to repentance, hoping their eyes might be opened and find God's gracious salvation. We preach repentance so sinners might be saved, refreshed, and renewed by God.

DESERVING OF DEATH

Though they know God's righteous decree that those who practice such things deserve to die, they not only do them but give approval to those who practice them (v. 32).

There is no middle ground. There are true servants and followers of Christ who proclaim the truth of God's Word and follow Jesus unashamedly. They will be saved and will gain eternal life. And then there are some who reject or are ashamed of the words of God in His Word and who live according to their desires. They will be destroyed. There is not a third group of people. There is no place for nominal Christians.

If you reject what the Bible says, it means God will be ashamed of you when He comes into the presence of His Holy Father. This is the Word of God preached in the book of Romans. It says, "The wrath of God will not only be poured out on those who practice such things but also those who approve of such things." Jesus said, "'Whoever is not with me is against me'" (Matt. 12:30).

Society is unraveling because we have rejected God, and now we are paying the price in an ever-increasing way. Can our culture be saved? I do not know the answer to that question, but I do know that "'everyone who calls upon the name of the Lord will be saved'" (Rom. 10:13). So whether America survives or not, there are millions of people here perishing who can be saved if we are brave and bold enough to tell them the truth. Some will dismiss, reject, and even mock our message; but some will repent and be saved! We must preach the gospel to a lost and dying world. We must tell people to repent because Jesus died for them. He wants to free them from the destruction of the world. If there is hope for this country, it will be because righteous men and women boldly proclaimed the power of the gospel. We must stand in open opposition to the immorality of this culture—done in Christ's love and Christ's truth.

STAND AND BE COUNTED

A message was given to Israel that we can apply to our day: "If my people who are called by my name humble themselves, and pray and seek my face and turn from their wicked ways" (2 Chron. 7:14a)—not just turn from their wicked ways but stop endorsing those who are evil and stand up and be counted as righteous. Remember, "the righteous shall live by faith" (Rom. 1:17). The verse continues, "Then I will hear from heaven and will forgive their sin and heal their land" (2 Chron. 7:14b). This Scripture does not refer to all or most people. It says "if *my* people"—if godly people—who proclaim to be Christians would humble themselves, pray, and cry out to God. Suppose they would humble themselves and turn from their wicked ways. Suppose they would combat the culture and speak the truth of the gospel. Then God says, "I will hear from heaven, and I will heal their land."

Here is a concluding Scripture:

> And now, brothers, I know that you acted in ignorance, as did also your rulers. But what God foretold by the mouth of all the prophets, that his Christ would suffer, he thus fulfilled. Repent therefore, and turn back, that your sins may be blotted out, that times of refreshing may come from the presence of the Lord, and that he may send the Christ appointed for you, Jesus, whom heaven must receive until the time for restoring all the things about which God spoke by the mouth of his holy prophets long ago (Acts 3:17-21).

The gospel is a message of repentance and salvation. But it is also a message of condemnation and judgment for those who reject Jesus. We cannot preach the gospel without coming into conflict with a lost and dying culture. There are preachers and Christians who are getting quieter and quieter about the wickedness of the world. Soon, nothing will be left to discuss except how Jesus loves you, quietly spoken from a small corner of your church.

In some countries, people are arrested for preaching in the streets. These countries do not need tolerant people. They need those willing to go into the streets and say, "I am not ashamed of the gospel, for it is the power of God for salvation to everyone who believes" (Rom. 1:16). What do abortion clinics need? They need men and women standing outside on the sidewalk saying, "Do not walk into that building. I know you are scared, but we will help you and your baby."

We are to be a people who deny ourselves, pick up our cross, and follow Him. On the other side of repentance is refreshment in the presence of the Lord, a clear conscience, peace with God, unbounded love, unmeasurable grace, peace, happiness, and eternal life. We are meant to give that to a lost and dying culture, but we cannot provide it without the message of repentance. Repent, stand up, and be counted because "'the righteous shall live by his faith'" (Hab. 2:4).

4

THE KINDNESS OF GOD THAT LEADS TO REPENTANCE

ROMANS 2:1–11

Therefore you have no excuse, O man, every one of you who judges. For in passing judgment on another you condemn yourself, because you, the judge, practice the very same things. We know that the judgment of God rightly falls on those who practice such things. Do you suppose, O man—you who judge those who practice such things and yet do them yourself—that you will escape the judgment of God? Or do you presume on the riches of his kindness and forbearance and patience, not knowing that God's kindness is meant to lead you to repentance? But because of your hard and impenitent heart you are storing up wrath for yourself on the day of wrath when God's righteous judgment will be revealed.

He will render to each one according to his works: to those who by patience in well-doing seek for glory and honor and immortality, he will give eternal life; but for those who are self-seeking and do not obey the truth, but obey unrighteousness, there will be wrath and fury. There will be tribulation and distress for every human being who does evil, the Jew first and also the Greek, but glory and honor and peace for everyone who does good, the Jew first and also the Greek. For God shows no partiality.

IN ROMANS CHAPTER ONE, WE read about God's righteous judgment on humanity and on cultures that reject God. We discussed how the judgment of God is being played out in our society today. However, it is important to understand that these Scriptures are not prophetic utterances toward America. God is speaking to the Gentile nations, explaining what will happen to *all* nations who reject God—nations who suppress the truth of righteousness for the sake of their sin. Since Christ's ascension over two thousand years ago, this rejection has played out repeatedly among the nations.

I have heard it said that it is unfair to say that one culture is better than another. I am not referring to a high-minded patriotic notion about one's country. However, there are differences between cultures; and the more a culture is patterned after the Word of God and the law of God, the better it will be. Even when the nation of Israel was following idols and turning away from God, there was a pattern laid out for them that they could return to. God was patient and kind as He tried to woo them back to Him repeatedly. As we know from biblical history, Israel did not listen; and eventually, God judged them. And this same pattern is happening in our culture today.

Cultures that strive to live according to God's principles are blessed even with imperfect and corrupt people. Many people today hate norms and established or traditional beliefs. They want to tear them down and say they are all evil. Not all progress is good, and not all change is good. But there is a pattern of blessing in the Bible; and the closer we live according to it, the better off we will be. However, this does not equate to salvation. Benefiting from a godly system in which you live or living a moral life does not make you right with God, and Paul is about to address this point regarding the Jews.

In Romans 1, Paul rebukes the Gentile nations. I am sure many Jews who listened to Paul's teaching agreed, saying, "Oh, yes, those Gentiles are immoral and wicked people." Nevertheless, Paul is about to address the Jews to remind them that they cannot be saved by the law either.

Proper worship of God means giving Him the fullness of your life as a being He created for His glory and His purposes. Paul says, "I appeal to you therefore, brothers, by the mercies of God, to present your bodies as a living sacrifice, holy and acceptable to God, which is your spiritual worship" (Rom. 12:1). However, because they did not serve God in this way, He turned them over to the futility of their wicked minds and hearts. They were cut off from the Source of knowledge. God turned them over to their debased minds and let them revel in their sin. He also let them revel in the consequences of their sin. They heaped more judgment and wrath on themselves to the point where people were confused about reality.

A prime example of this today is the rejection of God's created order regarding biological gender. This is "disorder" at its most fundamental level. To reject God as revealed in nature—or, more specifically, to reject His Word— is to deny knowledge, truth, reality, and the very Source of life.

GOD'S BENEVOLENCE

"Or do you presume on the riches of his kindness and forbearance and patience, not knowing that God's kindness is meant to lead you to repentance?" (v. 4)

As we begin Romans 2, let's examine verse four independently. These eleven verses are stated in the negative because they concern God's judgment. Nevertheless, we can assume some positive things here. It is often said, "It is the goodness or kindness of God that draws people to repentance." If we do not presume on the riches of God's kindness and patience, if we do heed the words of Scripture, and if we follow God, then that means God's kindness led us to repentance. The fact that God does not immediately judge us for our sins but allows us the opportunity to turn from our sins is the kindness and patience of God that is meant to lead us to repentance.

The benevolence of God means that His default disposition is kind, patient, loving, forbearing, giving, and good. God's judgment and wrath are being stored up for those who reject God, but it is equally important to understand that He is not just a God of wrath. He could have exacted judgment at any moment. He could have rightfully extinguished my life and called in my debts immediately. Some people get mad because they owe a debt they have not paid, and their account is sent to a collection agency. Often people get angry and bitter at bill collectors, forgetting that it is because they still owe the debt that they are being contacted.

Isn't this just like the twisted, wickedness of our minds? We are so used to God's forbearance and patience that we do not recognize it. We do not see the depths of our sinfulness nor realize how our best intentions or deeds are not good enough. God has extended charity toward humankind, but there is a price to pay for sin. God explained this to Moses in the wilderness on Mount Sinai:

> "The LORD descended in the cloud and stood with him there, and proclaimed the name of the LORD. The LORD passed before him and proclaimed, "The LORD, the LORD, a God merciful and gracious, slow to anger, and abounding in steadfast love and faithfulness, keeping steadfast love for thousands, forgiving iniquity and transgression and sin, but who will by no means clear the guilty, visiting the iniquity of the fathers on the children and the children's children, to the third and the fourth generation" (Exod. 34:5-7).

The gospel does not pardon our sins because God did not punish them. God punished them in His Son instead of in us. Understand, He still exacted His righteous justice and wrath. However, it was all centered on Christ instead of us. There is no time or situation when God's justice will not be satisfied. The question is if we will pay it as we suffer the consequences of our sin, which is death or benefit from the atoning work of Christ as He died on our behalf. There is no place where truth will not ultimately prevail. This is why we can only come to God humbly. We have done nothing, nor could we ever do enough to deserve His love or grace.

In the Sermon on the Mount, Jesus taught the crowd:

> You have heard that it was said, "You shall love your neighbor and hate your enemy." But I say to you, Love your enemies and pray for those who persecute you, so that you may be sons of your Father who is in heaven. For he makes his sun rise on the evil and on the good, and sends rain on the just and on the unjust. For if you love those who love you, what reward do you have? Do not even the tax collectors do the same? And if you greet only your brothers, what more are you doing than others? Do not even the Gentiles do the same? You therefore must be perfect, as your heavenly Father is perfect (Matt. 5:43-48).

God allows the rain to fall and produce crops from the ground for the just and the unjust. Even the Gentiles benefitted from the sun rising and the rain that watered their crops. God extends an immense amount of grace, known as common grace. In theology, there is a distinction between common grace and saving grace. The common grace of God allows us to have air pumping through our lungs and blood flowing through our veins and beating our hearts while we are God's enemies. Common grace implies that if we sow, we will reap. The sun and the rain will nourish the seeds we plant. Even wicked people benefit from common grace.

Those who do not believe in God often demand instant justice when they have been wronged. They get fixated on justice in this life because they do not believe in a future day of reckoning. People are interested in getting justice when they are the ones who have been wronged. But our posture changes drastically regarding our wrongdoing when we are in need of grace.

People who quote or paraphrase Romans 2:4 say, "It is the goodness of God that draws people to repentance." Typically, they are saying this to discourage people from discussing the hard truths in the Bible, such as the judgment of God, Heaven, and Hell. But this verse is sandwiched between a section of Scripture that is all about the wrath and judgment of God. I intend to state this positively because if we read it the way it is written, it is negative, not positive. It says, "You presume on the riches of God. You presume on the grace of God; and therefore, because of that, God's going to turn you over to an unrepentant or an impenitent heart." The first four chapters of Romans are heavy and somber, but we have to truly understand the holiness of God, the grievousness of sin, and just how desperate our situation is for us to value the saving grace of God in the gospel.

OH, HYPOCRITE!

"Therefore you have no excuse, O man, every one of you who judges.
For in passing judgment on another you condemn yourself, because you,
the judge, practice the very same things" (v. 1).

The word "therefore" in Scripture means we need to pay attention to what was previously written. In Romans 1, Paul gave a dissertation on God's wrath and judgment stored up for humanity for those who do not repent and follow God. Here, he is making it clear that those who consider themselves less depraved or more moral should not give themselves a free pass. A modern-day example is someone who embezzles money from his company while thinking a bank robber is a criminal, but not him. Isn't that what we do? We frame our sins in a way that lets us sleep at night. Paul is writing, "Be careful not to pass judgment on others for the same kinds of sins you practice." This is reminiscent of the words of Jesus:

> "Judge not, that you be not judged. For with the judgment you pronounce you will be judged, and with the measure you use it will be measured to you. Why do you see the speck that is in your brother's eye, but do not notice the log that is in your own eye? Or how can you say to your brother, 'Let me take the speck out of your eye,' when there is the log in your own eye? You hypocrite,

first take the log out of your own eye, and then you will see clearly
to take the speck out of your brother's eye."(Matt. 7:1-5).

We live in a culture that says you are judgmental if you speak the truth.
We all make judgments, but the Bible tells us to make righteous judgments.
There are two different types of judgment in Scripture—righteous and
truthful judgments according to God's Word and condemnation. Speaking
the truth of God's Word is not judgmental in the sense that it is wrong. We
are to proclaim the truth, but it is God Who administers condemnation.
Those who respond to the conviction of the Spirit will avoid condemnation.

In Matthew 7, Jesus says not to make hypocritical judgments. In other
words, do not call someone sexually immoral when you are living a sexually
immoral lifestyle. We cannot remove a little piece of sawdust from someone's
eye if a log obstructs our view. In other words, do not be a hypocrite! We
must make sure we are doing everything with the right heart and according
to God's Word. Christian living is examining our hearts, applying Scripture
to our lives, and living it out. Our words have more value when our lives bear
witness to the truth. The Jews were judging the Gentiles based on their lack
of moral law-keeping, but Paul is about to shatter this notion.

HYPOCRITICAL JUDGMENT

*"We know that the judgment of God rightly falls on those who practice such things.
Do you suppose, O man—you who judge those who practice such things and yet do
them yourself—that you will escape the judgment of God?" (vv. 2-3).*

These verses are about hypocritical judgments, including external
wickedness and internal and private evil-doing. Paul uses the word "know"
in verse two, translated from the Greek word *oda* or *odia*, implying formal
knowledge. He is making sure that the Jewish listeners understand that what

he is saying is not only for the Gentiles. Righteous wrath is being stored up for those who do wicked things. The Gentiles were without excuse because of the natural order of creation, which bears witness that there is a God. However, the Jews have a clearer indictment. They have the Law and the Prophets that revealed God's commands and the consequences for those who disobeyed.

NO ESCAPE

"Or do you presume on the riches of his kindness and forbearance and patience, not knowing that God's kindness is meant to lead you to repentance?" (v. 4).

Matthew Henry said, "There is in every willful sin an interpretive contempt of the goodness of God."[6] Willful sin shows evidence of our contempt for God. The King James translation uses the word "goodness" of God in Romans 2:4 instead of "kindness." That translation difference is because the meaning of the word "good" has changed since the King James Version was translated four hundred years ago. The goodness of God meant moral perfection. Everything God does, He does for the right reasons. Perfection and goodness are tied together. Nevertheless, do not mistake God's loving kindness for weakness. The wicked see the grace of God as an opportunity to continue in their sin. Yet a truly converted person understands the severity of God and His judgment, which gives an appreciation for God's grace. The true knowledge of God will produce holiness in one's life.

The word "holiness" means being set apart for God and His holy purposes. Israel was an example to the world as God's holy people. They were set apart and were supposed to be a peculiar people who stood out because they lived for God. So, we, too, are to be set apart. But there will come a day when every wicked thought, every deed, and everything we have ever done will be exposed. The apostle Peter writes:

> The Lord is not slow to fulfill his promise as some count slowness, but is patient toward you, not wishing that any should perish, but that all should reach repentance. But the day of the Lord will come like a thief, and then the heavens will pass away with a roar, and the heavenly bodies will be burned up and dissolved, and the earth and the works that are done on it will be exposed (2 Peter 3:9-10).

Many of the people Peter was ministering to seemed question the validity of the Lord's return. They wanted to know, when was this supposed day of the Lord coming? Peter responds by reminding them of the Great Flood of Noah's day. He says do not mistake God's loving kindness for slowness to keep His promised judgment or as weakness. In other words, do not "presume on the riches of his kindness and forbearance and patience" (Rom. 2:4). Many of us have spent our lives presuming on the riches of God's mercy. We go one more day, sin one more time, and tomorrow we will ask for forgiveness. God postponed judgment before the flood just as He does in the case of our lives today. He is loving and kind; but in the end, once His grace is rejected, there is no hope left—only the full measure of His wrath and judgment.

> For if we go on sinning deliberately after receiving the knowledge of the truth, there no longer remains a sacrifice for sins, but a fearful expectation of judgment, and a fury of fire that will consume the adversaries. Anyone who has set aside the law of Moses dies without mercy on the evidence of two or three witnesses. How much worse punishment, do you think, will be deserved by the one who has trampled underfoot the Son of God and has profaned the blood of the covenant by which he was sanctified and has outraged the Spirit of grace? For we know him who said, "Vengeance is mine; I will repay." And again, "The Lord will judge his people." It is a fearful thing to fall into the hands of the living God (Heb. 10:26-31).

In the law of Moses, if two or three witnesses testified against someone, that person could be put to death without question. To many people today, that seems like a harsh judgment. Often, we compare God's grace in the New Testament to what we perceive as harshness in the Old Testament. However, Hebrews 10 questions, "If those who did not have the full revelation of God and had not seen Christ could be judged so severely, how extreme will the judgment be for those who had access to the full revelation of Christ?" How severe will judgment be for those who reject the gospel of grace—those who go on sinning as they trample His precious blood, who reject God and the means of His grace—what a fearful and dreadful day that will be!

A PARADIGM SHIFT

In a letter to the Corinthians, Paul wrote, "Behold, now is the favorable time; behold, now is the day of salvation" (2 Cor. 6:2). God's mercies are renewed every day for us. Today is the day of truth and salvation. R.C. Sproul said, "The justice of God is so just that even the damned will not be able to deny the justice of his righteous judgment."[7] Hebrews 4:13 says, "And no creature is hidden from his sight, but all are naked and exposed to the eyes of him to whom we must give account." God's loving-kindness, goodness, and patience are meant to draw us to repentance.

The word repentance is from the Greek word *metanoia*, which means to have a change of mind or heart. This is not a frivolous change of mind but something that leads to a paradigm shift in action. The direction of one's life is completely changed. They were blind, but now they see; they were dead, but now they are alive. *Metanoia* means we have repented from our sin and have seen the error of our ways, not because of the consequences of our sin but because we have offended a holy God Who extends love, mercy, and grace to us. John MacArthur writes, "The purpose of the kindness of God is not to excuse men of their sin, but instead to convict them of it and lead them to repentance."[8] MacArthur refers to *metanoia* as a change of one's mind about sin, from loving it to renouncing it and turning to God for forgiveness.

To the church in Thessalonica, Paul wrote: "For they themselves report concerning us the kind of reception we had among you, and how you turned to God from idols to serve the living and true God, and to wait for his Son from heaven, whom he raised from the dead, Jesus who delivers us from the wrath to come" (1 Thess. 1:9-10). Paul is referring to the evidence that the gospel has transformed someone's life. A person who truly knows and fears the Lord will repent of their sins, discard their idols, and follow God. True repentance brings a change in life and a change in action. It is not about perfection; it is about a changed mind. The sin we once loved, we now hate.

THE GOODNESS OF GOD

"But because of your hard and impenitent heart you are storing up wrath for yourself on the day of wrath when God's righteous judgment will be revealed" (v. 5).

It is important to reread Romans 2:4 along with this verse. The "goodness of God" is the opportunity to repent. If repentance is not a part of the gospel we proclaim, then we distort the truth of the gospel. Repentance is what the gospel is meant to produce in our lives. If the gospel is merely reciting a prayer to receive salvation without understanding the life change needed to serve God, then the prayer is in vain. Those who take verse four out of context distort the truth that the goodness of God is the ability and opportunity He has given us to repent. Those who distance the message of judgment and wrath from the goodness of God completely pervert Scripture. The New American Standard Bible translates the term unrepentant instead as "impenitent." Both words have the same meaning, and Paul refers to the opposite of being repentant over sin.

FROM HOPELESSNESS TO REPENTANCE

"He will render to each one according to his works: to those who by patience in well-doing seek for glory and honor and immortality, he will give eternal life; but for those who are self-seeking and do not obey the truth, but obey unrighteousness, there will be wrath and fury" (vv. 6-8).

Once we forsake the only means of grace that God has given us in the gospel of Jesus Christ and trample the blood that Christ shed for us, there is nothing left to save us. All that is left is a hardening of our hearts and fearful expectation of the wrath that is to come. Charles Spurgeon noted:

> I believe the gospel makes some men in this world more miserable than they would be. The drunkard could drink and could revel in his intoxication with greater joy, if he did not hear it said, "All drunkards shall have their portion in the lake that burneth with fire and brimstone." How jovially the Sabbath-breaker would riot through his Sabbaths if the Bible did not say, "Remember the Sabbath day to keep it holy!" And how happily could the libertine and licentious man drive on his mad career if he were not told, "The wages of sin is death and after death the judgment!" But the truth put the bitter in his cup; the warnings of God freeze the current of his soul.
>
> The truth of the gospel in the Scripture shines bright as the midday sun. And let us remember it's the same sun that melts the wax that also hardens the clay and the same gospel that melts some persons to repentance hardens others in their sin.[9]

NO PARTIALITY

"There will be tribulation and distress for every human being who does evil, the Jew first and also the Greek, but glory and honor and peace for everyone who does good, the Jew first and also the Greek. For God shows no partiality" (vv. 9-11).

Paul addresses every individual, which is bad news for those seeking God through worldly wisdom, as the Greeks did. It is terrible news for the Jews who demand signs. Paul is creating despair and building up to a point where he will eventually say, "For all have sinned and fall short of the glory of God" (Rom. 3:23). It is hopelessness apart from Christ, first for the Jew but also for the Gentile. We will never come to the saving knowledge of the gospel until we see the hopelessness of our personal goodness. Paul is referring to the Gentiles who are reveling in sin and also the religious law-keeping Jews who think they are better than the Gentiles.

> But now the righteousness of God has been manifested apart from the law, although the Law and the Prophets bear witness to it—the righteousness of God through faith in Jesus Christ for all who believe. For there is no distinction: for all have sinned and fall short of the glory of God, and are justified by his grace as a gift, through the redemption that is in Christ Jesus, whom God put forward as a propitiation by his blood, to be received by faith. This was to show God's righteousness, because in his divine forbearance he had passed over former sins. It was to show his righteousness at the present time, so that he might be just and the justifier of the one who has faith in Jesus (Rom. 3:21-26).

This is why Paul says, "For I am not ashamed of the gospel, for it is the power of God for salvation to everyone who believes, to the Jew first and also to the Greek" (Rom. 1:16). In this chapter, it says that there is hopelessness; and there will be wrath and judgment first for the Jew and then the Greek. Paul is talking to the whole world, and he is going to build a stronger and stronger case against the Gentiles and the Jews. But the good news is that we see that God shows no partiality in judgment or in salvation. God is not a respecter of persons. He is a respecter of the principles of His gospel and His Word. All who call upon the name of the Lord will be saved. "For in Christ Jesus you are all sons of God, through faith. For as many of you as were baptized into Christ have put on

Christ. There is neither Jew nor Greek, there is neither slave nor free, there is no male and female, for you are all one in Christ Jesus. And if you are Christ's, then you are Abraham's offspring, heirs according to promise" (Gal. 3:26-29).

The promise that God gave Abraham is not only for ethnic and geographical Jews. It is for the true descendants of Abraham who are grafted in through Christ. Here, we see the consistent principles of the perfect law of the Lord. God is not wavering. He is unchanging, perfect in judgment, perfect in justice, and rich in mercy. The more we see God's justice and judgment, the more beautiful and precious the grace of God in the gospel becomes. The true Christian does not despise the law. He loves it because it is the character of a holy God. The law of God is meant to show us our need for the grace of God. We cannot despise the law of God because it is evidence of his holy perfection.

The more we understand the law of God, the more correctly we can apply the gospel of God. No one conceptualizes this better than Charles Spurgeon: "I do not believe that any man can preach the gospel who does not preach the law. The law is the needle, and you cannot draw the silken thread of the gospel through a man's heart unless you have first pierced it with the needle of the law to make way for it."[10]

In the first part of Romans, Paul asks this question of *all* of us: "Do you presume on the riches and the kindness and forbearance and patience of God, not knowing that God's kindness is meant to lead you to repentance?" (Rom. 2:4). If the Word of God does not pierce our hearts, there is no room for the gospel. The gospel cannot be applied externally; it must be applied internally. It is not about our good works but about being broken before a holy God and repenting. It is about seeing God for Who He is and, in light of that, seeing ourselves for who we are. Once the gospel has taken hold of our hearts, we will begin to change and become less self-serving, self-seeking, and selfishly ambitious. We will start to emulate the character of God: love, joy, peace, patience, kindness, goodness, faithfulness, gentleness, and self-control. We must God's kindness lead us to repentance.

5

BROUGHT TO DESPAIR UNDER THE LAW

ROMANS 2:12-29

For all who have sinned without the law will also perish without the law, and all who have sinned under the law will be judged by the law. For it is not the hearers of the law who are righteous before God, but the doers of the law who will be justified. For when Gentiles, who do not have the law, by nature do what the law requires, they are a law to themselves, even though they do not have the law. They show that the work of the law is written on their hearts, while their conscience also bears witness, and their conflicting thoughts accuse or even excuse them on that day when, according to my gospel, God judges the secrets of men by Christ Jesus.

But if you call yourself a Jew and rely on the law and boast in God and know his will and approve what is excellent, because you are instructed from the law; and if you are sure that you yourself are a guide to the blind, a light to those who are in darkness, an instructor of the foolish, a teacher of children, having in the law the embodiment of knowledge and truth—you then who teach others, do you not teach yourself? While you preach against stealing, do you steal? You who say that one must not commit adultery, do you commit adultery? You who abhor idols, do you rob temples? You who boast in the law dishonor God by breaking the law. For, as it is written, "The name of God is blasphemed among the Gentiles because of you."

For circumcision indeed is of value if you obey the law, but if you break the law, your circumcision becomes uncircumcision. So, if a man who is uncircumcised keeps the precepts of the law, will not his uncircumcision be regarded as circumcision? Then he who is physically uncircumcised but keeps the law will condemn you who have the written code and circumcision but break the law. For no one is a Jew who is merely one outwardly, nor is circumcision outward and physical. But a Jew is one inwardly, and circumcision is a matter of the heart, by the Spirit, not by the letter. His praise is not from man but from God.

APOSTLE PAUL HAS GUIDED US through the first two chapters of Romans, focusing on God's patience, kindness, and goodness that lead us to repentance. God's law demonstrates His goodness in that He does not exact judgment instantaneously. We all live on borrowed time or credit from God, but many live in the midst of His goodness while not experiencing its fullness. Often, we only look to God when we want or need something, when we hope He can make us feel better, or in the hope that He will validate or justify our actions. But when it comes to the reality of what God's righteous character demands from humanity, we suppress that knowledge. Romans 1 explains that we do this so that we can live and engage in sin while pretending to have a "clear conscience." Yet our conscience is not clear and gets darker the more we suppress the truth of God. When we remove ourselves from the reality and knowledge of God, nature, our hearts, and our conscience remind us that we were made in the image of God. Our purpose in life is to worship and glorify Him. When we live outside of honoring God with our lives, we deny Him; and our hearts begin to harden toward Him.

People often question the existence of evil in the world and wonder why God does not immediately eradicate evil and sin from the world. We often look at horrific sins committed in our world and ask, where is God's justice? However, if we truly processed that question, we would understand that if God exacted His justice immediately, we would *all* perish. We often deceive ourselves into believing that our sin is somehow less wicked than others; but all sin comes from the same root, and "the wages of [all] sin is death" (Rom. 6:23).

In conversation, someone asked why I do not refer to the love of God more when I talk about the gospel. I explained that the gospel *is* the love of God. When we want God to approve of our sins or accept us outside of the purpose we were created for, that is not love. Doing what someone wants to make them feel good is not love. Love is doing what is right for someone, no matter the cost. It is reprimanding your son or daughter for playing in a busy street because you do not want them to get hurt. Sometimes, love is encouragement; sometimes, it is telling someone no; but it is always doing what is right—and never at the expense of the truth. That is what love is all about.

When God corrects and reproves us and points us to the way of righteousness, He does it because He loves us. He knows where we will find satisfaction in life and where we will be complete. He knows what we need in our hearts to stop chasing the frivolity and the perishing treasures of this world.

In our lives before Christ and in the lives of others who have not yet been saved and regenerated, God's goodness, patience, and loving kindness postpone judgment in hopes that men and women will be drawn to repentance. Paul ends chapter two, verse eleven by explaining that "God shows no partiality," which launches us into the following verses.

THE LAW SET IN MOTION

"For all who have sinned without the law will also perish without the law, and all who have sinned under the law will be judged by the law" (v. 12).

Paul is not saying that the law is unimportant. He is explaining that the mechanism set in place by the curse—in contrast to the law of God—will naturally occur whether or not we know why it is happening. A person who has studied physics understands the why and how of our planet's gravitational pull. If we jump off a house, the pull of gravity will bring us to the ground. The physics will work in this situation whether or not we understand why we are being pulled down. This is the same with the law of God. The moral law of God is the character of a holy God. The law of God in the Ten Commandments in Exodus 20 is proposed to us in negatives: "'you shall not steal'" (v. 15); "'you shall not murder'" (v. 13); "you shall have no other gods before me" (v. 3); and so on. But the positive side is what we should be doing. We should love and obey God and show love to those around us. The curse brought selfishness, self-centeredness, and a disconnection from God. God wants us to live in fellowship with Him and harmony with others.

Jesus agreed when the law was summarized: "'Love the Lord your God with all your heart and with all your soul and with all your strength and with all your mind, and your neighbor as yourself'" (Luke 10:27). This summarizes the law; yet in our fallen minds, we think that as long as we love God and try to be nice to people, we can keep the law perfectly. No! There has never been a person who has loved the Lord their God with "all [their] heart and with all [their] soul and with all of [their] strength and with all of [their] mind." There has never been a person who has "loved [their] neighbor as [themselves]" for every moment of their life. There may be moments when we have loved our neighbors or given ourselves sacrificially; but inside, it is a battle to live this way at all times, even toward those we love dearly. To perfectly keep the law, we have to keep it at all points.

When Paul talks about the law being a law unto itself for the Gentiles, he is not saying that they would be justified by it, just like there was no possibility that the Jews would be justified by it. Nevertheless, he is saying that there are times when the Gentiles can do what is right because the law is written in their hearts, they have consciences, and they are made in the image of God. Even though they are corrupted by sin, they still have the imprint of the Creator on them. God does not show partiality in His administration of justice.

The symbol of our American legal system is a woman blindfolded, holding the scales of justice in her hand. Those administering justice in our culture are not perfect, but the goal is to administer justice without partiality. It is a lofty goal because we are imperfect people; but when our society was founded, the idea was that justice and truth would decide right from wrong. The blindfold represents that there should be no partiality in our judicial system. Considering all of the circumstances, we should do our best to administer the law justly and fairly to everyone. God always administers justice fairly and properly. He is a just Judge. The evidence of our faith is when we realize that we have entrusted ourselves to the Judge Who judges justly. God is sovereign and has us in the palm of His hand.

The apostle Peter said, "If you call on him as Father who judges impartially according to each one's deeds, conduct yourselves with fear throughout the time of your exile" (1 Peter 1:17). Peter is referring to our temporary life. We are not building a kingdom here; this is not our home. We are exiles; and if we understand that God judges each of us according to our deeds, we will live in reverent fear of God. He is a just God Who takes into consideration the knowledge we have, and He judges us accordingly. Those who have the law will be judged more harshly because they have more access to the truth.

In America, we are out of excuses. Everyone has access to the Bible and to finding the truth. Many are living in a false dichotomy, claiming God is nowhere to be found. The truth is God has sought them and sought them, but they have hardened their hearts. Many profess, "I want a different way. Give me a religion that affirms my identity and how I want to live my life." That is the idolatrous religion of America—the ministry of prosperity, the church of self-love and self-centeredness. Do we understand that our biggest problem as humans is being self-centered? When God says, "'Love the Lord your God with all your heart . . . soul . . . and with all your mind, and your neighbor as yourself'" (Luke 10:27), it does not mean first to love yourself and cut out toxic people. No, He says, "Seek his kingdom" (Luke 12:31). When we spend our lives worrying about comfort and success, it will leave us empty, lost, and broken. Seek His kingdom and let God worry about you.

There is a fallacy that says people who have not heard the Word of God will not be judged according to the law of God. Some foolishly Believe people who live in far-off cultures who have not heard about God are safe for God's righteous wrath and judgement. I do not entirely understand how God disseminates the gospel according to His sovereign will. However, if that thinking is true, we have done a great disservice to the world by sending missionaries all around the globe. Then, was Jesus wrong when He said, "'Go therefore and make disciples of all nations, baptizing them in the name of the Father and of the Son and of the Holy Spirit'" (Matt. 28:19)?

We should not worry about how God administers justice to other people; instead, we need to be faithful witnesses of God. It is a way of thinking that is looking for a loophole to escape God's justice when we believe the person on an island somewhere who does not hear the name of Jesus will not be judged fairly. We have to search our hearts. If we are concerned because that person might perish and go to Hell, then why aren't we on a boat headed that way? We must examine our intentions and motives when we question God's goodness or try to pit it against God's justice.

EVIDENCE OF FAITH

"For it is not the hearers of the law who are righteous before God,
but the doers of the law who will be justified" (v. 13).

This means that while the Jewish people of Paul's day and age had heard the law and had lived according to the law to some extent, they will not be justified by the law. To be justified by the law, we must be doers of it, which means doers in perfection. Remember, justification through the law differs from justification by grace through faith in Christ. To be justified through the law, we must live according to it perfectly. To be justified by Christ and grace, we must have a heart willing to be transformed.

In the gospel, God is transforming us to live according to the law, but no one on this side of Heaven is living up to it perfectly. Understand that our good deeds or following God's precepts are insufficient to earn justification or receive a place in Heaven. Still, our good works are evidence that we have been transformed. Some preachers fear this teaching because it may lead sinners to run amok in their sins. But if someone has been reborn in Christ, they will want to live for God. If they do not, it might indicate they are not saved. As a preacher of God's Word, I cannot change you; all I can do is preach the truth.

> If you really fulfill the royal law according to the Scripture, "You shall love your neighbor as yourself," you are doing well. But if you show partiality, you are committing sin and are convicted by the law as transgressors. For whoever keeps the whole law but fails in one point has become guilty of all of it. For he who said, "Do not commit adultery," also said, "Do not murder." If you do not commit adultery but do murder, you have become a transgressor of the law. So speak and so act as those who are to be judged under the law of liberty. For judgment is without mercy to one who has shown no mercy. Mercy triumphs over judgment (James 2:8-13).

Jesus also addressed this in Matthew 5 when he referred to adultery and murder. If you even look at a woman with lust or you have been angry with someone, the sin has been committed in the heart. God is not just concerned with the bright, shiny fruit on the end of the tree; He is equally concerned with the root that produces that fruit. We already know God's default disposition—mercy triumphs over judgment. God has gone to great lengths to show us mercy. The law is meant to be a mirror to show us how sinful and needy we are. We often feel pretty good about ourselves until we are compared to the perfection of God. That is precisely the purpose of the moral law of God.

King David referred to the law of God as a heavy weight that crushed him, and yet he contrasted the law as bringing him liberty and happiness, exclaiming, "Oh how I love your law!" (Psalm 119:97). David wanted to live up to the law because he loved God, but he realized that he could not.

James describes what the law of God is supposed to do in our lives:

> But be doers of the word, and not hearers only, deceiving yourselves. For if anyone is a hearer of the word and not a doer, he is like a man who looks intently at his natural face in a mirror. For he looks at himself and goes away and at once forgets what he was like. But the one who looks into the perfect law, the law of liberty, and perseveres, being no hearer who forgets but a doer who acts, he will be blessed in his doing (James 1:22-25).

If we do not see God as holy and ourselves as sinful, we will never see grace as a precious lifeline. He is our only means of salvation. For those who are saved by grace through faith in Christ, being doers of the Word is evidence that we are saved, not a means to salvation. Jesus concludes the Sermon on the Mount with these powerful words:

> "Everyone then who hears these words of mine and does them will be like a wise man who built his house on the rock. And the rain fell, and the floods came, and the winds blew and beat on that house, but it did not fall, because it had been founded on the rock. And everyone who hears these words of mine and does not do them will be like a foolish man who built his house on the sand. And the rain fell, and the floods came, and the winds blew and beat against that house, and it fell, and great was the fall of it" (Matt. 7:24-27).

In Matthew 5-7, Jesus pointed to Himself as the narrow way to salvation. He told the crowd that He did not come to abolish the law but to fulfill it perfectly. The narrow way "leads to life," and only a few will find it (Matt. 7:13-14). It is not in the universe or through a perception or idea. Christ is revealed in the Scripture. Jesus says throughout the Gospel of John, "'I am the door'" (10:9); "'I am the good shepherd'" (10:11); "'I am the way, and the truth, and the life. No one comes through the Father except through me'" (14:6). Jesus is the only Way. From Genesis to Revelation, we must build our lives on this promise of Christ and His Word. The evidence of our faith is that we can withstand the storms of life and persevere to the end because our lives are built on Christ.

Paul wants the Jews to understand that the law was not meant to save them but instead to make them despair so they would recognize their need for salvation that is only found through faith in Christ. His was the purpose of all the types and shadows of the Old Covenant. They were meant to point us to Christ. Overcoming trials as we put our faith and trust in God is evidence of our salvation. This does not mean we will never fall into temptation. However, when tempted, we realize that part of our lives is not built on the Rock. So we repent and continue to follow Jesus. This is sanctification, and it is a messy and lifelong process. Charles Spurgeon said, "The law is for the self-righteous to humble their pride and the gospel is for the lost to remove their despair."[11]

Someone might think their goodness is good enough: the Jew who follows the law or the middle-class American who attends church their whole life and gives to charity. But if their lives are not firmly built on the rock of Christ, they have to come to despair before they can benefit from the gospel. They have to compare their lives to God, realizing they are lost and sinful and that their good deeds are like filthy rags. Salvation begins with the fear of the Lord. "The fear of the Lord is the beginning of wisdom, and the knowledge of the Holy One is insight" (Prov. 9:10). The self-righteous must be brought to despair before being brought to grace.

THE WORK OF THE LAW

"For when Gentiles, who do not have the law, by nature do what the law requires,

they are a law to themselves, even though they do not have the law. They show that the

work of the law is written on their hearts, while their conscience also bears witness,

and their conflicting thoughts accuse or even excuse them on that day when,

according to my gospel, God judges the secrets of men by Christ Jesus" (vv. 14-16).

The Jew is condemned directly by the law of God, but the Gentile is condemned because they reject the knowledge of God displayed in creation. Because we are made in the very image of God, the law is written on our hearts; and our conscience bears witness to our sins. The Gentiles have reasoning minds, yet they purposely ignore their consciences. When we go down the wrong path, we willfully ignore our conscience. The first lie, the first thing stolen, the first lustful stare—it starts a process, but the nature of corruption was already there. It is a process of stifling and silencing our conscience and reasoning ourselves into all kinds of sins. The Gentiles are without excuse, but the Jews are entirely without excuse because the law is not only written on their hearts but also was revealed to them in the Scripture.

In verse sixteen, Paul says, "God judges the secrets of men by Jesus Christ." On the day of judgment, our motives will be exposed. God rightfully and accurately judges our sinful motives. In our legal system, the court judges based on evidence; all we have to do is prove our innocence beyond a reasonable doubt to be acquitted. However, God will judge our intentions and our secrets. Those in Christ will want the truth exposed so we can live in forgiveness and freedom from our sins.

When Jesus was preaching to a group of Jews, He said, "'Blessed are the poor in spirit, for theirs is the kingdom of heaven'" (Matt. 5:3). To be poor in spirit means that we recognize that we are spiritually desperate and needy and have no remedy to fix this. "'Blessed are those who mourn, for they shall be comforted'" (Matt. 5:4). The Pharisees were known as keepers of the law. Why would they need to mourn? But Jesus is teaching that *only* those who mourn and lament over their sin will be comforted on the day of judgment.

"'Blessed are the meek, for they shall inherit the earth'" (Matt. 5:5). The person who meekly puts their trust in God will inherit the earth along with Christ as his co-heir. Before God fills us and satisfies us in Himself, we must first come to despair by seeing the reality of our situation. Pastor John Piper refers to this as a state of holy emptiness.

This is what the first three Beatitudes are about in Matthew 5. We see and acknowledge we are poor and needy, mourn, lament, and repent over our sins, and meekly put our trust in God. God promised that those who come to this place of holy emptiness will hunger and thirst to be right with Him, and they will be satisfied. They will find satisfaction in Christ. "'Blessed are those who hunger and thirst for righteousness, for they will be satisfied'" (Matt. 5:6).

To be saved from the wrath and judgment of God, you must want to be right with God. Those who believe they are right with themselves or right with the universe and do not have faith in Christ alone are in a terrible and desperate situation. Faith in anything other than the exclusive nature of the cross of Christ is despair; those who do not recognize that despair will never come to the cross humbly. Grace is for the humble. There will not be proud people in Heaven—only thankful, grateful, saved people. Nothing is worse than denying the truth and finding false security in something untrue, especially when eternity is at stake.

DECEIVED BY RELIGION

But if you call yourself a Jew and rely on the law and boast in God and know his will and approve what is excellent, because you are instructed from the law; and if you are sure that you yourself are a guide to the blind, a light to those who are in darkness, an instructor of the foolish, a teacher of children, having in the law the embodiment of knowledge and truth—you then who teach others, do you not teach yourself? While you preach against stealing, do you steal? You who say that one must not commit adultery,

do you commit adultery? You who abhor idols, do you rob temples? You who boast in

the law dishonor God by breaking the law. For, as it is written, "The name of God is

blasphemed among the Gentiles because of you" (vv. 17-24).

The Pharisees exacted a legalistic and harsh brand of religious observance on the people, which neither the people nor even they could live up to. Paul essentially told them the same thing Jesus did: "You are so worried about cleaning the outside of the cup, but shouldn't we clean the inside first?" (Matt. 23:26). We have to think about these verses in context. Paul is talking to the Jews who think their goodness is good enough. He is trying to bring them to despair by looking at the perfection of the law, showing them Who God is, and wanting them to look at themselves in contrast. He knows that if the law is not humbling them, they are not looking at it properly. There is something distorted in their minds.

Legalism produces two kinds of people. In those who are self-deceived about themselves, it produces proud Pharisees; and in those who are honest, it produces despair. The difference between the type of despair legalism produces and the kind a proper administration of law produces is this: legalism produces despair without hope, and a proper understanding of the law produces despair that magnifies our need for Christ.

Although the Jews were God's set apart and chosen people through whom many wonderful and godly things were given to us, they were also very self-deceived as a people, as we all are. Anytime we disobey and think we know better than God's Word, we will find ourselves in a bad situation. This was the reason why they wandered for forty years in the wilderness. The book of Judges details how the people "did what was right in his own eyes" (Judges 17:6). They rejected God as King to have a human king like the Gentile nations. Their continual rejection of the very Word of God through the prophets and their idolatry led to captivity and slavery. They even rejected God Himself when Jesus took on flesh to bring salvation first to the Jews and then to the Gentiles. The Jews rejected Him; they hated Him; and they murdered Him.

Paul is intentional in his examination of the Jews. They are God's chosen people. They are the keepers of the oracles of the law, set apart for God's glory; but they needed a Savior every bit as much as the Gentiles did, and this was always God's plan. If the Jewish people who had the law needed a Savior, then how much more do *we* need salvation? Paul is teaching the Jews that they are just as desperate and needy as the Gentiles. The Jews believed that they were better *than*, more theological *than*, and closer to God *than* the Gentiles. But Paul is saying that even if Jews have good orthodoxy, they do not have good orthopraxy. They are hearers and teachers of the Word but not doers of the Word.

In verse twenty-four, Paul quotes the prophet Isaiah: "'The name of God is blasphemed among the Gentiles because of you'" (Rom. 2:24). What is worse than doing evil? Doing evil in God's name. This is why Jesus was so harsh to the Pharisees, and it is why we need to expose false teachers who are like wolves in sheep's clothing. They use God to empower themselves and blaspheme His name to deceive people and sheer His precious sheep.

Psalm 50 warns:

> But to the wicked God says: "What right have you to recite my statutes or take my covenant on your lips? For you hate discipline, and you cast my words behind you. If you see a thief, you are pleased with him, and you keep company with adulterers. You give your mouth free rein for evil, and your tongue frames deceit. You sit and speak against your brother; you slander your own mother's son. These things you have done, and I have been silent; you thought that I was one like yourself. But now I rebuke you and lay the charge before you. "Mark this, then, you who forget God, lest I tear you apart, and there be none to deliver! The one who offers thanksgiving as his sacrifice glorifies me; to one who orders his way rightly I will show the salvation of God" (vv. 16-23).

Those thankful to God for their lives will have the proper perspective of who they are. The truth sets them free (John 8:32), and thankfulness and gratitude are evidence of that. Those people have experienced God's salvation and are living for others, not for themselves. Paul points out two main problems with how the Jews viewed and used the law. First, they were hypocrites; and second, they misunderstood its purpose.

Jesus had the same problem with the Pharisees and the ruling council. He did not have a problem with the law but with the hypocritical nature in which they administered it. They harshly and dogmatically applied it to the people but not to themselves, demonstrating that they misunderstood the purpose of the law. Rightly applying the law to oneself will bring humility, not pride. In turn, one will administer the law with humility and not pride. If the law of God's holy perfection makes us prideful, it shows that we are blind to God's holy perfection and our own wretched sinfulness. If we are students of the Bible and it is not producing humility in us, it is evidence that we are not understanding who God is.

The Jews were falsely secure in their heritage, knowledge, and religious ceremonies. They were puffed up and conceited rather than brought low in humility. They referred to the Gentiles as the "uncircumcised." The Jews had the physical symbol of circumcision, which meant they belonged to God. They arrogantly said, "See, we are God's people." However, Paul responds that it is not as much about the outward symbol of being circumcised but whether we are circumcised in our hearts.

There may be evidence of being set apart for God on the outside, but what about on the inside? Holiness means to be set apart for God. Like baptism, we have to decide that when we are raised up from that water, we leave our old life behind and are raised in Christ. It is a symbolic gesture professing to society that our lives are not our own—we are dead to sin but alive in Christ. However, our security is not in baptism or any good deeds. Our security rightly applies the law to our lives, and we are humbled—finding grace, love, and peace in Christ alone.

CIRCUMCISION OF THE HEART

For circumcision indeed is of value if you obey the law, but if you break the law, your circumcision becomes uncircumcision. So, if a man who is uncircumcised keeps the precepts of the law, will not his uncircumcision be regarded as circumcision? Then he who is physically uncircumcised but keeps the law will condemn you who have the written code and circumcision but break the law. For no one is a Jew who is merely one outwardly, nor is circumcision outward and physical. But a Jew is one inwardly, and circumcision is a matter of the heart, by the Spirit, not by the letter. His praise is not from man but from God (vv. 25-29).

Paul is referring to circumcision as symbolic and reminding them not to live by the letter of the law while forgetting the spirit of the law. The law was meant to bring the Jews to despair. God commanded Abraham and all of his descendants to be circumcised as an outward symbol that they were God's chosen people and set apart. It reminded them of their sinfulness and that the seed of corruption and sin was to be made right through living in holiness. It was supposed to be an act of holiness and humbling; instead, it made them prideful.

The law was meant to bring the Jews to despair and to cause them to lament, mourn, and repent of their sins. God promises He will comfort this type of person in the gospel. What good is the outward symbolism if it doesn't make us lament our sins? What good is water baptism if it is not the beginning of a life lived for Christ, if it is not representative of an inner man who is dead to sin and alive in Christ? Why take the bread and wine of communion if we are not truly doing it in remembrance of His broken body and His shed blood? Remember, Jesus said, "Do this in remembrance of me'" (Luke 22:19).

Many of the Jews had become so arrogant and prideful in themselves that the symbolism and the ceremonial law had become more important than the actual meaning of it. Circumcision had become something that made them feel superior instead of humbling them and causing them to lament their sins and focus on being set apart for the glory of God. The civic law was to keep peace and order in the land. The moral law was meant to bring us to despair in ourselves so that we would long for a Savior, and every part of the ceremonial law was meant to point us to that Savior.

There is no righteousness in law-keeping in and of itself. The answer is not inside us, our good works, or our church membership. Meditating on the law will bring the realization that we cannot keep it. Therefore, we cannot be saved by it. But gazing and meditating on Jesus shows us that one Man did perfectly keep the law—fulfilling it and proving that He is God and worthy of our lives and our praise.

The law should bring despair, so a person can rightly receive the gospel of grace. Then, that person will graciously administer the gospel to others. We need the law to break our hearts so that we can receive the grace of God. The apostle Paul wants the Jews to recognize this grace, call upon the Lord, and be saved. Both Jews and Gentiles alike must see the law of God as the diagnosis and the gospel of Jesus Christ as the only cure for what ails the heart of man.

6

EXPOSING THE TRUE HEART OF HUMANITY

ROMANS 3:1-20

Then what advantage has the Jew? Or what is the value of circumcision? Much in every

way. To begin with, the Jews were entrusted with the oracles of God. What if some were

unfaithful? Does their faithlessness nullify the faithfulness of God? By no means! Let

God be true though every one were a liar, as it is written, "That you may be justified in

your words, and prevail when you are judged." But if our unrighteousness serves to show

the righteousness of God, what shall we say? That God is unrighteous to inflict wrath on

us? (I speak in a human way.) By no means! For then how could God judge the world?

But if through my lie God's truth abounds to his glory, why am I still being condemned

as a sinner? And why not do evil that good may come?—as some people slanderously

charge us with saying. Their condemnation is just. What then? Are we Jews any better

off? No, not at all. For we have already charged that all, both Jews and Greeks, are

under sin, as it is written: "None is righteous, no, not one; no one understands; no one

seeks for God. All have turned aside; together they have become worthless; no one does

good, not even one." Their throat is an open grave; they use their tongues to deceive.

The venom of asps is under their lips. Their mouth is full of curses and bitterness. Their

feet are swift to shed blood; in their paths are ruin and misery, and the way of peace

they have not known. There is no fear of God before their eyes. Now we know that

whatever the law says it speaks to those who are under the law, so that every mouth

may be stopped, and the whole world may be held accountable to God. For by works
of the law no human being will be justified in his sight, since through the law comes
knowledge of sin.

AS I MENTIONED IN THE previous chapter, the first part of Romans conveys some heavy topics. Still, it is imperative that we lay out these doctrines sufficiently to understand just how good the good news of the gospel really is. Romans 3 begins with a deep look into the state of the human heart and humanity's sinful nature. Up to this point, the apostle Paul has established the gospel as the power of God unto salvation, explaining that its scope and power include Jews and Gentiles alike. He explains the unavoidable reality of God's looming judgment on the Gentiles and Jews by saying, "Gentiles will die outside the law, while Jews will die under the law. No one can be saved under the law because that was never its purpose. It was meant to point us toward the only one who can save us.

Some professed Christians believe that God had an original plan for humanity; but because Adam and Eve fell, that plan was scrapped because we couldn't live up to it. So God returned to the "drawing board" to figure out another way. However, it is important to understand that the gospel was not the backup plan; it was always the plan. If the gospel was not the plan, then God is not sovereign and cannot see the end from the beginning. But God is sovereign, and there is nothing that He does not know—past, present, and future. The reason some Christians question this is because we judge God because of the wickedness and evil in the world, trying to explain away the wickedness of our own hearts. I hope I have communicated clearly up to this point that God allows wickedness and evil to exist because He is kind, longsuffering, and merciful, not wishing that any would perish but that all would repent and receive eternal life. No Jew nor Gentile nor any person will be saved outside of God's grace—all are damned outside of the gospel of Jesus Christ.

THE VALUE OF CIRCUMCISION

The Jews accused Paul of being a lawbreaker and teaching others to be lawbreakers, too. Some Jewish leaders tried to perpetuate the idea that Paul was teaching that the law was unimportant, but this was not true. Both Paul and Jesus communicated that the law was like a road marker that pointed toward something. Yes, it exposes the holiness of God and the sinfulness of men, but the ceremonial practices of the law had another specific purpose—to point us toward the Perfect. The law was a foreshadowing, a sort of preview of Christ and His coming kingdom. When Jesus arrived, there was no more need for animal sacrifices, an imperfect human priest, or a temple divided into three sections. Christ came as a bridge meant to reconcile man to God. He is our Prophet, Priest, and King.

Paul was a devout Jew and obeyed the Jewish law, even after he became a Christian. He even personally circumcised his devoted ministry partner Timothy because Timothy's mother was Jewish. Paul was not a lawbreaker, but he taught that the law was unable to save because that was never its purpose. He explains that the Gentiles would die outside the law, and the Jews would die under the law. In Romans 3, Paul anticipates some questions the Jews might ask regarding this teaching. He begins by asking, "Then what advantage has the Jew? Or what is the value of circumcision?" (v. 1). Circumcision was meant to be a sign that God had set apart the Jews to reflect His glory in the world, a physical representation that God had made a covenant with His people. It also served as a reminder of the sinfulness of man. Paul is rhetorically asking the question: If salvation is not found in the law, then is there any value in being a Jew or in circumcision? Then he answers his own question by saying, "Much in every way. To begin with, the Jews were entrusted with the oracles of God" (v. 2).

The Jewish people had a very important purpose in redemptive history. However, by the first century, the Jewish religious system had forsaken the actual purpose of their set-apartness. They were not living toward the law of God and even added more rabbinical commandments to the law, which they continually debated over. The Jewish priesthood, which was supposed to draw men to God, was putting heavy burdens on men. They used their position to distance the people from God rather than drawing them to Him. People in power and authority sometimes do this when they use their position for personal gain rather than to serve. They misuse their power to raise themselves at the expense of others. That is not the point of authority.

There is nothing evil about authority itself; the concept of authority is biblical. Godly authority is meant to be administered justly. The priesthood in Jesus' day did not use their authority to serve but rather to be served. Some priests and kings were godly in the Old Testament. However, we primarily see the symptomatic nature of humanity's depravity playing out from the beginning of time until today—that man is not good. Humans are easily self-deceived when it comes to the state of our goodness.

The Bible teaches that humanity is totally depraved and completely corrupt. However, this does not mean that men are *utterly* depraved. There is a difference. Total depravity means that there is not a part of us that has not been corrupted or touched by sin. While utter depravity means that there is no possibility of doing anything good and no goodness left in us, total depravity means that our intentions, thoughts, and flesh have been tainted by sin; but we can still do good deeds. But in comparison to a Holy God, our good deeds are like filthy rags (Isa. 64:6) and could never come close to justifying us.

When Paul mentions in verse two that the Jews were entrusted with God's oracles, he means the sacred words of Scripture. But they were often unfaithful to God's Word. There are examples of this unfaithfulness throughout the Old Testament, but one stands out in the book of 2 Chronicles. The Jews had misplaced the Book of the Law; and for decades, it was not taught in the temple. The purpose of the temple's construction was to be where God's presence dwelled and where His sacred law was taught. But they neglected the words of God; and eventually, the book went missing.

One day, the high priest Hilkiah found the book of the Law during the restoration of the temple, and the people began to observe the ceremonies and commandments of God once again. However, this is just one of many examples of how inconsistent and unfaithful they were in honoring and obeying God. And their renewed obedience to the law was only for a short time under the reign of King Josiah.

The idea that Israel was faithful to God is a pretty sketchy argument. There had been faithful men; but mostly, we see the symptoms of a fallen humanity whose heart is far from God. We have seen this play in every culture since the beginning, including our own culture. Either a culture doesn't know God and is living completely opposed to His law; or they are a culture that acknowledges God but is continually falling away, living in rebellion, and worshiping idols. From the beginning of time, no one has been consistently faithful to God. There have been men like Abraham and Moses and women like Sarah and Esther who were looking forward to their future reward, but even their faithfulness was imperfect and could not justify them before God. Hebrews 11 tells us that they, too, were justified by faith.

God had blessed the Jews far above other nations; but time and time again, they enjoyed the blessings and privileges of being God's chosen people while neglecting their responsibilities. During Paul's day, the Jewish ruling council was so corrupt and focused on modern, man-made rabbinical traditions and interpretations that they completely neglected the true spirit of the law. The letter of the law kills; and the spirit of the law is meant to lead us to Christ, and this is what they neglected.

Here is an analogy I hope explains the difference between the letter of the law and the spirit of the law. There was a wealthy man who was kind and generous. He became sad when he noticed many children playing and wandering in the streets of the neighborhood where he worked. There was a lot of crime and violence in this community. It was dirty, rundown, and unsafe. Since there was no clean and safe place for the children to play, this kind man decided to build a place where they could go after school instead of playing in the dangerous streets. The motto was "a clean and safe place to hang out and play." This wealthy man hired a manager to run the location, and he told him that the motto should govern everything he did and every decision he made in managing the program.

When the facility opened, many children began to hang out and play. However, when the children entered the building, the manager noticed they brought in dirt and grime. The toys would get dirty, and he and the staff had to clean the building and the toys every night. One day, a window was accidentally broken by one of the children; and while cleaning up the glass, he became frustrated. Thinking of the motto's words, he concluded that the only way to keep the place "clean and safe" was to kick the children out of the building and lock it up. He put a chain on the door and thought, *Now, this place will remain clean and safe.* This is an example of enforcing the letter of the law at the expense of the spirit of the law. His solution did keep the place clean and safe, but it completely undermined the original purpose of why it was constructed in the first place.

The Jews were doing this very thing in the first century. They had no heart for the people and did not act as God's servants. They put heavy burdens on people's backs that they could not carry. If the scribes and Pharisees had rightly applied the law of God first to their hearts and lives, it would have made them more humble and graceful in their implementation and administration of it. More than anyone else, they should have understood the meaning and magnitude of why they were circumcised and why animals had to be sacrificed in the temple. All that bloodshed was also for their sin; they, too, were sinners who needed atonement for their sins.

This train of thought also applies to pastors. Pastors are not above the people but are one among many in a congregation performing a particular function. Like the Jewish leaders of the temple, they are God's under-shepherds and do have authority and responsibility; but the pastor of a church needs grace, the forgiveness of sin, and the Word of God just as much as the people he is serving.

THE PROMISE OF GOD

"What if some were unfaithful? Does their faithlessness nullify the faithfulness of God?" (v. 3).

The objection Paul was preemptively answering was, "Is there no value in circumcision or in being a Jew?" However, Paul says there is much value when understood from the right perspective. They were thinking about it the wrong way. Paul makes it clear that man's imperfections and failings cannot thwart the sovereign purposes of God. Throughout the Old Testament, we witness how humanity's unfaithfulness in no way nullifies the faithfulness and promises of God. Men like Moses and Abraham, with all their imperfections and failures, could not thwart God's faithfulness. Even when Israel was completely corrupt, God's promises endured. If God has ordained something to happen, it will take place. Nothing can change God's sovereign will or cause His promises to go unfulfilled.

Paul builds his case to discourage them from finding false security in the works of the flesh and themselves. He wants them to understand that those in Christ cannot be separated from the love of God. Nothing, absolutely nothing, can separate you from God if you are in Christ! When God makes a promise, He keeps it. Outside of Christ, we are on our own; but in Christ, nothing can separate us from His love and salvation. Paul confirms this when he says, "For I am sure that neither death nor life, nor angels nor rulers, nor things present nor things to come, nor powers, nor height nor depth, nor anything else in all creation, will be able to separate us from the love of God that is in Christ Jesus our Lord" (Rom. 8:38-39).

God sent His Son to fulfill the law. There was never a moment when the possibility existed that Jesus might not accomplish His mission. There was never a chance that God's will would not come to pass. The self-righteous or the spiritually blind will claim that God is on their side. But truly righteous people are concerned with whether or not they are on God's side. The question is, "Am I living my life and worshipping Him according to His Word?" These are the right questions, posture, and disposition to approach God. Salvation is a gift; and upon salvation, a true believer will be justified. And over the course of their life, they will be sanctified by and through the Holy Spirit. The reorientation of our hearts and the change in what we crave and desire are also gifts from God.

UNDEFILED TRUTH

By no means! Let God be true though every one were a liar, as it is written,
"That you may be justified in your words, and prevail when you are judged" (v. 4).

The Jews were confused about God's promises to them. Because of their geographical and ethnic lineage as Jews, they thought this somehow entitled them to salvation. However, Paul makes it clear that the promises God made to Israel as a nation have nothing to do with the salvation of the individual man. This is good news because being under the law and the old system as a nation meant they were subjected to the blessings as well as the curses that God would pour out on the third and fourth generations of the sons and daughters of those who came after them. However, the book of Jeremiah reveals that a prophet will come to ensure that each man stands on his own. This reminds us that we must stand before God *in Christ* or on the merit of our own life.

Verse four is a powerful statement that can be applied to every other part of Christianity. People often try to pit science, philosophy, or some other fleshly wisdom against the knowledge of God. If someone questions our faith in the Word of God, our response should be, "Let God be true, and all men be liars." These words should be seared and branded deep inside our hearts and minds. We have not only missed the boat if we look for validation from the world instead of God, but we have also missed the entire ocean. We cannot look for human validation if we truly believe in God. Christianity is not primarily scientific or philosophical but far above and beyond that. It originated with and was initiated by God, and we are convinced because He has transformed us. This is the lens through which we should see *all* of God's Word. Anything that does not line up with Scripture is a lie, plain and simple. Subjecting God's Word to validation through human means, be it science, psychology, or modern cultural wisdom, is not only wrong but also wicked.

There is no need to suspend logic because the Bible is logical, coherent, and consistent. There is no worldview that does not require faith. There is faith in science, atheism, and every other worldview. But "'the righteous shall live by faith'" (Rom. 1:17) in God, which comes by hearing the Word of the Lord. Those with saving faith believe that God is true and that all men—systems of thought, perceived knowledge, or wisdom that conflict with the truth of God's word— are liars.

In the last part of verse four, Paul quotes Amos 3:2, when the prophet Amos tells the Jewish people that God's promises are for those who have faith in Him and obey His Word. This chapter in Amos exposes Israel's guilt for not obeying God and the punishment coming from their disobedience.

CONDEMNED FOR OUR SINS

But if our unrighteousness serves to show the righteousness of God, what shall we say? That God is unrighteous to inflict wrath on us? (I speak in a human way.) By no means! For then how could God judge the world? But if through my lie God's truth abounds to his glory, why am I still being condemned as a sinner? And why not do evil that good may come?—as some people slanderously charge us with saying. Their condemnation is just (vv. 5-8).

Here, Paul anticipates another objection to the gospel: "If God controls everything and works everything out for good, then how can we be condemned for our sins?" Paul wants us to understand that this is a foolish way of thinking. The fact that we cannot understand how God can take something evil and bring about good does not give us a right to sin. Instead, this exposes the corrupt nature of our hearts. If we live for God and have forsaken sin, we will look back in awe of the good God has done in our lives and the plan of salvation. But this does not mean we should keep on living in sin. Spiritual regeneration puts the love of God into our hearts and changes our desires and affections.

The person who has been made right by God wants to do right. He hungers and thirsts to be right with God. The fact that we fall short and use that as an excuse to sin shows that the Spirit of God probably does not live in us. A faithful Christian strives for righteousness but falls short. A righteous person falls seven times but gets back up because he truly knows, loves, and fears the Lord. Proverbs 9:10 says, "The fear of the LORD is the beginning of wisdom, and the knowledge of the Holy One is insight." We obey God not to gain His mercy and grace; but through Christ, we have been saved by His mercy and grace.

FOR GOD'S GLORY

Paul addresses another objection by answering the following questions: If we are unable to be saved by the law, isn't it unfair that we are condemned under it? Does that make God unrighteous for inflicting wrath on us for not keeping the law? Even today, people ask this same question. However, it is interesting that when the Gentiles were condemned, the Jews did not object in the same way. We often do the same thing. We are fine when other people get what they deserve, but oh, how we underestimate our wretchedness! The Jews had no problem with the Gentiles being condemned to Hell forever because they had not applied the law to themselves. When we hear the Word of God, the first thing we should consider is how it applies to us, not how it applies to others. Remember, the law of God reveals and magnifies two things: the holiness of God and the sinfulness of man. The gospel of Jesus Christ reveals the love, mercy, and grace of God while upholding the holiness, justice, and perfection of God.

The set-apartness of the Jews and the revelation of the law was about bringing glory to God. We often misunderstand this; and instead of glorifying God, we question His goodness when we do not get the good things we think we deserve. Why did this happen to me? How is this fair? If God is good, then why am I going through this trial? In the book of John, Jesus' disciples questioned why a man they encountered was born blind.

They asked, "'Rabbi, who sinned, this man or his parents, that he was born blind?' Jesus answered, 'It was not that this man sinned, or his parents, but that the works of God might be displayed in him'" (John 9:3).

All things are for the glory of God. Once we comprehend this as Christians, our life struggles become much easier to accept. We will not be asking the question, "Why me, God?" The law and the gospel are not exclusively for the benefit of man. They are for the glory of God! "We walk by faith, not by sight" (2 Cor. 5:7), trusting in the Lord, knowing that despite what our circumstances look like, He is working all things together for our good (Rom. 8:28).

LIVING IN GOD'S BLESSING

What then? Are we Jews any better off? No, not at all. For we have already charged that all, both Jews and Greeks, are under sin (v. 9).

We need to understand the flow of Paul's progressive logic here. In a worldly sense, the Jews were better off because they had God's commands of blessing and cursing, so they had the potential to live in God's blessing. They had access to God through the oracles of God, the Law and the Prophets, and the wisdom literature. In the same way, if a person does not know God in a saving way but applies proverbial wisdom to their life and lives according to the wisdom of God in the Old Testament, they will most likely live a better life on earth. The book of Proverbs says not to gamble or squander your money. If someone follows this wisdom and is a good steward of their money, they will probably end up in a better financial position than people who do not. All proverbial wisdom is from God. The Jewish way of life was undoubtedly better, but Paul says salvation is not based on doing good. Morality does not bring salvation; it might make for a better life, but Christ alone saves us.

When it comes to individual salvation, the Jews were no better off than the Gentiles. There is no way for Gentiles to be saved differently from the Jews, and there is no way that Jews will be saved differently from the Gentiles. In the book of Acts, Peter told the Jewish ruling council, "'This Jesus is the stone that was rejected by you, the builders, which has become the cornerstone. And there is salvation in no one else, for there is no other name under heaven given among men by which we must be saved'" (Acts 4:11-12). They rejected the Cornerstone; so Peter is talking to the Jews, including the High Priest, the Levites, and the entire priesthood, saying there is no other way of salvation. Paul wants to clearly explain that both Jews and Greeks are sinners, and both need a Savior. Because of the corruption of the Fall, they are not good. The law was not meant to save them but merely to magnify God's holiness and expose humankind's sinfulness.

PROVEN GUILTY!

As it is written: "None is righteous, no, not one; no one understands; no one seeks for
God. All have turned aside; together they have become worthless; no one does good, not
even one. Their throat is an open grave; they use their tongues to deceive. The venom of
asps is under their lips. Their mouth is full of curses and bitterness. Their feet are swift
to shed blood; in their paths are ruin and misery, and the way of peace they have not
known. There is no fear of God before their eyes" (vv. 10-18).

This basic biblical presupposition about the human condition must be understood to see how desperately we need the gospel. This is one reason why Christianity is in opposition to every other worldview. Christianity is completely opposed to the false idea that most people are basically good. Paul uses the Old Testament to argue that the opposite is true. He's saying no one is good. Our mouths are vile instruments of wickedness that tell lies, and our throats are open graves filled with death because we are all dead in sin and trespass against a holy God.

Today's self-help culture tells us it is wrong to feel guilt and that we should focus only on positive things. There is some truth to the idea that we should not carry guilt and shame from our past if we are in Christ. But our guilt serves a vital purpose. It is meant to reveal that we are estranged from a holy God Who made us in His image. We have to come face to face with our guilt, and Paul wants the Jews and the Gentiles he is writing to come face to face with their guilt. The world tells us to focus only on positive things, but the reality of our guilt makes us aware of a future and coming judgment; it steers us toward seeing our need for God's saving grace. When we look inside ourselves using the law as a flashlight, we realize there is too much guilt; and we cannot overcome it. We need help! As Christians, we do not have to carry the guilt of our past. We must repent of our sins as we put our faith in Christ, and He promises He will be faithful to forgive us.

People spend much time trying to minimize, numb, and escape guilt. But the guilt of our sins is inescapable because, as Romans 2 mentions, we have the law of God written on our hearts. This is why, instead of just living lawless lives, people long to have a person who is a perceived authority tell them that they are all right. We desperately need to be validated to feel justified in our sins. But deep down inside, our conscience is telling us something different. This is why some go to psychologists who say we are not at fault. They tell us to blame our parents, our environment, or some other outside source. We pretend like a person's drug addiction is a disease and not their fault. Adultery is sexual addiction, and it is not our fault. This is what drives people to listen to preachers who only speak of positive things. This is why therapeutic-style self-help theology is so very popular. We do not want to feel bad or guilty. It is the same reason why there are so many false religions in the world. False religions exist to try and pacify our conscience instead of pointing to the true law of God. Without a repentant heart, there is no forgiveness of sin!

Paul is trying to communicate that all humanity is guilty. No one is righteous. When he writes, "It is written," he means it is true according to God's inerrant, established, unchanging Word. It is the modern-day version of saying, "The Bible says . . ." It is true in every generation, civilization, nation, and person.

No one has ever been—nor will anyone ever be—right with God apart from Christ. Ecclesiastes says, "As you do not know the way the spirit comes to the bones in the womb of a woman with child, so you do not know the work of God who makes everything" (Eccl. 11:5). We cannot understand anything apart from knowledge revealed through God the Creator of all things. That simple truth should reveal that we have no right to tell God what is real and what is true. Scientists can give us a detailed analysis of what is involved in the process of life, but they do not know *how* it happens. How does the seed of a man turn into a life with a soul, a mind, and intellect? Humanity does not understand.

This is why the secular world is so desperate to cling to the lie of Darwinian evolution. They are desperate to explain the origin of life in a way that doesn't hold them guilty before the law of God. The Lord declares:

- "For as the heavens are higher than the earth, so are my ways higher than your ways and my thoughts than your thoughts" (Isa. 55:9).
- "Have you not known? Have you not heard? The LORD is the everlasting God, the Creator of the ends of the earth. He does not faint or grow weary; his understanding is unsearchable" (Isa. 40:28).

What we know about God is what has been revealed to us through the world He created and His Word. Many churches today are consumed with catering to lost people who they believe are desperately looking for God. So they try to get the music right and make the sermons short and positive, thinking maybe people will find God if they aren't "turned off" by Christianity. But the Bible says "no one seeks for God" (Rom. 3:11).

Do you know Who the seeker is? God! He is the One Who speaks to a heart that has turned away from Him and says, "'Come to me . . . For my yoke is easy, and my burden is light'" (Matt. 11:28-30). The church gets this confused because people are seeking what God alone can provide. We all want peace, love, blessings, hope, and health. But we do not want it at the expense of bowing our knees to God and calling Him Lord. Jeremiah 29:13 says, "You will seek me and find me, when you seek me with all your heart." Anyone who has truly sought God will find Him.

In the Sermon on the Mount, Jesus said:

> "Ask, and it will be given to you; seek, and you will find; knock, and it will be opened to you. For everyone who asks receives, and the one who seeks finds, and to the one who knocks it will be opened. Or which one of you, if his son asks him for bread, will give him a stone? Or if he asks for a fish, will give him a serpent? If you then, who are evil, know how to give good gifts to your children, how much more will your Father who is in heaven give good things to those who ask him!" (Matt. 7:7-11).

This is not about monetary prosperity; it is about the gospel. Jesus said, "'Blessed are those who hunger and thirst for righteousness, for they shall be satisfied'" (Matt. 5:6). If we want to be right with God, He will meet us where we are. Many of us want this but do not want it on God's terms. Yet it is all or nothing.

Romans 3:12 says, "All have turned aside; together they have become worthless; no one does good, not even one.'" The phrase "all have turned aside" means we have gone our own way. We resist the narrow path that leads to life. "Together, they have become worthless" means we serve no purpose. We do not serve the purpose we were created for: to worship and glorify God with our hearts and lives. The New American Standard Bible says "useless" instead of "worthless." It is like a dead twig that is not connected to a tree rooted in the ground, which gives life to the branches that are connected to it. It is good for nothing but to be thrown into the fire, like kindling, and burned. It is like salt that has lost its saltiness, so it is thrown on the ground to be trampled upon. This is the state and condition of mankind apart from Christ.

Paul then restates his original statement for emphasis: "No one does good, not even one." This is the internal state of all humankind—the deceitful and corrupt heart of man. Since the tree is corrupt, its actions and fruit will be corrupt. Paul talks about our inner condition and then states what it produces. "'Their throat is an open grave; they use their tongues to deceive. The venom of asps is under their lips. Their mouth is full of curses and bitterness'" (vv. 13-14). We are dead in our sin and trespasses, and Paul is saying our mouths are the means to see inside of us. It shows that we are an open grave. What is inside of us? Death that leads to death. Our mouths are full of deceit and lies. Jesus taught regarding this:

- "Do you not see that whatever goes into the mouth passes into the stomach and is expelled? But what comes out of the mouth proceeds from the heart, and this defiles a person. For out of the heart come evil thoughts, murder, adultery, sexual immorality, theft, false witness, slander. These are what defile a person. But to eat with unwashed hands does not defile anyone" (Matt. 15:17-20).
- "For no good tree bears bad fruit, nor again does a bad tree bear good fruit, for each tree is known by its own fruit. For figs are not gathered from thornbushes, nor are grapes picked from a bramble bush. The good person out of the good treasure of his heart produces good, and the evil person out of his evil treasure produces evil, for out of the abundance of the heart his mouth speaks (Matt. 6:43-45).

Jesus is teaching that from the abundance of the heart, the mouth speaks. In other words, we have not been afflicted with wickedness and self-centeredness; we were born with these things. This is the difference between Christianity and every other religion—we are not good. "'Their feet are swift to shed blood; in their paths are ruin and misery, and the way of peace they have not known'" (Rom. 3:15-17). These verses speak of the state of humanity throughout the ages. We do not know the way of peace or the way to peace. We only know the way of war and bloodshed, and every nation has fallen into war.

There is no peace in the world. There are only "wars and rumors of wars" (Matt. 24:6). We are always living between wars; and in our individual lives, we see people shedding blood and living for themselves. No matter how hard we try, we cannot bring peace to the world. There are periods without all-out war, but this is not the same thing as true peace. Humanity cannot find lasting external peace because our hearts are not at peace. People say, "If only we could fix this one thing or solve this one problem, then we would have peace; and then we could finally live in utopia." However, the problem is that humanity is wicked; no matter what we do to improve things, we will find a way to mess it up.

Paul says this is all true because "there is no fear of God before their eyes" (Rom. 3:18). We live wicked lives because we ignore the looming and inescapable truth of our future judgment. We live this way because we do not believe we will stand before a holy God one day. We would live differently if we were truly aware of the coming day of the Lord and His righteous wrath and judgment. Proverbs 14:27 says, "The fear of the LORD is a fountain of life, that one may turn away from the snares of death."

THE LAW

Now we know that whatever the law says it speaks to those who are under the law, so

that every mouth may be stopped, and the whole world may be held accountable to

*God. For by works of the law no human being will be justified in his sight, since through
the law comes knowledge of sin (vv. 19-20).*

The law reveals the holiness of God, which logically gives us the knowledge of sin. A person who does not realize that they are a wretched, unclean sinner has never known God. When the prophet Isaiah, a man who did know and fear the Lord, saw just the train of God's robe, he was compelled by his wretchedness. He said, "'Woe is me! For I am lost; for I am a man of unclean lips, and I dwell in the midst of a people of unclean lips" (Isa. 6:5).

Coming into the presence of the holy, perfect, undefiled God will show us who we really are. This is an imperative part of the gospel, which is why our nation is full of false converts. The Church has removed the preaching of sin because it makes people feel bad about themselves, and they believe fewer people will fill the pews if we preach this way. But preaching that does not address the reality of sin never reveals our need for the gospel. If our sin has not brought us to despair, we do not know the one true God. Many churches refuse to preach on sin and the total depravity of man. But the law of God speaks so that *every* mouth be stopped, that *every* excuse be silenced. The Word of God calls everything into subjection. Let every man, every mouth be stopped. Let God be true and every man a liar.

To preach the true, complete, and biblical gospel, we must also preach the law, which exposes man's sin. We must preach repentance from sin and the exclusivity of the narrow way that is Jesus Christ. No one will ever be justified by ignoring the guilt of their sin. A moral lifestyle will justify no one. No one is good—no, not one! Justification comes through Christ. *All* things outside of Christ will be subject to judgment and condemnation. No one will be justified before God apart from the atoning work of Christ on the cross. If our sins do not bring us to that conclusion, then we are trampling on the sacrifice of God's only begotten Son. We cannot preach the good news without first preaching the bad news. Narrow is the way that leads to life, and only a few will find it (Matt. 7:14).

7

JUSTIFIED BY THE GIFT OF GOD'S GRACE

ROMANS 3:21-31

But now the righteousness of God has been manifested apart from the law, although the Law and the Prophets bear witness to it—the righteousness of God through faith in Jesus Christ for all who believe. For there is no distinction: for all have sinned and fall short of the glory of God, and are justified by his grace as a gift, through the redemption that is in Christ Jesus, whom God put forward as a propitiation by his blood, to be received by faith. This was to show God's righteousness, because in his divine forbearance he had passed over former sins. It was to show his righteousness at the present time, so that he might be just and the justifier of the one who has faith in Jesus. Then what becomes of our boasting? It is excluded. By what kind of law? By a law of works? No, but by the law of faith. For we hold that one is justified by faith apart from works of the law. Or is God the God of Jews only? Is he not the God of Gentiles also? Yes, of Gentiles also, since God is one—who will justify the circumcised by faith and the uncircumcised through faith. Do we then overthrow the law by this faith? By no means! On the contrary, we uphold the law.

ONE OF THE MOST IMPORTANT themes throughout Romans is righteousness—a holy righteousness. Holy righteousness means that God is completely just, perfect, and set apart from humankind in all of His ways. To be counted as righteous in God's sight we must also be perfect as he is perfect. And here lies the problem: we are not and far from it. If God is holy, just, and perfect in all His ways and we are not, then how can we be made right with God? There is a stark contrast between God's righteousness and the state of man because none of us are righteous. No, not even one!

CAPTIVATED BY GOD'S HOLY RIGHTEOUSNESS

Mediating and deeply gazing into the righteousness of God is what reveals our own sinfulness and our need for salvation. Many people get emotionally excited about God's grace and love; but if we do not see how desperate we truly are in light of God's holy righteousness, we cannot comprehend our need for or the value of God's saving grace and the beauty of the gospel. We cannot know what it means to follow Jesus apart from understanding Who He is and what He did for us. The gate is narrow, and it is found in only one place. We must look intently at Who God is and come to despair over who we are so that we see grace as a precious, unearned gift. The grace of God saves us; but not only that, it changes us and assures us of our faith through the Holy Spirit.

As Christians, we are to understand two things: apart from God, we can do nothing; but through Him, "all things are possible" (Mark 10:27). That Scripture is not meant to apply to a softball team's win or a person finding employment. No, it means God is saving our eternal soul and working all things together for our good (Rom. 8:28) if we are truly in Christ. All things are possible with Him.

We measure what is right and just in every area of our lives according to God's supreme righteousness. Today, our culture has many voices that tell us otherwise. Many people try to superimpose what they feel is right or wrong on God, and the reason they do this is because that person does not know God and is not being saved by Him. We come to God to see what is righteous, just, holy, and good. We measure all things by the righteousness of God. God's holy, righteous perfection should make us despair in ourselves but also make us sure of our justification in Christ. Everything God does is perfectly just and good. The justice of God for those wretched sins that we have committed and those wretched lives we once lived are now forgiven and hidden in Christ.

Romans 1:17 says, "'The righteous shall live by faith,'" which means that those who are right with God because of Christ take Him at His word and live their lives accordingly. We must understand that this speaks of saving faith that cannot be divorced from the gospel. When Scripture says, "Without faith, it is impossible to please him" (Heb. 11:6), it does not mean to go and do something bold for God. No, it means it is impossible to please God without salvific faith. When the Bible speaks of faith, it means saving faith. How many Scriptures regarding faith have been wrongly applied without seeing them through the lens of the gospel? Faith is knowing we stand justified before God based on Christ, and God will keep the promises He made to us in His Holy Word.

"'The righteous shall live by faith'" (Rom. 1:17) and "the wrath of God is revealed from heaven against all ungodliness and all unrighteousness of men" (Rom. 1:18). Most people are not right with God and do not want to be right with God. They prefer instead to go their own way, gratifying their sinful desires. Because of that, God's righteous judgment is revealed and laid upon them. It is a burden that they will not be able to bear, not just in the final judgment but throughout their lives. They will become darker, more depraved, and more disconnected from the light of God's knowledge and reality. "He will render to each one according to his works: to those who by patience in well-doing seek for glory and honor and immortality, he will give eternal life; but for those who are self-seeking and do not obey the truth, but obey unrighteousness, there will be wrath and fury" (Rom. 2:6-8).

There are only two groups of people in the world: those who live aware of a coming day of judgment with the expectation of standing before God and those who live for themselves and live as if there is no future day of judgment. This is why many people fall into false religious legalistic systems of belief. Religious systems, like Roman Catholicism, are appealing to people because, in it, you can still live for yourself; but with the illusion, while doing so, you can still be right with God. A priest offers forgiveness after someone confesses their list of sins and requires some act of penance or a good deed. Then that person goes on with their everyday life living for themselves. However, the Christian life is not compartmentalized. It is not divided into a Sunday version of yourself and then back again to a Monday version of yourself. It is being reborn with a new nature with new affections and desires.

As Christians, we live differently because we know that one day, we will stand before God, Who sees and knows all but also because our hearts now love Him and want to please Him. Yes, we still battle sin and fall short, but we now hate the sin we once loved because we truly love God. Through the Holy Spirit, we gain a real awareness of God and become more concerned about being right with Him than what the world thinks of us.

A true Christian will value the truth more than the consequences of living in that truth. If living in God's truth is not important to someone, the Spirit of God is not living in them. We cannot be more concerned with this temporary life than we are with our eternal souls. A Christian hates sin, feels conviction of sin, and wants to come out of the darkness and into the light. Jesus said, "For everyone who does wicked things hates the light and does not come to the light, lest his works should be exposed" (John 3:20). A Christian wants to be free of the burden of sin and be right with God. This is not about the works we do; it is about the evidence of our salvation. Looking intently into God's righteousness exposes our sins and reveals our unrighteousness.

THE AGE-OLD QUESTION

All men and women who the Bible says are counted as righteous before God in the Old and New Testaments are counted as so based on faith. Often, people foolishly believe that people saved in the Old Testament were saved through the

Old Covenant and that we, after the New Testament, are saved because of the New Covenant; but this is simply untrue. We are all saved the same way.

In the history of humankind, there has never been one person saved who was not saved according to faith in God. All who were counted as righteous in the sight of God were counted so not because they met God's holy standard of perfection but because they truly knew God, which exposed their need for Him. They saw God for Who He is, revered His Word, and lived by it. This did not earn them anything; it proved they had faith in God. No one in the history of the world has ever been saved apart from Christ's sacrifice on the cross. Some were justified as they looked forward toward a future Messiah, while others looked back into history at the work of a risen Messiah; but all who are saved and will be saved are so based on faith.

Remember, Hebrews tells us it is impossible to please God without faith. This does not mean giving a huge faith offering at church or doing something daring for Christ. It means it is impossible to please God unless we have saving faith and are connected to the Vine. This narrow and exclusive means of salvation has always been the only way.

In the book of Job, a man named Bildad asks: "How then can man be in the right before God? How can he who is born of woman be pure?" (Job 25:4). While Job is in despair, Bildad asks, "How can a man be right before God?" The book of Job is one of the oldest texts of the Bible. Here, Bildad asks the enduring and vital question that has hung over humankind ever since the fall in the Garden of Eden. In Job's suffering, he was concerned about being right with God. However, his friends questioned whether he had done enough good deeds for God to take away all his troubles.

We hear the same question today in some Christian circles: if someone is not healthy, blessed, and prosperous, we wonder if they not doing enough good works. Do they have secret sin? Do they have enough faith? Yet this is a flawed, foolish, and unbiblical way to view things, especially in Job's case. God considered him the most righteous man in the world, but trouble still fell upon him; and we know from the text that all of his problems were initiated by the hand of God. But they weren't pointless; they had a purpose. All the hardships he experienced exposed Who God was to Job. That is why when his wife said, "'Curse God and die'" (Job 2:9), he would not listen to her. Instead, he held fast to the words of God, and he lived by faith.

How can a man be approved in God's sight? How can he gain favor with God? How can he be right before a holy God? These questions are pondered throughout the Old and even in the New Testament. It is what the multitudes asked John the Baptist when he was preaching a message of repentance and God's coming judgment. "Tell us what to do." This is the effect true gospel preaching should have on those who hear it. The message must be so clear and direct that it leaves those who hear it either rejecting God, knowing exactly what they are rejecting, or, like many who heard Peter's gospel message on the day of Pentecost, asking, "What then must we do to be saved?" (Acts 2).

The gospel brings conviction to the lost sinner and surety to the true believer. It is not just some beginner's thing; it is everything. The preaching of the gospel causes us to live in the reality of Christ's glory, beauty, and power forever. The gospel brings comfort and peace to the believer because we know that Christ is saving us; and to the lost, we hope it draws them to His salvation and eternal life. The message of God's salvation was prominent and present in the Old Testament as well as in the New Testament. Many people who saw Jesus' mighty works asked, "What must we do to be saved and have eternal life?" Sometimes, this was an insincere and mocking question from the teachers of the law. Still, other times, it was a good and sincere question, like when the rich, young ruler asked, "'Good Teacher, what must I do to inherit eternal life?'" (Mark 10:17). The problem was that, in this instance, while the question was sincere, the young ruler didn't like Jesus' answer.

The story of the rich, young ruler starts with this man asking Jesus a sincere question. He asked the right person the right question, and the Bible indicates he did it with the right attitude. Everything was right except one thing: he didn't see God as valuable enough to give his life up for, and he didn't see Jesus as his only way to God. He didn't truly see his own rightness and goodness in light of God's holy perfection. After the rich ruler asked the question, Jesus looked at him, loved him, and said, "'You lack one thing: go, sell all that you have and give to the poor, then and you will have treasure in heaven; and come, follow me'" (Mark 10:21). Jesus is not telling him that he had to earn eternal life by doing something. He is saying, "Do you see Who I am?" The man said he wanted eternal life; so Jesus told him to sell his possessions, give to the poor, and come and follow Him. However, it says the man went away sad because he wanted eternal life without repentance, obedience, and following Jesus. He didn't see Christ as a treasure whose value is incomparable. We cannot have eternal life apart from surrendering our lives and following Jesus.

This same call from Jesus persuaded Matthew to leave his tax collector's booth to follow Him. He, too, was a man of wealth; but instead of going away sad, he followed. It prompted Peter and John to leave their fishing boats and follow Him. Although the young ruler had a vague idea of Who God was, he didn't see Jesus as God; and he didn't see himself as in need of a Savior.

This is just as true today as it was then. People are so desperate to hold on to the illusion that they are in control of their lives and the fleeting treasures of this world that they ignore the most valuable treasure of all. We want eternal life and God's blessings, but we want them on our terms. This isn't a negotiation; it's a command: "'Lay down your life and follow me!'"

WHOSE WORD WILL YOU BELIEVE?

But now the righteousness of God has been manifested apart from the law,
although the Law and the Prophets bear witness to it (v. 21).

In Romans 1, Paul says the righteous judgment of God is being stored up to be poured out on those who do not acknowledge God according to the law. But now Paul says that God has manifested His righteousness apart from the law, by grace in the person and the gospel of Jesus Christ. There is a way of escape for us! The first word of the verse—"But,"—implies a stark and important transition. The righteousness of God has been manifested not only in His righteous judgment of sinners but also in saving sinners through grace by pouring that punishment out on His Son. The Law of God and the prophets of God were never meant to be a means of salvation. They were merely meant to point us toward the One Who can make us right with God. This is Divine grace—a gift we cannot earn.

A legalistic person thinks very little of God but thinks much of themselves because they believe they can work their way to God. The Jewish legalists thought they could earn salvation by keeping the law. There are two ditches on either side of the narrow gospel road of grace. First is legalism—salvation by works. This is believing that your works somehow contribute to your salvation. The second is antinomianism, which means lawlessness. This is the belief that we can live as we please because of God's grace. This is using the idea of God's grace to live lawlessly, rather than as a means to live in obedience to God's law.

Both of these views of God's grace are completely wrong. In the book of Matthew, Jesus said, "*I never knew you; depart from me, you workers of lawlessness*" (Matt. 7:23). The indictment against the Jewish leaders of His day was this: "You had the Law; but from it, you did not know Me." Paul makes the same accusation that Jesus did. Paul tells them that the Gentiles will die apart from the Law, and the Jews will die under the Law. To the Gentiles, Jesus says, "You lawless evildoers, I never knew you." But to the Jews, He says, "You had the Law and the Prophets; how could you not know me?"

The Jews thought they could approach God based on their knowledge of the law and the ethnic lineage they shared with Noah, Isaiah, Moses, and Abraham. But how could they think that was even possible? Remember, the patriarchs and heroes that the Jews revered were all saved by faith, which was "counted to [them] as righteousness" (Rom. 4:3). The point where man departed from God's favor was when they did not take Him at His word in the garden. In Genesis, God told man to enjoy and subdue the earth, be fruitful, and multiply. He gave one warning: "'You may surely eat of every tree of the garden, but of the tree of the knowledge of good and evil you shall not eat, for in the day that you eat of it you shall surely die'" (Gen. 2:16-17). What happened? The enemy of their soul got them to ask the question, "Did God really say . . . " (Gen. 3:1). This is the question that the devil got Adam and Eve to ask, which ultimately caused all mankind to fall into sin. It is the same question that causes us to continue in sin to this very day.

Taking God at His Word is the only means by which men are saved. Yes, it was atoned for and paid for based on what Christ did on the cross, but that can only be applied to your life by believing by faith and living as if it is true. "'The righteous shall live by faith'" (Rom. 1:17), and it is impossible to please God without faith. "Now faith is the assurance of things hoped for, the conviction of things not seen. For by it the people of old received their commendation. By faith we understand that the universe was created by the word of God, so that what is seen was not made out of things that are visible" (Heb. 11:1-3). This verse is not about being rich in this world but about the assurance of living for eternity's future reward.

Faith starts with Genesis and believing that God created the world in six days. If we cannot believe that, how can we believe anything else? Today, many say, "But I have all this other evidence." But whose word are you going to believe? Like the rich young ruler, many fear God's answer may not align with their life plan or perception of reality. But Hebrews 11:6-7 says:

> Without faith it is impossible to please him, for whoever would draw near to God must believe that he exists and that he rewards those who seek him. By faith Noah, being warned by God concerning events as yet unseen, in reverent fear constructed an ark for the saving of his household. By this he condemned

the world and became an heir of the righteousness that comes by faith.

God told Noah that He was going to condemn and destroy the world and instructed him to build an ark for the salvation of his family. Noah received God's word, and what did he do with it? Did Noah falter and question God? No, he believed God and took Him at His word. What did that obedience produce in Noah's life? Salvation for him and his family. What a picture of the gospel in the Old Testament! There is only condemnation for those outside the ark and, in our case, those outside Christ. Our lives will look different if we live by faith. Actions will not save us, but they bear witness to the fact that we believe God's Word and live according to it by faith.

Scripture refers to men like Noah, Abraham, and Moses, saying, "These all died in faith, not having received the things promised, but having seen them and greeted them from afar, and having acknowledged that they were strangers and exiles on the earth" (Heb. 11:13). What this means is that they were looking for salvation from a future Christ. They had no problem being saved by the promise that God would send a propitiation for their sin. We have the same sort of faith. We look back to what God did in history's past, and that is what we are being saved by.

THE FREE GIFT OF GOD'S GRACE

The righteousness of God through faith in Jesus Christ for all who believe. For there is no distinction: for all have sinned and fall short of the glory of God (vv. 22-23).

If the Law and the Prophets merely point toward and bear witness to the righteousness of God but don't fully reveal it, then what does? Up to this point, Paul has backed all of humanity into a dark and hopeless corner. Now, he reveals the light of the world, and this is how the gospel must always be presented. Paul presents the holiness of God and the absolute despair of man because of sin, and then he introduces the grace of God. When we are aware we are in darkness, this grace looks like a beautiful, bright, and shining light. It is an oasis of water for those parched and dying of thirst in the desert. It is a precious, beautiful reward we cannot earn, but it was given to us through Christ on the cross.

The righteousness of God is revealed perfectly in the Son, Jesus Christ, and more specifically in the gospel of Jesus Christ. His law-fulfilling and perfect life, His sacrificial and atoning death, and His resurrection validate him as God and King of kings and Lord of lords—not just because He is perfectly righteous and perfectly just but because He overcame death. Christ fulfilled the law in two ways. He lived a perfect life and fulfilled the righteous requirement of the law; and because of this, He was the only One qualified to atone for and pay the price of our sins. The cost of sin is death, which must be paid for, either by us or by Christ.

True faith in Jesus is life-changing and transformative. It is not merely knowledge of who He is, for Scripture acknowledges, "Even the demons believe—and shudder!" (James 2:19). Saving faith is not about merely aspiring to a mental knowledge of Who God is. It is life! Transformational saving faith produces obedience, and it yields followers of Jesus. A.W Tozer describes what happened to the doctrine of justification:

> The faith of Paul and Luther was a revolutionizing thing. It upset the whole life of an individual and made him into another person altogether. It laid hold of the life and brought it into obedience to Christ. It took up its cross and followed along after Jesus with no intention of going back. It said good-bye to its old friends as certainly as Elijah when he stepped onto a fiery chair and went away in a whirlwind. It had a finality about it. It snapped shut on a man's heart like a trap; it captured the man and made him from that moment forward, a happy love-servant of his Lord.[12]

This is the gospel in our hearts—immovable, happily in service to God. If we have decided to follow Jesus, there is no turning back. Nothing will ever take us off course if we have truly seen the value of the reward.

There is no distinction between Jews and Gentiles. All are condemned and subject to judgment because "all have sinned and fall short of the glory of God" (Rom. 3:23). However, Paul also says there is no distinction in salvation. There is righteousness in the sight of God for *all* who put their faith in Christ Jesus. The whole world should despair because of sin, but the entire world should rejoice because of the salvation found in Christ. "For God so loved the world that he gave his only Son, that whoever believes in him should not perish but have eternal life" (John 3:16). Paul reiterates this teaching in Romans 10:9-13:

> Because, if you confess with your mouth that Jesus is Lord and believe in your heart that God raised him from the dead, you will be saved. For with the heart one believes and is justified, and with the mouth one confesses and is saved. For the Scripture says, "Everyone who believes in him will not be put to shame." For there is no distinction between Jew and Greek; for the same Lord is Lord of all, bestowing his riches on *all who call on him*. For "everyone who calls on the name of the Lord will be saved" (emphasis added).

COVERED BY INNOCENT BLOOD

And are justified by his grace as a gift, through the redemption that is in Christ Jesus, whom God put forward as a propitiation by his blood, to be received by faith. This was to show God's righteousness, because in his divine forbearance he had passed over former sins (vv. 24-25).

Salvation is a gift that is fully funded by God's grace. We are justified before God on the basis of Christ. The word "propitiation" refers to God and how He atoned for our sins. In other words, propitiation was trading His innocence for our guilt. Only God was qualified to do that.

God is perfectly just in eternity, so He cannot leave sin unpunished. The only reason we think that God should leave sin unpunished is because we are a wicked and twisted people without justice in our hearts. But God is perfectly just; He cannot leave wrong undone or sin unpunished. "For the wages of sin is death, but the free gift of God is eternal life in Christ Jesus our Lord" (Rom. 6:23).

God's justice demands that we die; and after death (described as the second death in the Bible), there will be eternal judgment and condemnation for God's enemies. Verse twenty-five says God "passed over former sins" until His righteousness was revealed. Christ made propitiation for us, which means he made atonement for our sins, which only He could do. Truly innocent blood is more valuable than all guilty blood in the history of the world. It would be better for a hundred guilty men to go free than to risk executing one innocent man.

Our law system today is not perfect, and innocent people have been convicted and most likely even put to death. But in principle, we would never willfully take the chance of putting someone to death who is even potentially innocent. This is why men on death row have years of appeals and incarceration before they are executed. This is also why we do not convict someone to death without proven and corroborating evidence that goes beyond any reasonable doubt. But when it comes to humankind transgressing God, no one is innocent. The sacrifice of something truly innocent is so valuable that we cannot comprehend it. Men who go to court because they have been charged with a crime might be acquitted because they are not guilty of that particular crime, but everyone is guilty of sin. This is why sacrificing Christ could atone for the sins of all mankind; He is the only truly innocent Person in history.

The sacrifices in the Old Testament on the Day of Atonement could not forgive sin. It was merely a placeholder and reminder that the true day of atonement would come when the Messiah arrived. This is why its purpose was for the remission of sins, not the forgiveness of sins. Pastor John MacArthur explains it this way:

> The Mercy Seat in the Holy of Holies [was] where the high priest went once a year, on the Day of Atonement, to make a sacrifice on behalf of the people. On that occasion he sprinkled blood on the Mercy Seat, symbolizing the payment of the penalty for his own sins and the sins of the people. But that yearly act, although divinely prescribed and honored, had no power to remove or pay the penalty for a single sin. It could only point to the true and effective "offering of the body of Jesus Christ once and for all."[13]

Everything comes down to the gift of grace secured for us in the act of Christ dying and rising again. This is evidenced in the book of Hebrews:

> When he said above, "You have neither desired nor taken pleasure in sacrifices and offerings and burnt offerings and sin offerings" (these are offered according to the law), then he added, "Behold, I have come to do your will." He does away with the first in order to establish the second. And by that will we have been sanctified through the offering of the body of Jesus Christ once for all. And every priest stands daily at his service, offering repeatedly the same sacrifices, which can never take away sins. But when Christ had offered for all time a single sacrifice for sins, he sat down at the right hand of God, waiting from that time until his enemies should be made a footstool for his feet. For by a single offering he has perfected for all time those who are being sanctified (Heb. 10:8-14).

COMPLETELY AND PERFECTLY JUST

It was to show his righteousness at the present time, so that he might be just and the justifier of the one who has faith in Jesus (v. 26).

The paradox of this statement is that God needed to remain completely and perfectly just. At the same time, He was the Justifier of sinners. How can you justify sinners and remain perfectly just? The answer is the cross because God had to punish sin to be just. He cannot leave sin unpunished; but out of His love for us, He made a way to justify us.

The ultimate purpose of the cross was to reveal the righteousness of God. Beyond everything else, the purpose of the cross is to glorify God. The chief end of man and the chief end of creation is to glorify God, and we are the benefactors of His grace. Ephesians explains grace through faith:

> But God, being rich in mercy, because of the great love with which he loved us, even when we were dead in our trespasses, made us alive together with Christ—by grace you have been saved—and raised us up with him and seated us with him in the heavenly places in Christ Jesus, so that in the coming ages he might show the immeasurable riches of his grace in kindness toward us in Christ Jesus. For by grace you have been saved through faith. And this is not your own doing; it is the gift of God, not a result of works, so that no one may boast. For we are his workmanship, created in Christ Jesus for good works, which God prepared beforehand, that we should walk in them (Eph. 2:4-10).

In other words, no one can boast or be proud. All of us are saved by grace if we are truly saved. We are not better than the person who is dying in their sins. The reason we are not going to Hell is because, by faith, we have been covered by the blood of the Lamb. Our debt has been paid. In the justice of God, He did not leave a tiny part of it unpaid. It is paid in full. When we act as if God did not pay it in full, we trample the very blood of God—His goodness, power, and justice.

THE JUSTIFICATION OF THE CROSS

Then what becomes of our boasting? It is excluded. By what kind of law? By a law of works? No, but by the law of faith. For we hold that one is justified by faith apart from works of the law. Or is God the God of Jews only? Is he not the God of Gentiles also? Yes, of Gentiles also, since God is one—who will justify the circumcised by faith and the uncircumcised through faith. Do we then overthrow the law by this faith? By no means! On the contrary, we uphold the law (vv. 27-31).

The prophet Jeremiah said, "The heart is deceitful above all things, and desperately sick; who can understand it?" (Jer. 17:9). Under the inspiration of the Holy Spirit, Paul does an autopsy on Jeremiah's diagnosis of the heart. He has confirmed that man's heart is desperately sick and wicked. No one is good. No, not one! Paul asks, "Do we overthrow the law by this faith?" He answers: "By no means! On the contrary, we uphold the law." We could never be justified according to God's perfect law or anything in and of ourselves. We are justified by His grace as a gift through redemption in Christ Jesus alone—by the cross.

The cross confirms the law in three ways. First, it confirms it by paying the penalty of death, which the law demanded for our failure to follow its righteous requirements perfectly. Jesus fulfilled the law by His perfect and sinless life and by bearing the sin of humankind. He kept the law in His own life and then paid the debt of the law in our lives. Second, the cross confirms the law by pointing men to their need for faith in Christ. Remember, the righteousness of God was not fully revealed in the Law and the Prophets but in Christ. The Law and the Prophets were merely meant to bear witness to Him. Lastly, the cross confirms the Law by enabling us to fulfill it because of Christ in us.

There is therefore now no condemnation for those who are in Christ Jesus. For the law of the Spirit of life has set you free in Christ Jesus from the law of sin and death. For God has done what the law, weakened by the flesh, could not do. By sending his own Son in the likeness of sinful flesh and for sin, he condemned sin in the flesh, in order that the righteous requirement of the law might be fulfilled in us, who walk not according to the flesh but according to the Spirit (Rom. 8:1-4).

While our works are not saving us, they are bearing witness to Christ and the propitiatory work of Christ— that we are being transformed into His very image. Saving faith is knowing and living as though we stand justified before God on the basis of the gift of grace provided to us through the cross of Christ. Because of this, we live according to His Word. In regeneration, we grow to know and love God and believe His Word. Therefore, we live in obedience to it. Jesus said, "If you love me, you will keep my commandments" (John 14:15). In regeneration, our heart toward the law changes. In Psalm 119, David writes about how perfect, beautiful, and pure the law is. We love the law because it is the character of God.

These verses in Romans should dig a deep trench in our hearts, filling us with a reservoir of grace. As we elevate and see the truth about man's sinfulness and God's holiness, we elevate the value of grace. Many people today, maybe sincerely but foolishly, are afraid to tell sinners that they are sinners. All they want to tell them is about God's grace. However, this cheapens grace. The Word of God is the mystery and treasure of all the ages because it reveals us to the gospel. The only way to know and perceive this is to elevate God and see who we are compared to Him. Then, we will see the beautiful, immeasurable riches of God's grace that are available to us today and will be given to us in its fullness in the future. This is what we are living for in Christ!

8

ABRAHAM: A LIFE JUSTIFIED BY FAITH

ROMANS 4:1–12

What then shall we say was gained by Abraham, our forefather according to the flesh? For if Abraham was justified by works, he has something to boast about, but not before God. For what does the Scripture say? "Abraham believed God, and it was counted to him as righteousness." Now to the one who works, his wages are not counted as a gift but as his due. And to the one who does not work but believes in him who justifies the ungodly, his faith is counted as righteousness, just as David also speaks of the blessing of the one to whom God counts righteousness apart from works:

"Blessed are those whose lawless deeds are forgiven, and whose sins are covered; blessed is the man against whom the Lord will not count his sin."

Is this blessing then only for the circumcised, or also for the uncircumcised? For we say that faith was counted to Abraham as righteousness. How then was it counted to him? Was it before or after he had been circumcised? It was not after, but before he was circumcised. He received the sign of circumcision as a seal of the righteousness that he had by faith while he was still uncircumcised. The purpose was to make him the father of all who believe without being circumcised, so that righteousness would be counted to them as well, and to make him the father of the circumcised who are not merely circumcised but who also walk in the footsteps of the faith that our father Abraham had before he was circumcised.

THERE HAS NEVER BEEN ANYONE in the history of the world who was saved by any other means than by faith and the gift of grace given by God. No good person has risen to the level of being good enough for God, not because God judges us harshly but because God is holy. There is a chasm between the holiness and the goodness of God and His fallen and sinful created beings. So God, in His love for us, made a way for us. Paul uses the life of Abraham—saved and justified by God according to faith—to illustrate this.

The Jews considered Abraham the most righteous and revered man in Jewish history. He is the father of the nation of Israel and is considered the father of faith because he received the promise of God. From his seed, there would be a blessing for all people of all nations. Israel's heritage came through Abraham, his son Isaac, and his grandson Jacob, who was later renamed Israel. From Jacob's sons would come the twelve tribes of the nation of Israel.

In Romans 4, Paul communicates three things about Abraham. First, he espouses that Abraham was saved and justified before God based on faith, not works (vv. 1-8). Second, he was justified by grace, not by law (vv. 9-17). Lastly, Abraham was justified by God's power, not man's power (vv. 18-25).

Throughout the history of Israel, there are many heroes the Jewish people remember and admire; but there are three that stand out as the greatest and most revered: Abraham, the father of many nations; Moses, who led the Hebrews out of Egypt into the Promised Land and was given the law by God; and King David, the greatest king in Israel's history. If we look deeper at these three heroes of the Jewish faith and Paul's three points in Romans 4, we will see some interesting comparisons. For example, Abraham is not only the father of faith but also a person who needed to be justified before God. Moses was the giver of the Law, yet the Law did not save him. And when it comes to the power of men versus the power of God, King David was not the obvious choice among earthly men and thrones to replace King Saul. So what do we see with these three chosen men? We see grace, justification, and salvation given by God. All of this is through the power of God, not the power of man.

The Jews cite Abraham as an example of righteousness under the law or works of righteousness. However, Abraham's life is one of the greatest examples of a life justified by faith. He predates the giving of the law, and we have already established that no one is good based on God's standard of goodness. No, not one! This includes Abraham.

It does not say no one is good except Abraham, Moses, and David. All we have to do is study the Bible to realize Abraham was not perfect. He lied and was a coward when he pretended that his wife was his sister for fear that someone would harm him or try to kill him. Abraham was not completely faithful to the promise God had given to him. His lack of faith led to him fathering Ishmael, the son of his wife's handmaid, Hagar. We see this same imperfection in Moses, who grew weary of the Israelites and disobeyed God, costing him entrance into the Promised Land. King David, who was a man after God's own heart, engaged in adultery, used his power as king to get what he wanted and ordered murder to cover up his sin. Yet David was one of the greatest examples of God's grace worked out in a person's life. For those who truly understand God's holiness, Abraham, Moses, and King David's failings should be an encouragement.

The book of Galatians points back to Abraham's life: "And the Scripture, foreseeing that God would justify the Gentiles by faith, preached the gospel beforehand to Abraham, saying, 'In you shall all the nations be blessed'" (Gal. 3:8). How amazing that God preached the gospel to Abraham in the Old Testament. The promise given to Abraham was not only to bless Israel. Yes, there is a nation called Israel with ethnic Jews God brought into the Promised Land; and they were given specific promises, benedictions, and assurances in the Old Testament. Ultimately, however, Abraham was not merely the father of the Jewish nation; he was the father of faith.

We know this because Jesus rebukes the high priests and teachers of the Law in the New Testament and tells them that they are not the children of Abraham. This rebuke was driven by the fact that they did not have true faith in God. They didn't want God; they didn't love or fear Him; and they did not know Him because when God showed up face to face, they rejected and killed Him.

The promise given to Abraham wasn't just a mere geographical and ethnic promise given to a group of people. It was a spiritual promise that would be a blessing to all people, of all tribes, of all nations—anyone who would align themselves with the kingdom that will never pass away.

IMPUTED RIGHTEOUSNESS

What then shall we say was gained by Abraham, our forefather according to the flesh? For if Abraham was justified by works, he has something to boast about, but not before God (vv. 1-2).

There is no doubt Scripture tells us that Abraham was a man justified in the sight of God. He was a righteous man. The Bible conveys this about Abraham and others who predate him. From the very beginning, Scripture references people who knew and feared the sovereign God of the universe. In Hebrews 11, there is a list of those saved and justified by faith, beginning with Abel, Adam's son, whose sacrifice God approved. Enoch is also an example of one who pleased God.

Hebrews 11 lists both Jews and Gentiles who are justified by saving faith. The prostitute Rahab believed what Joshua told her; she hid his spies in Jericho, and God "counted it as righteousness" (Josh. 6:25). Rahab had faith in God. Scripture says, "And without faith it is impossible to please him, for whoever would draw near to God must believe that he exists and that he rewards those who seek him" (Heb. 11:6). Genuine faith acknowledges the God of the universe. If we believe in a God who created the world in six days and that there is no God except the God of the Bible, we will live a different kind of life. The lives of Abraham, Joshua, Rahab, and everyone else saved by faith in the Old Testament had evidence they were looking forward to and living toward God's salvation.

Why was Abraham counted as justified and righteous? What did he do? Why was Abraham pleasing in God's sight? Abraham took God at His word. He was made righteous because of his faith. Faith is knowing that we stand justified before God on the basis of Christ and that God will keep His promises. In Abraham's case, it was based on a future Messiah. Hebrews 11:39 says, "Though commended through their faith, did not receive what was promised." Abraham only greeted that blessing from far off.

Abraham received God's imputed righteousness. The theological word *imputed* means "superimposed, given, or put into." It is not something to find or earn. Imputed means it is applied to you. As Christians, our debt has been paid; and we are blessed because we are now sons and daughters of God. The gospel is not about anything we have done but what Christ did on the cross. All we do is believe by faith; and somehow, supernaturally, if it is a true belief, it transforms our lives. The gospel changes us and gives us a new heart.

If Paul were saying that God blessed Abraham because he was a righteous man, he would have something to boast about. However, Paul ends verse two by saying, "Not before God," which means works did not justify Abraham. Paul is making a distinction between the flesh and the Spirit. According to the flesh, Abraham was the father of the Jewish nation; and he was righteous and good. All ethnic Jews can trace their lineage back to him. But this has nothing to do with salvation. Salvation is from God—accomplished and secured by Christ on every level. It is by faith that we are saved. This includes Jews, Gentiles, and Abraham, the father of the Jewish nation.

COUNTED FOR RIGHTEOUSNESS

For what does the Scripture say? "Abraham believed God,
and it was counted to him as righteousness" (v. 3).

The Jews in Paul's day used Abraham as an example of a life to emulate. It was an unobtainable example or standard based on good works. Paul corrects this self-centered and flawed theology of the Jews who are teaching salvation by works. He uses Abraham as an example as he quotes from the Torah in Genesis 15:6: "And he believed the Lord, and he counted it to him as righteousness." In the beginning, long before Abraham was circumcised or anything significant was done through him, it says he believed God and was justified. He believed in the word of God.

Paul's teaching of faith over works is essential to recognize because adding any condition or requirement other than faith in Christ damages the gospel. If people think their good works add to their salvation, they have lost sight of the gospel. The most important thing to God is your eternal soul, and He will use any means necessary to conform you to the image of Christ. Paul points to this theme in other areas of Scripture with this rebuke to the Galatians:

> O foolish Galatians! Who has bewitched you? It was before your eyes that Jesus Christ was publicly portrayed as crucified. Let me ask you only this: Did you receive the Spirit by works of the law or by hearing with faith? Are you so foolish? Having begun by the Spirit, are you now being perfected by the flesh? Did you suffer so many things in vain—if indeed it was in vain? Does he who supplies the Spirit to you and works miracles among you do so by works of the law, or by hearing with faith—just as Abraham "believed God, and it was counted to him as righteousness"? Know then that it is those of faith who are the sons of Abraham. And the Scripture, foreseeing that God would justify the Gentiles by faith, preached the gospel beforehand to Abraham, saying, "In you shall all the nations be blessed." So then, those who are of faith are blessed along with Abraham, the man of faith (Gal. 3:1-9).

Anything we add to the gospel of Jesus Christ damages the all-sufficient work of Christ on the cross and God's sovereignty. Abraham is the father of the Jews in the flesh because all ethnic Jews descended from him. But more importantly, Abraham was counted as righteous because he *believed* in God's word. Paul is using a real-life example to teach against the legalism of his day. Abraham took God at His word, which is what imputed righteousness is all about. Faith is believing God's word. The true spiritual sons of Abraham are not those who descended from him ethnically but those who believe that they are saved by faith in God and trust Him with their life on earth and in eternity.

Faith is giving up control and the plan for this life, trusting God's Word, obeying it, and trusting God's promise for our eternity. Many want to go to Heaven, but they do not want to apply biblical faith to their lives now. Jesus addressed this when He said, "Whoever finds his life will lose it, and whoever loses his life for my sake will find it" (Matt. 10:39). Paul wants the Jews to understand that apart from God, Abraham's obedience and good deeds were like filthy rags regarding making him right before God. If Abraham was saved and justified by faith, then this applied to the Jews; and it applies to us today.

RIGHTEOUSNESS CREDITED BY FAITH

Now to the one who works, his wages are not counted as a gift but as his due.
And to the one who does not work but believes in him who justifies the ungodly,
his faith is counted as righteousness (vv. 4-5).

Faith is required for salvation, but it is not faith that saves us. It is *Who* our faith is in that saves us—and what He did to secure salvation as a free and unearned gift. This is why Paul rebuked the Galatians harshly because if man had anything to do with salvation, it would not be a gift.

Many Christian pastors and teachers present a mixture or a hybrid of works of righteousness and gospel. However, Paul gives a clear example of how these contradict each other. It is either a gift or not. A modern-day example is a person who makes thirty dollars an hour, works fifty-five hours, and receives a nice paycheck at the end of the week. But that paycheck is not a gift; it was earned. If we earn something, it is not a gift.

Paul teaches that we are wrong if we think we deserve salvation based on anything we have done. If we work for something, it is a wage. It is not grace. But for those who accept the gift of grace given to us in the gospel, God imputes the righteousness of Christ as a free and unearned gift because He loves us! Not because of anything we have done. This is true faith, and it changes and transforms us. It produces a gratefulness in our lives. To those who accept the free gift of grace given in the gospel, God will impute the righteousness of Christ. Paul also teaches this to the church in Ephesus:

> And you were dead in the trespasses and sins in which you once walked, following the course of this world, following the prince of the power of the air, the spirit that is now at work in the sons of disobedience—among whom we all once lived in the passions of our flesh, carrying out the desires of the body and the mind, and were by nature children of wrath, like the rest of mankind. But God, being rich in mercy, because of the great love with which he loved us, even when we were dead in our trespasses, made us alive together with Christ—by grace you have been saved—and raised us up with him and seated us with him in the heavenly places in Christ Jesus, so that in the coming ages he might show the immeasurable riches of his grace in kindness toward us in Christ Jesus. For by grace you have been saved through faith. And this is not your own doing; it is the gift of God, not a result of works, so that no one may boast. For we are his workmanship, created in Christ Jesus for good works, which God prepared beforehand, that we should walk in them (Eph. 2:1-10).

We will be humble and grateful if God's grace has saved us. We will find the secret of being content because, like Paul, we will realize that we "can do all things through him who strengthens [us]" (Phil. 4:13). We live for a future city because, by faith, we know immeasurable blessings and riches await us in Christ. If we do not see Christ as valuable, we will not live for Him. Denying ourselves in this life for His sake will seem foolish to a watching world that does not perceive the value of the treasure. Scripture says we deserve death: "For the wages of sin is death, but the free gift of God is eternal life in Christ Jesus our Lord" (Rom. 6:23). We are owed death, judgment, and condemnation. But because of the love of God in Christ, He took the punishment we deserved to satisfy the perfect justice of God; and He endured the wrath of God. The payment was made, and our accounts were made right. Not only did God give mercy, which means we are not subject to the penalty of our past, but He also gave grace, which provides us with an eternal future. John MacArthur writes, "Because God credits the believer's sin to Christ's account, He can credit Christ's righteousness to the believer's account. God could not have justly credited righteousness to Abraham had not Abraham's sin, like every believer's sin, been paid for by the sacrifice of Christ's own blood."[14]

Christ shed His blood for our benefit, and that blood covers us. This means nothing can separate us from God's love, His immeasurable riches, and eternity in His presence. We live by faith because we believe it. This was true for Abraham, the Jewish hero of the faith, and the Gentile prostitute Rahab. "Without faith it is impossible to please him" (Heb. 11:6).

WHO IS BLESSED?

Just as David also speaks of the blessing of the one to whom God counts righteousness apart from works: "Blessed are those whose lawless deeds are forgiven, and whose sins are covered; blessed is the man against whom the Lord will not count his sin" (vv. 6-8).

Previously, Paul used the words of Abraham, and now he quotes King David from Psalm 32. This is the psalm that David wrote after he was caught in adultery with Bathsheba and murdered her husband. The prophet Nathan confronted David with his sin, and he was humbled before the Lord and repented. David cried out in his brokenness, "Blessed is the one whose transgression is forgiven, whose sin is covered. Blessed is the man against whom the LORD counts no iniquity" (Psalm 32:1-2). David understood that our righteousness comes from outside of ourselves. He uses the word "blessed" in a salvific or eternal way. David is a part of Abraham's seed and a part of the lineage of Jesus; but he is blessed because of God, not for anything he did. When David was confronted with the truth of his sin, he repented before the Lord because he, too, was a man whose faith was credited to him as righteousness. Even in this grievous act of sin, David demonstrates that it was through faith that righteousness was credited to him.

THE SYMBOL OF CIRCUMCISION

Is this blessing then only for the circumcised, or also for the uncircumcised? For we say that faith was counted to Abraham as righteousness. How then was it counted to him? Was it before or after he had been circumcised? It was not after, but before he was circumcised (vv. 9-10).

The symbol of circumcision did not make Abraham mighty or righteous. Scripture says, "[Abraham] believed the LORD, and he accounted it to him for righteousness" (Gen. 15:6). This was years before he was circumcised. We know this because Ishmael was thirteen when Abraham and all his family were circumcised. Many years had passed, but the circumcision was a symbol of the faith that he had in God.

Again, the term "blessing" refers to salvation and eternal life. Another way to ask the question is this: who are God's people? Is it the Jews? Is it those who, like Abraham, have faith in the word of God; and because of it, they are counted as right before God? Paul says the true Jew is the one who has faith in God, and in Romans 3, he explains what that looks like and how it was accomplished through the work of Christ on the cross.

Abraham received God's promise long before he was circumcised. Circumcision was important because God had commanded Abraham and the Jews to be set apart as His covenant people. But what the legalistic Jews of Paul's day misunderstood was that circumcision was evidence of God's covenant with

Abraham, not the other way around. Like baptism, one can be baptized in water and not be a Christian; and Paul is saying that you can also be circumcised and not be a true son of Abraham. The symbolism does not save; it is merely an outward expression of an inward covenant. In the same way, faith itself does not save; our salvation is found in the Person in Whom our faith is directed. This is what baptism should represent and what circumcision was supposed to mean. Symbols do not save a person; only the word of God—the promise God made to us—a promise that was paid in full on the cross.

A SEAL OF RIGHTEOUSNESS

He received the sign of circumcision as a seal of the righteousness that he had by faith while he was still uncircumcised. The purpose was to make him the father of all who believe without being circumcised, so that righteousness would be counted to them as well, and to make him the father of the circumcised who are not merely circumcised but who also walk in the footsteps of the faith that our father Abraham had before he was circumcised (vv. 11-12).

The grace of God saved Abraham because he had faith in God. Scripture reminds us, "And without faith it is impossible to please him, for whoever would draw near to God must believe that he exists and that he rewards those who seek him" (Heb. 11:6). We have to take God at His Word. Anything that contradicts God's Word is a lie. It is not about perfectly walking it out. It is about being convinced, like Abraham when he took his son Isaac to the altar to sacrifice him in obedience to God. It's about being convinced, like Noah when he redirected his entire life to build the ark for decades and decades because the word of God had produced in him reverent fear. It's about being convinced, like Rahab, when she was willing to hide God's people at risk of death because she took the promise to heart. It is about believing in God; true belief will produce action and change a life.

Jews were commanded to be circumcised just like we, as Christians, are commanded to be water-baptized and observe the Lord's Supper. But without saving faith, these things are meaningless. We find another example of this in the book of Exodus. Why did the Angel of Death pass over the house of the Jews who put the blood of a lamb on their doorposts? Was it because they were Jews? No, it was because they obeyed God. If some of the Egyptians had known about this and had also put the blood over their doorposts, the Angel of Death would have passed over them, too.

The Jews did not lose their firstborn children. The Angel of Death passed over them because they had faith in what God said through His prophet Moses, and they obeyed. Faith in God has always been the means of being justified before God. In the first century, God revealed how He permanently accomplished His administration of truth and justice in the life of the believer, and that was through the penal substitutionary atonement and death of Christ. This was always God's plan, and the prophet Jeremiah confirms it:

> Thus says the Lord: "Let not the wise man boast in his wisdom, let not the mighty man boast in his might, let not the rich man boast in his riches, but let him who boasts boast in this, that he understands and knows me, that I am the LORD who practices steadfast love, justice, and righteousness in the earth. For in these things I delight, declares the Lord."

> "Behold, the days are coming, declares the LORD, when I will punish all those who are circumcised merely in the flesh—Egypt, Judah, Edom, the sons of Ammon, Moab, and all who dwell in the desert who cut the corners of their hair, for all these nations are uncircumcised, and all the house of Israel are uncircumcised *in heart*" (Jer. 9:23-26, emphasis added).

What makes us blessed and right before God? Is it through symbols like circumcision, baptism, or the Lord's Supper? Is it our good works? No, we are right before God through the blood of Christ—if we have faith in its power.

A ceremonial dip into a baptismal tank and physical circumcision cannot make us right with God. We need our scarlet red hearts washed white as snow, and we need circumcision of our hearts, which is only possible through the gospel of Jesus Christ. The lives of Abraham, Moses, and King David in the Old Testament are meant to lead us to the conclusion that we need a better covenant, Prophet, Priest, and King. We are foreigners, exiles, and sojourners merely passing through, and we are "looking forward to the city that has foundations, whose designer and builder is God" (Heb. 11:10).

9

THE PROMISE OF GRACE RECEIVED BY FAITH

ROMANS 4:13-25

For the promise to Abraham and his offspring that he would be heir of the world did not come through the law but through the righteousness of faith. For if it is the adherents of the law who are to be the heirs, faith is null and the promise is void. For the law brings wrath, but where there is no law there is no transgression.

That is why it depends on faith, in order that the promise may rest on grace and be guaranteed to all his offspring—not only to the adherent of the law but also to the one who shares the faith of Abraham, who is the father of us all, as it is written, "I have made you the father of many nations"—in the presence of the God in whom he believed, who gives life to the dead and calls into existence the things that do not exist. In hope he believed against hope, that he should become the father of many nations, as he had been told, "So shall your offspring be." He did not weaken in faith when he considered his own body, which was as good as dead (since he was about a hundred years old), or when he considered the barrenness of Sarah's womb. No unbelief made him waver concerning the promise of God, but he grew strong in his faith as he gave glory to God, fully convinced that God was able to do what he had promised. That is why his faith was "counted to him as righteousness." But the words "it was counted to him" were not written for his sake alone, but for ours also. It will be counted to us who believe in him

who raised from the dead Jesus our Lord, who was delivered up for our trespasses and
raised for our justification.

THERE IS A STARK CONTRAST between true religion, which worships the one true God, and all other religions. Most false religion is human-centered, whereas the Christian faith is entirely God-centered. True Christianity is based on what God has done and the promises that He has made, not on the works of man. Nearly every other religion in the world is focused on fulfilling rights, rituals, and ordinances so God might approve man. In contrast, Christianity is entirely dependent on the promises of God and, more specifically, a promise that God made to Abraham; and God has fulfilled this promise in every way. He is a God of covenant and promise. This is why Christianity is wholly built around and subordinate to the Word of God. Christianity depends entirely on God, and we are merely benefactors by faith. We know all of this from God's Word and through the power of the Holy Spirit, Who works to fulfill the covenant promises of His Word.

THE COVENANT AND PROMISE

When the prophet Jeremiah was called, the Lord said to him, "'You have seen well, for I am watching over my word to perform it'" (Jer. 1:12). God is a God of covenant and promise, and He will not waver in His word. This is why we must diligently study, read, and learn Scripture. We must study to show ourselves approved. This is not religious legalism. It is a foolish proposition to try and pit the study and comprehension of the Bible against the work of the Spirit because we study the words of God to know God, what He has commanded of us, what He expects of us, and what is promised to those who live by faith in His Word.

In the life of Abraham, we see promises made and fulfilled by God. Some were directly related to ethnic Israel; and some were made and fulfilled to

God's true and eternal children, both Jews and Gentiles. This is the gospel of grace, and we must focus on grace as an unmerited gift. God's grace in the gospel has zero to do with man's ability, ordinances, and the ability to live up to anything. It is about having faith in the belief that God creates and calls things into existence. God alone has the power to create life and to speak things into existence.

God's covenant promise with Abraham involves four different aspects. First, the promise included a people God would set apart for himself on the earth. These are the Jews, who were set apart to be the caretakers of the oracles of God, from which would rise up the prophets of God. Ultimately, a Savior and Redeemer would rise out of this group. The Jews were set apart to glorify God on earth and to point toward the Messiah, who would be the fulfillment of the promise of Abraham.

Second, the promise involved a literal piece of land. Although Abraham would not see it come to pass in his lifetime, nearly five hundred years later, they would possess the land God promised in a particular geographical location. Third, there was an eternal and spiritual purpose that would eventually bless the entire world. This is because the gospel of Jesus Christ is for everyone—all who "'[call] on the name of the Lord will be saved'" (Rom. 10:13). This includes Jews who understand and know the law, as well as the Gentiles who live their lives outside the law of God. The law was never meant to save us; it cannot save us. The law was meant to expose our sinfulness and magnify the righteousness and holiness of God.

Lastly, the ultimate fulfillment of God's covenant promise would be that a Redeemer would be given through the line of Abraham. He would make a way of salvation for all who believe. "And the Scripture, foreseeing that God would justify the Gentiles by faith, preached the gospel beforehand to Abraham, saying, 'In you shall all the nations be blessed'" (Gal. 3:8).

Some try to make the blessing of Abraham about temporal prosperity and power in this life. This is foolish thinking because Abraham's blessing has nothing to do with being successful or wealthy in this life. Yes, there is value in living according to the law of God and the proverbial wisdom of the Old Testament in this life. Paul mentions the earthly benefits of being a Jew, circumcised and living according to God's rules and ordinances. However, this is not what Abraham's blessing is about. It is about eternal life and salvation through Christ.

Abraham believed in God's promise by faith. He obeyed when God commanded him to sacrifice his son, the heir through whom the promise was supposed to be fulfilled. In Genesis 22, God told Abraham to take his son Isaac to the top of a mountain and sacrifice him. Scripture says that Abraham understood that even if he killed Isaac, God could raise him from the dead. This is saving faith! Believing that God would raise Isaac from the dead so that He could keep His word showed Abraham had a sound view of God's word.

Isaac questioned his father, "Where is the ram?"

Abraham responded, "God will provide the sacrifice." Although he did not know who Jesus was or how the gospel would come to fruition, he believed that God would send a sacrifice for the trespass and sin of mankind. This was counted to Abraham as righteousness.

The author of Hebrews gives a very concise summary of this event: "By faith Abraham, when he was tested, offered up Isaac, and he who had received the promises was in the act of offering up his only son, of whom it was said, 'Through Isaac shall your offspring be named.' He considered that God was able even to raise him from the dead, from which, figuratively speaking, he did receive him back" (Heb. 11:17-19).

God said that the promise of Abraham as the father of many nations would be fulfilled through Isaac and his descendants. Abraham believed God would keep His promise even if he had to kill Isaac. It is important to understand that for Abraham, Isaac was as good as dead because he had already made up his mind when he raised the dagger to plunge it into his body. He had reconciled himself to the fact that his son was going to die. This was the testing that proved Abraham's faith. Salvation is by grace alone, through faith alone, in Christ alone.

We find the most simplistic and practical understanding of this by answering this question: does the blessing come through obedience, or is obedience a fruit of the blessing? Many people teach that we will be right with God if we obey Him. While it is true that we must obey God, it is impossible to be right with God and receive the blessing of salvation promised to Abraham through good works because it is impossible for us to fulfill the law. Some people teach that if we want to be approved by God, we must obey Him. The only problem is we must live a perfect and sinless life; and because we are born into sin, this is impossible. In other words, we are not accepted by God because we obey; we obey because God has already accepted us completely. Obedience does not produce salvation; salvation produces obedience. This is by grace because of what Christ did on the cross. Coming to this realization produced Abraham's life of faith and every righteous man who has come after him. Our righteousness is imputed from Christ, not based on our good works.

This does not mean that we should live immoral and lawless lives. We should strive to obey God, do good, and live at peace with our neighbors. However, righteousness is a gift of grace imputed, implanted, and given to us by God. A life of obedience can indeed bring blessings and rewards in this life. Doing what is right will help us live in peace with others; but when it comes to being right with God, that is a gift of grace accomplished through the gospel of Jesus Christ. No one has ever been saved through keeping religious observances, rituals, or rights. This is the problem with the false religion of Roman Catholicism, as with many legalistic forms of religion in the world today. This was also the problem with the legalism of the Pharisees in the first century. They believed they were right with God by keeping the law, tithing, and not working on the Sabbath. They became so legalistic about these things because they thought their deeds were helping them be justified before God. That is why they did not know Him as God when Jesus showed up and took on flesh—full of grace and truth.

Abraham understood that nothing of man has the power to save. Jesus said, "Your father Abraham rejoiced that he would see my day. He saw it and was glad" (John 8:56). Although Abraham did not know who the Messiah would be, he knew that God would provide a sacrifice for the sins of the people. He lived his life in faith according to that fact. He knew God would make provision for the sins of men. The promise proceeded the law, which was merely a placeholder pointing to Christ, Who alone is our salvation. God is our salvation!

Nothing inside of us and nothing external has the power to save us except for Jesus Christ—His sinless life, His death on the cross, and the power that comes from His resurrection. This is why the way many people present the "salvation prayer" is so dangerous. We cannot reduce following God, repentance from sin, and having faith in a simple prayer or a religious ceremony. The evidence of a true, confessing Christian is the belief in our heart and what that produces in our lives. Good deeds will not save us, but they are evidence that we live a life of faith like Abraham.

For those who talk about finding success and worldly blessing through the law of God more than they do the gospel, the end of the tunnel for them is usually personal gain, worldly influence, and financial prosperity. "And they come to you as people come, and they sit before you as my people, and they hear what you say but they will not do it; for with lustful talk in their mouths they act; their heart is set on *their* gain" (Ezek. 33:31, emphasis added). This verse describes people who hear and even regurgitate God's words, but it is not in their hearts. They do not know Who God is or who they truly are. Their desperate need for the free, unearned, unmerited gift of grace is truly lost on them.

It says in the book of Isaiah, "And the Lord said: 'Because this people draw near with their mouth and honor me with their lips, while their hearts are far from me, and their fear of me is a commandment taught by men'"

(Isa. 29:13). Jesus paraphrased this same Scripture as he rebuked the Pharisees when He said, "'You hypocrites! Well did Isaiah prophesy of you, when he said: *This people honors me with their lips, but their heart is far from me; in vain do they worship me, teaching as doctrines the commandments of men*'" (Matt. 15:7-9).

Where does saving faith come from, and how is faith cultivated? Romans 10:17 says, "So faith comes by hearing, and hearing through the word of Christ." This is what our faith is built on—on what God has said—not what we hope in ourselves or want for ourselves, but what God has promised to those who love Him and diligently seek Him, not because we are trying to earn a place with him but because we understand the gravity of the gospel and the beautiful gift of grace.

THE DEEP CHASM

For the promise to Abraham and his offspring that he would be heir of the world did not come through the law but through the righteousness of faith. For if it is the adherents of the law who are to be the heirs, faith is null and the promise is void. For the law brings wrath, but where there is no law there is no transgression (vv. 13-15).

The promise of God to Abraham was not made by the law. It was a promise God made to Abraham that he received by faith. Abraham took God at His word. So much of Christianity is about taking God at His word. The law gives us what we deserve, which is justice; and there is no salvation in the law because no man will be justified by the law. We need grace! "All have sinned and fall short of the glory of God" (Rom. 3:23). Our good deeds are like filthy rag rags in the sight of God. "For the wages of sin is death, but the free gift of God is eternal life in Christ Jesus our Lord" (Rom. 6:23). It is only through Christ's perfection and sacrifice that justice is satisfied and mercy and grace are afforded.

God has not created multiple ways of escape. There is one way of escape from the consequences of our sin, and it is a narrow road that leads to life.

The narrow road is departure from the broad road of the world system of sin and self-reliance. That narrow road is Jesus Christ. The gospel does not look at what we should do; it looks at what God has done through His Son, Jesus Christ. By faith, we believe it; and God imputes righteousness to us.

The law gives us what we deserve. If salvation depended on us earning or getting the wages of what we deserve, there would be no reason for faith. God's promise to Abraham would be void because the law brings wrath and death; and after all, that is what we justly deserve. Mankind always wants to recenter on to "self" to find his footing and confidence in himself. Some people do it through business success. Some do it by feeling secure because they have a bank full of money or are in a relationship with the right person. Still, others find it in false religion as they observe ordinances and rights and go through the motions to make themselves feel like they have accomplished something. However, the law was never meant to save us. It cannot save us, but it does expose two crucial things. It magnifies and showcases that God is holy and righteous; because of that, it also shows that we are lost sinners who deserve wrath.

No one, including Abraham or any of his descendants, could live up to the law. Since the promise came before the law, it was given to Abraham as a gift. It is absurd to believe that God gave a conditional promise wherein it was impossible to achieve. That does not align with God's character because He is fully just, wise, honoring, and loving. God made a promise, to which He was the Guarantor. He gave the law to reveal His righteousness and man's sinfulness. The law can only bring wrath because it exposes how deep and wide the chasm is between God and man.

Paul says both those outside the law and under the law will die. We must understand this because if we do not, we will never truly have faith in the singularity of the gospel of Jesus Christ. The gospel is scandalous and offensive because it is the only way of salvation. All other ways lead to destruction. There is but one way, one truth, one life—"'no one comes to the Father except through [Him]," Jesus Christ (John 14:6). Paul further explains:

> What then shall we say? That the law is sin? By no means! Yet if it had not been for the law, I would not have known sin. For I would not have known what it is to covet if the law had not said, "You shall not covet." But sin, seizing an opportunity through the commandment, produced in me all kinds of covetousness. For apart from the law, sin lies dead. I was once alive apart from the law, but when the commandment came, sin came alive and I died. The very commandment that promised life proved to be death to me. For sin, seizing an opportunity through the commandment, deceived me and through it killed me (Rom. 7:7-11).

The law exposes sin. There is a chasm between God and us; but the law shines a light on just how wide and deep that chasm is, and grace is the bridge that unites one side with the other. The law demonstrates over and over again how depraved and wretched our hearts truly are. In Galatians, Paul rhetorically asked, "Why then the law? It was added because of transgressions, until the offspring should come to whom the promise had been made, and it was put in place through angels by an intermediary" (Gal. 3:19). Here Paul is conveying that the law is an intermediary until the one true Advocate arrives. Remember, the law was never meant to save us; instead, it was meant to be a tutor that leads us to Christ. The law was meant to bring us to despair and show us that there is no hope in this world or inside us apart from the gospel. Self-love is not the answer.

The only words that have the power to bring life is the truth of God's Word. Paul explains clearly:

> Now before faith came, we were held captive under the law, imprisoned until the coming faith would be revealed. So then,

the law was our guardian until Christ came, in order that we might be justified by faith. But now that faith has come, we are no longer under a guardian, for in Christ Jesus you are all sons of God, through faith. For as many of you as were baptized into Christ have put on Christ. There is neither Jew nor Greek, there is neither slave nor free, there is no male and female, for you are all one in Christ Jesus. And if you are Christ's, then you are Abraham's offspring, heirs according to promise (Gal. 3:23-29).

SPIRITUAL HEIRS

Before the foundation of the world, God had a plan in place. The law pointed us toward God and away from ourselves. It showed us that self-sufficiency was futile and pointless. Those who are heirs of Abraham are those who take God at His word, and these heirs are made up of all people: Jews, Gentiles, males, females, freemen, and slaves. From every demographic in the world, all "'who [call] upon the name of the Lord will be saved'" (Rom. 10:13). We are exiles and foreigners, and we are *not* meant to fit into this world. We are to live by faith according to the gospel of Jesus Christ, living our lives as if we are saved by grace alone through faith alone in Christ alone.

A PROMISE FOR EVERYONE

That is why it depends on faith, in order that the promise may rest on grace and be guaranteed to all his offspring—not only to the adherent of the law but also to the one who shares the faith of Abraham, who is the father of us all (v. 16).

Paul is using descriptive language to say the promise is not just for Jews. It is for Jews and Gentiles alike, united by one central truth—faith in Christ alone for salvation. He clarifies that he is speaking about Abraham's spiritual and eternal descendants. The blessing of Abraham is meant for his spiritual offspring. It is a promise that entirely depends on faith so that it might rest on the grace of God.

THE POWER OF LIFE

As it is written, "I have made you the father of many nations"—in the presence of the
God in whom he believed, who gives life to the dead and calls into existence the things
that do not exist (v. 17).

Only God has the power to give life to the dead and call things into existence. Under the inspiration of the Holy Spirit, Paul quotes scripture from Genesis 17:5. Abraham was not saved by works; he was saved by faith. He was not justified by law but by grace. The gift and promise made by God was despite Abraham's imperfection, and God fulfilled it.

MAN'S FAITH AND GOD'S GRACE

In hope he believed against hope, that he should become the father of many nations,
as he had been told, "So shall your offspring be." He did not weaken in faith when he
considered his own body, which was as good as dead (since he was about a hundred
years old), or when he considered the barrenness of Sarah's womb (vv. 18-19).

Man's faith and God's grace are both necessary ingredients for salvation but are not equal. Understand that man's faith is like a raindrop that falls into the ocean of God's grace. Yes, we must have faith in God to be saved. Scripture says, "With faith, it is impossible to please [God]" (Heb. 11:6); but it is not equal to grace because, like grace, faith is a gift from God.

Paul says, "In hope [Abraham] believed against hope" (Rom. 4:18). This was a poetic way of saying that Abraham believed when there was no natural reason to believe but only God's promise. Abraham was an old man, and Sarah was barren. No earthly circumstances could have convinced him that he would have an heir. The only thing that Abraham had was the word of God, and that was enough for him. Nothing has changed in our day. Those truly saved in Christ have faith, despite worldly wisdom or circumstances. This is righteousness counted to us based on faith. In hope, we believe against hope!

To be saved, we must believe that God has the power to raise the dead because if Christ is not raised, then neither shall we be. Our blessed hope is that we believe that we stand justified before God based on Christ. We believe that we will have abundant and eternal life in Him. We believe that the trespasses and stains of our sins have no bearing on our future because we have been made alive in Christ. Scripture says, "Therefore, if anyone is in Christ, he is a new creation. The old has passed away; behold, the new has come" (2 Cor. 5:17).

THE REPENTANCE BRIDGE

No unbelief made him waver concerning the promise of God, but he grew strong in his faith as he gave glory to God, fully convinced that God was able to do what he had promised. That is why his faith was "counted to him as righteousness" (vv. 20–22).

True faith will grow stronger and stronger as we become doers of the Word and see God's faithfulness in our own lives. Many in the church today deem that if they believe something is good or necessary for their life, God has promised it to them. Yet when it is not received, they lose faith because it is in something they wanted from God rather than God Himself and His word. Our faith will fail unless rooted and anchored in God's unwavering, unchanging, inerrant, and all-sufficient Word. However, there is a promise we can be sure of; it is that God will save all who trust Him in salvation through the life, death, and resurrection of Christ. True faith grows stronger. It does not waver. We will still face temptation and failure, but falling is not the same as giving up. If our faith is rooted in a proper understanding of God's promises in His Word, it will be tested, refined, pruned, and grow even stronger.

Abraham's belief in the promise God made him caused him to grow strong in faith, and it also caused him to give glory to God. Why did God give the blessing and promise to Abraham? "'God so loved the world, that he gave his one and only Son, that whoever believes in him should not perish but have eternal life'" (John 3:16). That is the fulfillment of the promise that God gave to Abraham. A Christian's faith rooted and anchored in God's Word will be tested, but it will stand the test and be strengthened and purified as silver or gold refined in the fire. Those with true saving faith will persevere to the end because Jesus is "the founder and perfecter of our faith" (Heb. 12:2).

IT WAS COUNTED

But the words "it was counted to him" were not written for his sake alone, but for ours also. It will be counted to us who believe in him who raised from the dead Jesus our Lord, who was delivered up for our trespasses and raised for our justification (vv. 23-25).

This part of the text is encouraging for all believers. Abraham is one of the greatest examples of faith in the Old Testament, yet he had the same avenue to salvation as we do. He took God at his word, lived by faith according to it, and it was counted to him as righteousness. That is salvation. We must live as if we believe in Him who raised Christ from the dead and that He did it for our trespasses and was raised for our justification. The qualification is repentance of our trespasses, which is evidence that we believe in all the imperatives of the gospel. This means we believe that God is holy, we are lost sinners unable to save ourselves, and that it is only through Christ's atoning work on the cross that we are justified before God.

Repentance does not make us right with God, but it is evidence of three essential things. First, repentance is evidence that we realize that we are not right with God and we need to be made right with Him. Second, it is evidence that we want to be made right with God. Realizing we are sinners is not enough. We have to acknowledge that we want to be made right by

God. Jesus said, "'Blessed are those who hunger and thirst for righteousness, for they shall be satisfied'" (Matt. 5:6). God promises that we will be satisfied. Lastly, repentance is evidence that we believe that through Christ, we can be made right with God. Through public confession of this faith, we are made right with God and stand justified because of Christ's perfect life, His atoning death, and justifying resurrection from the dead.

Repentance is evidence that we see the chasm between us and God and long for a bridge to reconcile us to Him. Christ is that Bridge; He is the Door; He is the Narrow Path; and He is the Way, the Truth, and the Life. Christ is our Salvation. Those who have committed their lives to Him have been made right with God based on Christ alone.

10

THE OUTPOURING AND THE INFILLING OF GOD'S LOVE

ROMANS 5:1–11

Therefore, since we have been justified by faith, we have peace with God through our Lord Jesus Christ. Through him we have also obtained access by faith into this grace in which we stand, and we rejoice in hope of the glory of God. Not only that, but we rejoice in our sufferings, knowing that suffering produces endurance, and endurance produces character, and character produces hope, and hope does not put us to shame, because God's love has been poured into our hearts through the Holy Spirit who has been given to us.

For while we were still weak, at the right time Christ died for the ungodly. For one will scarcely die for a righteous person—though perhaps for a good person one would dare even to die—but God shows his love for us in that while we were still sinners, Christ died for us. Since, therefore, we have now been justified by his blood, much more shall we be saved by him from the wrath of God. For if while we were enemies we were reconciled to God by the death of his Son, much more, now that we are reconciled, shall we be saved by his life. More than that, we also rejoice in God through our Lord Jesus Christ, through whom we have now received reconciliation.

THIS SECTION OF SCRIPTURE IS filled with assurance and encouragement for the true follower of Christ. Previously, Paul conveyed what qualifies us to rejoice in this great salvation. He did not go straight into the fact that God loves us or that there is grace in Christ. He first and foremost preached that we stand condemned before a holy God. This is an essential component of the gospel message that is often left out in our modern-day because we want people to feel good inside rather than bringing them to despair, which the law of God is designed to do. Here, Paul will explain why we can trust God's saving grace. He shares the depths and lengths God was willing to go to save those who believe by faith and how truly saved we are in the finished work of Christ.

COUNTED AND AT PEACE

Therefore, since we have been justified by faith, we have peace with God through our Lord Jesus Christ (v. 1).

Paul assumes that we understand what he communicated in Romans 4. Works do not save us; the law does not justify us; and no one will come to salvation under the power of man's effort. With this understanding, he says, "Therefore, since we . . . " His reference to "we" refers to all Christians who call upon the name of the Lord and are transformed and live for Him. All Christians throughout the history of the world have been justified by faith in what Christ has done, not in what we have done. The only part that man contributes is true faith in God.

Paul wants us to understand that when we are saved by faith, we are saved to the uttermost because God is doing the saving. There never comes a time when our salvation has anything to do with our effort. We are saved by faith in the finished work of Christ. God desires true faith. He wants us to take Him at His word, like Abraham did. To those who do, God promises He will save them fully and completely. "Looking to Jesus, the founder and perfecter of our faith, who for the joy that was set before him endured the cross, despising the shame, and is seated at the right hand of the throne of God" (Heb. 12:2). So, who began this work of salvation? God did. And if you are truly regenerated and justified, you are in the process of being sanctified. If God's salvation is truly at work in you, He will bring it to completion. As Philippians 1:6 says, "And I am sure of this, that he who began a good work in you will bring it to completion at the day of Jesus Christ."

> And we know that for those who love God all things work together for good, for those who are called according to his purpose. For those whom he foreknew he also predestined to be conformed to the image of his Son, in order that he might be the firstborn among many brothers. And those whom he predestined he also called, and those whom he called he also justified, and those whom he justified he also glorified.(Rom. 8:28).

These two verses declare that God started salvation and will continue to sanctify us throughout our lives. He says, "I will keep you, and I will ultimately glorify you." Glorification is the gift we receive at the end of our lives, where we will be free from sin and in the presence of God forever. You do not lose your salvation because you fall short; if that were the case, then no one would be saved. However, suppose someone is living in a long season of unrepentant sin. In that case, it may be confirmation that they were never really saved. Those whom he predestined he also called, and those whom he called, he also justified, and those whom he justified he also glorified" (Rom. 8:30). Understand that for those who truly want to follow God, He will keep them. He died for us; and ultimately, God is the One Who will glorify us.

We rejoice in God's peace, which this world cannot give or take away. The Bible describes it as a peace that surpasses human understanding (Phil. 4:7). Not only are we at peace with God, but it also says that we have access to God by faith through grace—the grace in which we now stand. This is the posture of the Christian life. We stand because of God's grace, and we stand in God's grace—and this is the life of faith. We stand righteous in the judgment of God. The judgment of God is coming, but here is the question: will we be judged on our merits, or will we be judged on the merits of Christ's life? The first psalm shares an example of someone living for God:

> Blessed is the man who walks not in the counsel of the wicked, nor stands in the way of sinners, nor sits in the seat of scoffers; but his delight is in the law of the LORD, and on his law he meditates day and night. He is like a tree planted by streams of water that yields its fruit in its season, and its leaf does not wither. In all that he does, he prospers. The wicked are not so, but are like chaff that the wind drives away. Therefore the wicked will not stand in the judgment, nor sinners in the congregation of the righteous; for the LORD knows the way of the righteous, but the way of the wicked will perish (Psalm 1:1-6).

The righteous person will bear the fruit or evidence of regeneration. God is changing him from the inside out because he is surrendered to God. He is living according to the law because Christ has saved him. But what does this psalm say about the wicked? "They will not stand in the judgment." They will not stand up and be counted as righteous, nor do they have access to the congregation of the righteous. In Romans, Paul tells us that we will stand not on our righteousness or achievements but in God's grace; because of that, we have access to the congregation of the righteous. We are counted as one of God's righteous children based on Christ, and we are at peace regarding the judgment of God.

LIVING AN INTERNAL TESTIMONY

Through him we have also obtained access by faith into this grace in which we stand,

and we rejoice in hope of the glory of God (v. 2).

We have joy in our blessed hope and the coming glory of God. Christ was truly and rightfully King in both His humiliation and exaltation; while He was living on earth as a baby; when He was beaten, whipped, and mocked; and when He bled and died on the cross. He was as much a King in those moments as now—exalted and sitting at the Father's right hand. The same applies to the Christian. If a person is "in Christ," they are as much a child of God right now as they will be on the day of glorification. Our debt is paid in full if we belong to Christ.

HOPE FOR FUTURE GLORY

Not only that, but we rejoice in our sufferings, knowing that suffering produces endurance, and endurance produces character, and character produces hope (v. 3-4).

We exalt Christ because of our hope for future glory—the glory of God. The refining fire of suffering accomplishes something in us that nothing else can. What does it do? It burns away other things we might be tempted to put our hope in. We say our hope is in Christ; but sometimes, upon further analysis, it becomes clear that it is really in money, a career, a relationship, or some external thing in your life. But suffering burns those things away and proves the genuineness of what is underneath. This is why the Old Testament message of gold or silver refined in a fire is so important.

When everything else is burned away, all that is left is pure and stronger than before. However, everything will be burned up if nothing precious and true is there. Suffering will burn everything else away to strengthen our hope in that future glory. The refining fire of suffering accomplishes something so crucial in the Christian. When it burns away money, status, health, and relationships, it builds assurance in the one thing that will never fail.

Suffering also produces endurance and perseverance. It helps us persevere by cleansing us of unrighteousness and proving what is pure, eternal, and real. "Endurance produces character, and character produces hope." God is going to judge us based on our character and faithfulness. Godly character is about our faithfulness to God. The beautiful part is that as God is refining us, He is forging the character of Christ in us. This is why when we suffer, we should rejoice and be glad. Suffering burns away all impurities, conforming us to the image of Christ until we are left with a purer and stronger hope than we started with.

HOPE THAT DOES NOT DISAPPOINT

And hope does not put us to shame, because God's love has been poured into our hearts through the Holy Spirit who has been given to us (v. 5).

The New American Standard Bible says, "And hope does not disappoint." If our hope is in God, we will not be disappointed or put to shame because the power of God in the gospel is an unbreakable promise. However, those who do not put their faith in God but in something else will find their faith stripped away. They will be put to shame. But Paul is saying that we will not be ashamed if our hope and affection are in God because God has poured His love into us.

We will stand in the judgment instead of being struck down. Some people will humbly bow in this life, and God will exalt them in the life to come. Others will boastfully and pridefully live for themselves in this life and will not stand in judgment because they will be struck down. Those of us in Christ will stand because of Christ.

Another powerful truth is that we will not only stand in the future, but we can also stand today because we have access to God. God has not left us alone looking toward the future. The word "access" in both Greek and English is in the present tense. It is not in the past tense or future tense. We have access to God now because of what Christ did in the past and the hope of glory we have in the future.

Our faith is not just a mental knowing or belief. If our lives are rooted in truth, there will be feelings, emotions, and experiences because the love of God is not just a concept. We experience God's love in salvation in this life, not just mentally but deep inside our hearts. It is the Spirit of God living in us. Our faith is rooted in knowing Who God is from His Word, which is the external testimony of God. Still, He also gives us an internal testimony. God has made external promises to those who believe in Christ for salvation. We are looking forward to a future event in a future city, but there is an internal reckoning and internal evidence in this life for those of us who are in Christ. This is the love of God! This fellowship we have with God is rooted in His love being "poured into our hearts through the Holy Spirit."

The first evidence of spiritual regeneration is the love of God that has been poured *into* you and now flows *through* you. This is why Jesus said, "'By this all people will know that you are my disciples, if you have love for one another'" (John 13:35). Love is the first evidence mentioned in the nine tenets of the fruit of the Spirit. The evidence that you are a Christian is "love, joy, peace, patience, kindness, goodness, faithfulness, gentleness, self-control (Galatians 5:22-23). When Jesus summed up the Ten Commandments in the New Testament, He said, "*Love the Lord your God with all your heart and with all your soul and with all your mind and with all your strength.* The second is this: *Love your neighbor as yourself.* There is no commandment greater than these'" (Mark 12:30-31).

The first four commandments on the first tablet of the Law are about our relationship with God, and the other six commandments on the second tablet of the Law are about our relationship with people. Jesus injects the law with the governing principle of love, turning what the Ten Commandments pose negatively into a positive statement. Instead of "thou shalt not" because of the love of God, "thou shalt do." We keep the commandments not out of a begrudging duty but out of our love for God because He has implanted His love inside of us.

GOD: LOVE DEFINED

For while we were still weak, at the right time Christ died for the ungodly.
For one will scarcely die for a righteous person—though perhaps for a good person one
would dare even to die—but God shows his love for us in that while we were still sinners,
Christ died for us (v. 6-8).

Why did God die for us? His reason was that He loves us, but the underlying cause was to save us. God saved us from God. Yes, Christ, being God, died for us to save us from God's righteous wrath and judgment. To be perfect in love, God also must be perfectly just. God had to rectify the sins of mankind with a perfect sacrifice, a sinless man—God in the flesh, Jesus. Scripture says, "For God so loved the world, that he gave his only Son, that whoever believes in him should not perish but have eternal life'" (John 3:16). We must know this to be saved, but Paul is teaching that we also must experience this in our relationship with Christ, which comes through the Spirit of God.

As previously mentioned, we cannot root our faith only in experiences, but a true, biblically rooted faith will have experience. An example is a Christian marriage, where the union is a godly commitment to a spouse. Love is dedication and produces feelings and experiences; but sometimes, we do not always have the same feelings we once did in marriage. Feelings ebb and flow; so to have a good marriage, we must hang on to the promise of our commitment to one another. The same is true in Christianity; and often, we will experience a purer and stronger love on the other side of a trial and refining. A biblically rooted faith will have expression, fellowship, and a relationship.

In verse eight, Paul mentions that God died for us "while we were still sinners"; but this is in the context of God pouring His love into us. Paul gives us an enduring example of love that cannot be surpassed. Someone might die for a noble person or cause. We witness this in our military, where people have died to save others. But this is an exception to the norm. Paul is describing a completely different type of love. The truest example of God's love is that "while we were still sinners, Christ died for us." The Bible says this makes God's love so beautiful and impactful. In a society that raises the banner of love as a god, we do not worship love; we worship God Who is love. God determines what love is, and genuine love is sacrificial and selfless.

God is Love, which is what love looks like in its purest form. Christ died for us, not because we had potential or because we would do great things for the kingdom but because He loved us. What kind of love is this? A love that died for us while we were still sinners, a love that saves, justifies, and transforms—a love that cannot fail. This is a redeeming, selfless love toward undeserving rebel sinners. God hates sin, but His love is extended to us without reservation during this life.

However, we cannot conflate or over-romanticize the word "love" to mean God's love is unending toward everyone for all eternity. People often say that God's love is the same for everyone forever and that He hates sin but loves the sinner. Well, the bad news is that God does not send sin to Hell; He sends unrepentant sinners to Hell. All of us are rebel sinners; we are outside of Christ and scheduled for a day of reckoning and judgment. Yet, throughout our lives, God has made a way for us to be saved. God sacrificed His precious and beautiful Son in His gracious love toward us.

If we reject the precious blood of Christ, the Lamb of God will judge us and torment us forever in the fire of Hell. The book of Revelation says, "The smoke of their torment goes up forever and ever" (Rev. 14:11). Either you will be part of the body of Christ, or you will be part of the footstool upon which He rests his feet. We are not worthy of the love of God! God is holding eternity and judgment back with one hand and reaching out to us with the other hand, and He is saying, "Come unto Me for forgiveness and salvation." But if we reject God in the gospel of Jesus Christ, at some point, He will drop both hands and let us go our own way, giving us what we deserve. Those who reject the love of God will be rightfully and justly subject to eternal wrath and judgment, not by the devil but by the Lamb of God.

FULLY SAVED

Since, therefore, we have now been justified by his blood, much more shall we be saved by him from the wrath of God (v. 9).

Here, Paul gets to the positive part of his statement. If we are saved by the blood of Christ, we are saved fully. We cannot save ourselves. But God keeps us, and Scripture says, "He who began a good work in you will bring it to completion at the day of Jesus Christ" (Phil. 1:6).

As Christians, we have been justified by the blood of Christ. If we are in Christ, we are hidden in Him. For those outside of Christ, their judgment is looming and is being compounded daily by their trespasses and their rejection of the blood of Christ. For those in Christ, the wrath they deserve has already been satisfied by Jesus dying on the cross. The love of God is poured out for us, and it changes who we are and how we live. Those who experience the saving love of God will be filled with joy—a joy the world cannot give you, and the world cannot take away. They will experience peace and be peaceable toward men because they are at peace with God. A person who is full of love, joy, and peace will also be a person who is patient, kind, good, faithful, and self-controlled in an ever-increasing way.

THE INFILLING OF THE SPIRIT

For if while we were enemies we were reconciled to God by the death of his Son, much more, now that we are reconciled, shall we be saved by his life. More than that, we also rejoice in God through our Lord Jesus Christ, through whom we have now received reconciliation (v. 10-11).

Those who gladly and joyously accept the outpouring of the love of God at the cross will receive the infilling of the love of God by His Spirit. Those who have been regenerated and saved through the gospel will bear fruit and evidence that the Spirit of God lives in them. By faith, we believe we are justified before God based on a past promise accomplished fully through a past event. Because of this, by faith, we live toward the blessed hope of a future event. But our surety in God is not only in these external things. It is experienced internally in a living and active fellowship with God.

We are God's external possession; but forevermore, starting at our conversion, we are in possession of the love of God, which has been given to us in the form of the Spirit of God—a love that provides us with surety of our salvation; that cannot be overcome by sin; that not only saves us but sanctifies and changes us; a love that disciplines, corrects, and encourages us as it refines us; a love that keeps no record of wrongs; a love filled with joy and peace; a love that is patient, kind, good, faithful, gentle, and self-controlled; a self-denying and self-sacrificial love. Like all the promises of God, it is a love that will never fail. "But God shows his love for us in that while we were *still* sinners, Christ died for us. Since, therefore, we have now been justified by his blood, much more shall we be saved by him from the wrath of God" (Rom. 5:8-9, emphasis added).

The love of God is lavish, beautiful, and extravagant. And what should be our rightful response to His love? To live our lives as a living sacrifice unto God. "If anyone would come after me, let him deny himself and take up his cross and follow me'" (Mark 8:34). Give up everything and follow Him because He is worthy!

11

THE GLORY OF GOD IN THE PERFECTION OF CHRIST

ROMANS 5:12-21

Therefore, just as sin came into the world through one man, and death through sin, and so death spread to all men because all sinned—for sin indeed was in the world before the law was given, but sin is not counted where there is no law. Yet death reigned from Adam to Moses, even over those whose sinning was not like the transgression of Adam, who was a type of the one who was to come.

But the free gift is not like the trespass. For if many died through one man's trespass, much more have the grace of God and the free gift by the grace of that one man Jesus Christ abounded for many. And the free gift is not like the result of that one man's sin. For the judgment following one trespass brought condemnation, but the free gift following many trespasses brought justification. For if, because of one man's trespass, death reigned through that one man, much more will those who receive the abundance of grace and the free gift of righteousness reign in life through the one man Jesus Christ.

Therefore, as one trespass led to condemnation for all men, so one act of righteousness leads to justification and life for all men. For as by the one man's disobedience the many were made sinners, so by the one man's obedience the many will be made righteous. Now the law came in to increase the trespass, but where sin increased, grace abounded all the more, so that, as sin reigned in death, grace also might reign through

righteousness leading to eternal life through Jesus Christ our Lord.

W E ARE JUSTIFIED BY FAITH in Christ alone. The Latin term *sola fide*—by faith alone—was one of the five *solas* of the Protestant Reformation. Our justification has been imputed to us, which means it has been put into us. We must understand that our justification has imputed Christ's righteousness into us. If we believe otherwise, it means we believe that we somehow obtained it on our own. Our faith is entirely about what Christ did on the cross. Most people who claim they belong to Christ would agree with that statement on the surface. However, when we see how many apply this practically to their lives, it becomes apparent that many who claim to believe this will contradict themselves.

Superficially, many of us will say that we are saved by faith in Christ; but as life and trouble come or as blessing and peace come, we begin to believe somehow that we are contributing to our salvation. We must understand this does not mean we should not do good works but instead realize those works cannot save us. The good works we do result from what Christ has done for us and in us. Christianity is about spiritual rebirth and regeneration. It is surrendering to Christ's Lordship and planting a new tree while the other tree is dying. To truly understand the depths of the gospel, the Father's love for us, and the unbreakable assurance of our salvation, we must first truly understand how wretched, wicked, and horrific sin is. That is why Paul belabors this point in the first three chapters of Romans. Misunderstanding the depth of God's love comes from not comprehending the depth of our sin. Many have a superficial understanding of the gospel of Jesus Christ because they do not look deeply into themselves and look intently at Who the God of the Bible is.

In Romans 1 and 2, Paul teaches us about original sin and man's total depravity; but he very plainly lays out sin's depth and power in Romans 3. Sometimes, people do not want to talk about the power and depth of sin for fear of giving too much glory to sin or Satan. But this is not the case because, by the end of Romans 5, it becomes clear that the law makes sure that we understand that as sin abounds, our knowledge of the depth of sin increases. When we look at sin the way God looks at sin, we are coming to grips with the reality that things are worse than we thought. But when we realize that sin is greater and deeper than we might have thought, we are assured that grace abounds even more. By looking intently at Who God is and how grievous sin is, we understand how great, beautiful, and valuable grace is.

The default disposition of mankind is being dead in sin and trespass; and until we truly understand that, we will not comprehend our need for a Savior. Jesus is the only Way to God, and Paul is doing what we all should do when we present the gospel. We cannot preach the gospel without talking about sin and the fact that we are all sinners, damned and condemned. We are all hopeless outside of Christ. Unless we understand this hopelessness, we will never see the beauty of Jesus and our need for a Savior. Jesus said, "Ask, and it will be given to you; seek, and you will find; knock, and it will be opened to you. For everyone who asks receives, and the one who seeks finds, and to the one who knocks it will be opened'" (Matt. 7:7-8). However, do not mistake seeking the things God provides as seeking God. There is no such thing as a seeker who looks for God but does not find Him. The Seeker in the story is God. He is the One Who died for us while we were yet sinners.

THE HIGH VIEW OF GOD

Therefore, just as sin came into the world through one man,
and death through sin, and so death spread to all men because all sinned (v. 12).

Paul explains how we became a race of people that fell under the curse of sin through Adam and how those who put their trust and faith in Christ alone become a redeemed race of people. The word "therefore" ties these verses to the previous ones:

But God shows his love for us in that while we were still sinners, Christ died for us. Since, therefore, we have now been justified by his blood, much more shall we be saved by him from the wrath of God. For if while we were enemies we were reconciled to God by the death of his Son, much more, now that we are reconciled, shall we be saved by his life. More than that, we also rejoice in God through our Lord Jesus Christ, through whom we have now received reconciliation (Rom. 5:8-11).

Understanding the grave nature of what we came out of is essential to recognize our weakness in sin. However, the positive side is that it will also increase dependence and faith, and our awareness of our need for God will grow. This is part of the sanctification process.

When I was a new Christian coming out of addiction, people began to notice that I was getting progressively better outwardly. That was true, and this is called bearing fruit. As Christ sanctifies us, we begin to change. But when the refining fire of trial comes, it exposes the validity of our faith. My family noticed a difference in me because the nature of Christ was growing in me.

However, internally, I began to realize I was much worse than I thought. Before Christ, I knew I needed some exterior changes in my life: getting off drugs, hoping I could secure a high-paying job, buying a house, and being a productive member of society. I obtained all of those things during my first stint of sobriety; but they did not satisfy me, nor did they last. God revealed a deficiency in me that was much deeper and more severe than I realized. Like Paul, I found the strength of Christ in my weakness. I realized I needed something all-sufficient and powerful. I didn't need to be refurbished; I needed to be remade.

People often have trouble believing that sin came into the world through one man. Some feel that it is unfair to have been subjected to the consequences of one man's sin. Most of our theological problems with the Bible come from our problem with evil and a flawed view of God's fairness or goodness. This comes from a low view of God and Scripture and a high view of mankind as we sit and judge God. This is not being a regenerated person. The beginning of life in Christ is realizing that He is God, and the Word of God is where we find all we need for life and godliness.

> He is the image of the invisible God, the firstborn of all creation. For by him all things were created, in heaven and on earth, visible and invisible, whether thrones or dominions or rulers or authorities— all things were created through him and for him. And he is before all things, and in him all things hold together. And he is the head of the body, the church. He is the beginning, the firstborn from the dead, that in everything he might be preeminent. For in him all the fullness of God was pleased to dwell, and through him to reconcile to himself all things, whether on earth or in heaven, making peace by the blood of his cross (Col. 1:15-20).

This Scripture reveals that all things were created by and for God. God is the Creator, and He made everything for His sovereign purposes. We cannot superimpose our idea of what we believe is fair or just on God. We do not deserve anything from God but condemnation and judgment. But we are blessed that He created us, reconciled us to Himself through the blood of His Son, and gave us eternal life and sonship.

Everything God grants us is grace. There are two kinds of grace: common grace and saving grace. Common grace is extended to all, including those living a rebellious life toward God, ignoring Him, or even blaspheming Him. They still get a daily allowance of air and food. The sun still shines down on them. If they plant a seed in the ground and water it, it grows; and they benefit from the earth's gravitational pull. God still extends common grace to them despite their sinful and rebellious hearts.

This is the common grace God extended to me while I was in addiction. I lived my life like there was no God in Heaven; but I could still eat, breathe, and live. But amazing, salvific grace is only granted to those who live by faith in the finished work of Christ on the cross. Christ died for the world, so all who believed in Him would be saved.

In verse twelve, when it says, "And so death spread to all men because all sinned," it means all men have sinned in Adam. We were damned before we committed one sin. We were born into sin and under a curse. Understanding this reality makes us find surety and confidence in what Christ did. One man brought sin into the world, and one Man eradicated sin and death. Adam was not subject to death before the Fall. He was given one prohibition: not to eat the fruit of the tree of the knowledge of good and evil. None of us had that benefit; we are all subject to death from birth. Every person born after Adam is subject to sin and the death that comes with it.

THE GLORIOUS PLAN OF THE CROSS

For sin indeed was in the world before the law was given, but sin is not counted where there is no law. Yet death reigned from Adam to Moses, even over those whose sinning was not like the transgression of Adam, who was a type of the one who was to come (vv. 13-14).

Paul is conveying that Adam disobeyed God's single prohibition, not eating from the tree of the knowledge of good and evil, causing sin to be passed down to all of his descendants, even though the law of God had not yet been given to Moses. We know this practically because all men from Adam on died and empirically because God's Word tells us so. The Bible says, "The wages of sin is death" (Rom. 6:23). Wages are something we earn; so we have not only been born into sin under the curse, but we are compounding our judgment as we live to commit willful and unwilful sins.

It says Adam was a type, which means he was a shadow of the One who was to come. Again, in Colossians 1:16 it says, "All things were created through him and for him." It goes on to say he would be "the firstborn from the dead, that in everything he might be preeminent" (Col. 1:18). The NIV says, "So that in everything he might have the supremacy." Jesus the Christ is God, and He created everything; and everything is subject to Him. All glory belongs to Him. But what Christ did and how the gospel reconciled us to Him made us something above other created beings. Christ tied Himself to human flesh and died a death like us and rose from the dead so that He might be the firstborn among many brethren from the dead. That is solidarity! We can have solidarity with people in this life, but we cannot have saving solidarity. The difference is Christ became like us so we could become like Him. Jesus is preeminent and supreme in all things.

Colossians 1:19-20 says, "For in him all the fullness of God was pleased to dwell, and through him to reconcile to himself all things, whether on earth or in heaven, making peace by the blood of his cross." The cross and the gospel were not in reaction to Adam's fall. God did not have a plan, and then we messed it up, so He had to go back to the drawing board to figure out a way to save us. No, it was so that God's glory, mercy, and power might be displayed on the earth. The cross was always the plan!

The Bible says before the foundation of the world, the names of the saints were written in the Lamb's Book of Life (Rev. 13:8). This was always the way. In light of God's supremacy and sovereignty, we must realize that all things are for God's glory; and He is worthy of all glory. He is worthy of whatever it costs.

The cross wasn't an afterthought; it was always the plan. God planned to give a people to His Son. Adam's failure was meant to magnify the glory of Christ. The imperfect sacrifices of the temple and the imperfect priesthood were meant to magnify the glory of Christ. The corrupt kingdoms that rise and fall in this world are only meant to magnify the one King Who will reign forever and ever as the saints gather around Him saying, "Holy is the Lord God Almighty. The earth is full of His glory. Hallelujah!" All things in creation are meant to glorify God. Anything that does not glorify and worship God is in rebellion against God.

Your life is not your own. You are not doing Jesus a favor by inviting him into your heart. He is not hanging around the door of your house waiting on bended knee, desperate for you to accept Him. No, He is a reigning King, and His kingdom is coming. He asks us to lay down our sword of rebellion and follow Him. Then, not only will He not hold our insurrection against us, but we will also become a part of His kingdom.

FREE AND UNDESERVED GIFT

But the free gift is not like the trespass. For if many died through one man's trespass, much more have the grace of God and the free gift by the grace of that one man Jesus Christ abounded for many. And the free gift is not like the result of that one man's sin. For the judgment following one trespass brought condemnation, but the free gift following many trespasses brought justification (vv. 15-16).

Adam's one act of disobedience brought sin, death, and condemnation to all mankind. The one seed of Adam's sin produced a tree that is replicating, branching off, and being compounded to this very day. That one sin brought much sin into the world. In contrast, Jesus, in His obedience and perfect innocence, put an axe to the root of that tree. This is why, at the beginning of Jesus' earthly ministry, His forerunner, John the Baptist, said, "The axe is laid to the root" (Matt. 3:10). The tree is dead, and it is lying to the side. Everyone connected to that tree is waiting to be thrown into the fire. John 15:4 says, "What good is a broken branch?" Jesus' one act was valuable enough to counteract the one act of sin that Adam committed. We are grafted into a new tree that is alive and gives us life because death has been overcome, and sin has been defeated at the source.

Christ was able to do what Adam did not do, and no one after him could do. Adam had the opportunity to live a life without sin and death. He didn't, but Christ did because He was not born of the seed of man but by the power of the Spirit when Mary conceived Him as a virgin. It had to be a supernatural birth because the seed of man is cursed. So, Jesus did what Adam didn't do and no one after Him has the ability to do, which is live in perfect obedience, which qualifies Him to be the perfect Sacrifice for our sins. His innocence was more valuable than all the guilt of all humankind's past, present, and future sins.

To have saving faith that gives us true fruit-bearing salvation, we must see Christ as valuable enough to rectify the sin of mankind. Christ's justification is far greater than Adam's transgression and our transgressions. We have confidence in our salvation by faith and through the Lordship and supremacy of Christ in all things. The justification we have in Christ is a free gift. We have done absolutely nothing to earn it. The clearer our view of the holiness of God, how wretchedly sinful we are, how truly damning sin is, and how much God hates and cannot coexist with sin, the more valuable the free gift of grace will be to us.

A casual and unrepentant life of sin shows a low view of God with little value of God's grace. Hebrews explains:

> For if we go on sinning deliberately after receiving the knowledge of the truth, there no longer remains a sacrifice for sins, but a fearful expectation of judgment, and a fury of fire that will consume the adversaries. Anyone who has set aside the law of Moses dies without mercy on the evidence of two or three witnesses. How much worse punishment, do you think, will be deserved by the one who has trampled underfoot the Son of God, and has profaned the blood of the covenant by which he was sanctified, and has outraged the Spirit of grace? For we know him who said, "Vengeance is mine; I will repay." And again, "The Lord will judge his people." It is a fearful thing to fall into the hands of the living God (Heb. 10:26-31).

This passage of Scripture refers to an unregenerate person living out their sins apart from Christ's salvation. True Christians are deeply concerned about their sins and mortify and fight to overcome them. We do not have to fight to be saved; we rest in our salvation. But from that place of rest, we battle against sin. Those who love God want to please Him and will fight the sin He hates because we are now part of a different kingdom.

The person who fears the Lord will seek God's mercy. Proverbs 9:10 says, "The fear of the Lord is the beginning of wisdom, and the knowledge of the Holy One is insight." But the person who thinks they deserve mercy proves they do not know God. They do not understand how grievous their sin is and how wicked their heart is. The preacher who never addresses sin or talks about the holiness of God has no idea what is in the heart. The prophet Jeremiah understood this and said, "The heart is deceitful above all things, and desperately sick; who can understand it?" (Jer. 17:9).

The problem is we think we know our hearts, but God knows us better than we know ourselves. "For the word of God is living and active, sharper than any two-edged sword, piercing to the division of soul and of spirit, of joints and of marrow, and discerning the thoughts and intentions of the heart" (Heb. 4:12). We come to the law of God to see who we are; and from there, we have the vantage point to see who Christ is, what He has done for us, and how desperate our need for Him is.

We are saved by grace alone, through faith alone, in Christ alone, according to the Scripture alone—all for the glory of God alone. The word *sola* in Latin creates a big contention between Roman Catholicism and true biblical Christianity. Catholics believe we are saved by faith and works, by Christ, other saints, and Mary. It is a hybrid of God and our works. But the Bible teaches in *sola* God—salvation is of God alone. In three verses, Paul says, "free gift" three times. We do not deserve it, and we did not earn it. It is a free gift. All for the glory of God!

THE GOSPEL TRICHOTOMY

For if, because of one man's trespass, death reigned through that one man,
much more will those who receive the abundance of grace and the free gift of
righteousness reign in life through the one man Jesus Christ (v. 17).

Paul is explaining the certainty for those who Christ truly justifies. The person who understands the trichotomy of God's holiness, the sinfulness of man, and the free gift of grace will have certainty and assurance in their justification. God wants us to turn our affection and gaze onto Him because He is the only sure Thing. This is why Jesus said unless your house is built on a sure foundation, it will fall (Matt. 7:25). In the full surety of salvation, Christ gets all of the glory, not us.

If our gospel is man-centered rather than God-centered, dependent on man's work rather than God's, and if the glory goes anywhere but to Jesus, it is a false gospel. There is no Jesus-plus. The gospel is the abundant life in Christ, and God is sovereign in all things—creation, salvation, and everything else. Because of this, He is worthy of all the honor and praise for the eternity of our lives in every situation. Even in our worst moments, God deserves glory. The person who thinks they deserve something or are entitled to something does not see God or fear the Lord. God has given us abundant grace; if we are in Christ, we are saved to the uttermost.

Through his death on the cross and resurrection from the dead, Christ gave us the gift of righteousness; and the righteous reign in life through one Man—Jesus Christ. If our faith is in Christ for salvation, we have surety in our salvation. But if it is not, instead of Christ ruling and reigning over us, sin and fear will rule and reign over us. If anything can break a person's faith—such as a failed marriage, the death of a child, or the loss of a job—that person never really had saving faith. If our faith is in Christ, it will not be broken no matter our suffering; and the Bible says, "You shall not be put to shame or confounded to all eternity" (Isa. 45:17).

THE CONTRAST BETWEEN ADAM AND CHRIST

Therefore, as one trespass led to condemnation for all men, so one act of righteousness leads to justification and life for all men. For as by the one man's disobedience the many were made sinners, so by the one man's obedience the many will be made righteous. Now the law came in to increase the trespass, but where sin increased, grace abounded all the more, so that, as sin reigned in death, grace also might reign through righteousness leading to eternal life through Jesus Christ our Lord (vv. 18-21).

The law of God reveals the perfection of God, which exposes the sinfulness of man, which exposes our need for salvation, which magnifies the perfection of Christ. Martin Luther said, "When I look at myself, I don't see how I can be saved; but when I look at Jesus, I don't see how I can be lost."[15] We must fix our eyes on Jesus.

> Therefore, since we are surrounded by so great a cloud of witnesses, let us also lay aside every weight, and sin which clings so closely, and let us run with endurance the race that is set before us, looking to Jesus, the founder and perfecter of our faith, who for the joy that was set before him endured the cross, despising the shame, and is seated at the right hand of the throne of God (Heb. 12:1-2).

We must preach the law of God. We must preach the Old and New Testament. We must preach the holiness of God. Every time we preach about the gospel, we must preach about sin. A gospel without sin is a gospel without a need for repentance. If there is no repentance, there is no salvation. What was the message that Jesus preached immediately when his ministry started?

"'Repent, for the kingdom of heaven is at hand'" (Matt. 4:17). This was the same message of the prophet Isaiah, the prophet Jeremiah, John the Baptist, Jesus, Peter, Paul, and every faithful saint from the beginning of the church—and will continue until Christ returns.

We must preach God's law and holiness, which is the light that magnifies man's sinfulness and helplessness. When we see God rightly, we understand Christ's incomparable value. Thus, we know the pricelessness of the free gift of His saving grace. We cannot convey the cost of the gospel when we do not preach sin. It is a free gift for us, but it was not free. Christ gave His life for it, and God the Father gave His Son for it. We will never be partakers if we do not see the immeasurable value of that. If we do not see the wretchedness and the grievousness of our sin and we do not apply the law to our lives, we will not see our need for the gospel.

God created the world for His glory. He allowed sin into the world for His glory. Jesus lived a perfect life, died a gruesome death, and was raised in victory from the dead; and this was for His glory. For those of us who are in Christ, God saved us from the consequences of our sins—for His glory. But understand, for those who reject God when He eternally punishes them, that, too, will be for God's glory. All things are for God's glory!

12

DEAD TO SIN, ALIVE IN CHRIST

ROMANS 6:1-14

What shall we say then? Are we to continue in sin that grace may abound? By no means! How can we who died to sin still live in it? Do you not know that all of us who have been baptized into Christ Jesus were baptized into his death? We were buried therefore with him by baptism into death, in order that, just as Christ was raised from the dead by the glory of the Father, we too might walk in newness of life.

For if we have been united with him in a death like his, we shall certainly be united with him in a resurrection like his. We know that our old self was crucified with him in order that the body of sin might be brought to nothing, so that we would no longer be enslaved to sin. For one who has died has been set free from sin. Now if we have died with Christ, we believe that we will also live with him. We know that Christ, being raised from the dead, will never die again; death no longer has dominion over him. For the death he died he died to sin, once for all, but the life he lives he lives to God. So you also must consider yourselves dead to sin and alive to God in Christ Jesus.

Let not sin therefore reign in your mortal body, to make you obey its passions. Do not present your members to sin as instruments for unrighteousness, but present yourselves to God as those who have been brought from death to life, and your members to God as instruments for righteousness. For sin will have no dominion over you, since you are not under law but under grace.

IN THE FIRST FIVE CHAPTERS, Paul extensively discusses God's holy nature, our depraved and sinful nature, and our redemption through Jesus Christ. But in Romans 6, Paul shifts the focus to the believer's life and the holiness we are called to. Paul wants us to understand that being a Christian does not mean we will never sin, but our nature toward sin has changed. We will still be tempted because we are still in a fallen body, cursed under Adam. However, if Christ truly lives in us, we have a new nature that doesn't merely mourn the consequences of sin but mourns sin itself.

Because the Spirit of God now lives inside of us, not only are we convicted when we sin but we also have the power to overcome the sin that once beset us. We have the desire and the ability to live a life of holiness. What does the word "holy" mean? We can look at it from two different perspectives. When referring to God, holy means completely set apart or "other." When we say "other," we mean God is completely unique. There is nothing in the universe like God. No one is like Him. He is preexistent, eternal, omnipresent, all-knowing, and all-powerful. So, God is perfect and pure in all his attributes. God is love. He is also fully just and perfect in all of His ways. Taking all the attributes of God and surmising them into one statement, we conclude that God is holy.

Being holy also means being *set apart* for God's purposes and His glory. We are not like God in His holiness, but we are set apart for His holy purposes. First Peter 2:9 says, "But you are a chosen race, a royal priesthood, a holy nation, a people for his own possession, that you may proclaim the excellencies of him who called you out of darkness into his marvelous light."

God has given us a new nature with the desire and ability to do something we could never do apart from Christ. We have been saved and set apart to live lives of obedience to God and His Word. God has not only called us to this, but He has also given us the power to walk it out through the Spirit of God. We were dead in our sins and trespasses. We were scheduled for destruction, which we deserved. Every person in history, from the very beginning of their lives, has earned eternity in Hell. Paul says, "'No one does good, not one'" (Rom. 3:12).

All have sinned and fallen short of the holy perfection of God. To understand this is to understand the value of grace. Our attitude toward His goodness toward us should fill us with thanksgiving and gratefulness. God has given us mercy and grace, which means He did not give us something we did deserve and instead gave us something we did not deserve—sonship and a place in the eternal family of God.

The gospel is like going before a judge in a court where you owe ten million dollars in fines. Since you only make fifty thousand a year, there is no possible way you will ever be able to pay it. If left unpaid, you would have to spend the rest of your life in prison. So, you go before the judge and say, "I deserve the punishment, but please have mercy on me." Then the judge says, "I will have mercy on you, and I will pay the fine for you out of my own fortune, so you don't owe your debt anymore." That's mercy. But as you are leaving the courtroom, the judge says, "Wait a moment. I will not only pay to free you from your past debt, but I will also provide for your future by adopting you and making you an heir of my fortune." That's grace. And that is the scandalous, offensive, and amazing nature of the gospel. God, in mercy, paid and pardoned our past, and in grace, gave us a future as a son and co-heir with Christ.

COME AND DIE

We are called to die to self and sin because we have been made alive in Christ. We are not earning our salvation by any stretch of the imagination. We are not doing good deeds so that we will go to Heaven. No, we live a life of holiness because God has truly changed us, and we have been made alive in Christ. This concept of living dead to sin and self is the theme of my book, *Come and Die: Dying to Self and Living for Christ*. I wrote on this topic specifically for new Christians to understand sanctification and how we overcome our sinful nature. Paul gives an excellent synopsis of this concept in his letter to the church of Galatia:

> But if, in our endeavor to be justified in Christ, we too were found to be sinners, is Christ then a servant of sin? Certainly not! For if I rebuild what I tore down, I prove myself to be a transgressor. For through the law I died to the law, so that I might live to God. I have been crucified with Christ. It is no longer I who live, but Christ who lives in me. And the life I now live in the flesh I live by faith in the Son of God, who loved me and gave himself for me. I do not nullify the grace of God, for if righteousness were through the law, then Christ died for no purpose (Gal. 2:17-21).

There are two important takeaways from Paul's words. First, he wants us to understand that if we could earn salvation, then Christ died for no reason. We should take great comfort in the fact that no person can earn salvation through the law. The law was never meant to save us. It was meant to expose the reality that we are not like God, we could never be like Him, and that we desperately need salvation.

Paul's other point is when he says, "For through the law I died to the law, so that I might live to God. I have been crucified with Christ. It is no longer I who live, but Christ who lives in me" (Gal. 2:19-20). There is a tendency among some Christians to celebrate because we are not subject to what they view as strict and outdated laws that are now meaningless because of grace. But Paul wants us to understand that we should strive to obey God's law, not for salvation but because we have been saved. We do not obey as a means to be justified before God; we obey because he has justified, saved, and accepted us. This is evidence that we are His children.

Christianity is not about giving up the stuff we do not like and keeping the things we do. It is about dying. Our old life is over. If someone never comes to this conclusion, they may not be a Christian. Jesus said to His disciples, "'If anyone would come after me, let him deny himself and take up his cross and follow me'" (Matt. 16:24). In the first century, when someone was fitted with a cross on their back, that was a one-way road to death. There was no turning back. Christ says, "Pick up that cross, deny yourself, and follow Me."

He continues, "For whoever will save his life will lose it, but whoever loses his life for my sake will find it" (Matt. 16:25).

NEW LIFE IN CHRIST

What shall we say then? Are we to continue in sin that grace may abound? By no means! How can we who died to sin still live in it? (vv. 1-2)

Paul begins here based on his previous statement in Romans 5:18-19: "Therefore, as one trespass led to condemnation for all men, so one act of righteousness leads to justification and life for all men. For as by the one man's disobedience the many were made sinners, so by the one man's obedience the many will be made righteous." He is referring to Adam's one sinful act that caused all of mankind to fall into sin and Jesus' one atoning act that causes men who call on His name to be saved. "Now the law came in to increase the trespass, but where sin increased, grace abounded all the more, so that, as sin reigned in death, grace also might reign through righteousness leading to eternal life through Jesus Christ our Lord" (Rom. 5:20-21). If we read this incorrectly, it might seem good if sin increases because it shows how much grace increases. But Paul is telling us not to read it that way. This is why he begins Romans 6, anticipating a question his critics would ask: does that mean we should continue in sin so that grace may abound? His response is, "No, of course not. But because we were once gripped by life-controlling sin, that is what magnifies the grace of God.

I am not proud of the fact that I once used and sold drugs. I robbed people and lived a debaucherous life, but I do not look back on it or draw attention to my past to bring any glory to it. No, the only reason I ever mention my dead, gross past life is to showcase the glory of God in the life I now live in Christ. If you had known me twenty-five years ago and saw me today, you would say, "How can it be?" But it is not only about being saved from a past of crime or addiction.

It is the same for anyone who has been saved. Even an eight-year-old girl attending Bible camp who realizes her desperate need for God and surrenders her life to Christ is a miracle of God. Both testimonies are equally miraculous. God uses and "work[s] all things together for those who are called according to his purpose (Rom. 8:28). We shouldn't be ashamed of the testimony of what God has brought us out of, but we also shouldn't use our testimony to glorify the past. Our testimony is merely a backdrop meant to showcase the glory and power of a God who saves!

Those who live under the law will die under the law, while those who live outside the law will die outside the law. It is like someone severely sick with Stage-4 lung cancer. Death will be the outcome for someone who never gets a diagnosis and for the one who gets the diagnosis but doesn't get treatment. Getting tests done that help determine the diagnosis doesn't help cure them, but getting those tests makes their prognosis definitive. In the same way, the law is not a means of salvation but our diagnosis. The law diagnoses what is wrong in us, and the gospel is the cure. Paul says there is a necessary component of the law, which is a diagnostic tool. It reveals how messed up we are. The standard that Jesus brings through the law is so high, nobody can live up to it. It diagnoses the dire nature of our situation. We should not engage in sin so that grace abounds (Rom. 5:20). Sin is there, regardless, and the law exposes just how bad it is. We see the magnification of the glory of grace when God saves us. As Ephesians 2:4-6 says, "But God, being rich in mercy, because of the great love with which he loved us, even when we were dead in our trespasses, made us alive together with Christ—by grace you have been saved— and raised us up with him and seated us with him in the heavenly places in Christ Jesus."

God used Paul, one of the greatest first-century persecutors of the church and one of the most legalistic Jews of his time, to become an instrument and servant of Christ, Whose ministry was aimed at the Gentile world. We can apply Paul's testimony to our own lives in Christ. How magnificent that God can use us despite who we once were and what we once did.

In the first two verses, Paul poses a question to the outsider and then directs a question to us: How can we live in sin if we have truly died to it? We may still sin and face temptation; but as true Christians, we will no longer love our sin. There may be times when our flesh rises up; but if the Spirit of God lives in us, we will be miserable in our sins. The sin we once loved, we will now hate. Paul makes a significant theological statement here about salvation: those who die to sin change their disposition toward sin. Our hearts change because our nature has changed.

Paul is doing something here that he often does in his writings: he anticipates the objections of his critics. His Jewish audience would have questioned whether being saved through Christ somehow makes one live a lawless life; and if so, what good can it be? This is why Paul wrote extensively about how no one could live up to the law. He is not speaking negatively about the law but explaining its purpose. We should not take the Old Testament, the Law, and the Prophets and throw them away. No, we are to apply them rightly to our Christian life. Paul explains that the law was meant to expose our depravity and show us our need for Christ. Those who are in Christ have died to sin and the nature of Adam and have been raised to new life in the nature of Christ. This is why Paul says, "For as by the one man's disobedience the many were made sinners, so by the one man's obedience the many will be made righteous" (Rom. 5:19).

THE SYMBOL OF A RESURRECTED LIFE

Do you not know that all of us who have been baptized into Christ Jesus were baptized into his death? (v. 3).

In modern American Christianity, everybody wants to talk about Christ's resurrection power and abundant life in Christ. Everyone wants the benefits of his resurrection, but no one wants to talk about dying. There is no resurrection to a life that is still lived unto sin, unto self, and unto this world.

We do not get the benefits of the resurrection until we decide to lay down our lives. The beginning of Christianity is giving up control of our lives. We cannot be lord over our life and serve and follow Jesus our Lord. We cannot call Him Savior if we do not call Him Lord!

Jesus is not waiting for us and begging us to ask Him into our hearts. Jesus is a reigning King Who died for us. If we want to be a part of His kingdom, we must lay down our lives. Our lives are like a heap of ashes next to the abundant life that Christ will give us. Many want to hold on to that bag of ash because it is familiar. But Christ is saying, "Give it to Me." If we love the things of this world, we better examine ourselves to see if we are in the faith.

John admonishes, "Do not love the world or the things in the world. If anyone loves the world, the love of the Father is not in him. For all that is in the world—the desires of the flesh and the desires of the eyes and pride of life—is not from the Father but is from the world. And the world is passing away along with its desires, but whoever does the will of God abides forever (1 John 2:15-17).

When John the Baptist, the forerunner of Christ, began to baptize, what was the point? It was a baptism unto repentance, a turning from sin. This is why most of the Pharisees rejected John the Baptist; they thought they were good and lived up to the law. They would not immerse themselves in the water before a crowd and acknowledge that they were sinners and needed to repent. Baptism was about identifying oneself as a sinner. We cannot repent of sins that we do not acknowledge. We have to see our lives as corrupt, helpless, hopeless, and lost without Christ. This is why the Jewish ruling council hated John the Baptist, and it is why later they would hate Jesus.

In the New Covenant, we are literally and permanently baptized into the death of Christ. When Paul says, "We have been baptized into Christ's death," he is explaining how we partake in His resurrection life. Christ will not die again. However, the beauty is that Christ did not have to die at all. He was God Who took on flesh so that He could die in our place, and He did this because of His great love for us. We are baptized in Christ to identify with Christ in His death and might also be able to identify with Him in His resurrection.

Like other apostles, Paul always mentioned water baptism when discussing salvation: repent and be baptized. But it is important to understand that being baptized does not make one saved. There is no mystical thing that happens in the water. It is merely symbolic. Being immersed in the water is simply obedience to God. It is an outward expression meant to accompany your open confession that you believe by faith you have been saved and reborn in Christ. It is about saying to the world, "I belong to Christ; my old life is dead."

In some American churches, baptism is performed casually and even irreverently. Yet baptism is a very reverent and symbolic event. In the Muslim culture, if someone decides to follow Christ and gets baptized, they are ostracized from society. Their family might treat them as dead because they know baptism has great significance. It should mean something in our culture, too. It means we are making a profession before the world. We are no longer bound to sin and no longer belong to the devil. Instead, we belong entirely to Christ. We are dead to sin and alive in Christ. We are buried and raised with Him. We did not become baptized into Christ by keeping the law but rather by Christ's sacrificial and atoning death on the cross.

DEAD AND RAISED

We were buried therefore with him by baptism into death, in order that,
just as Christ was raised from the dead by the glory of the Father, we too might
walk in newness of life (v. 4).

Since we have died with Christ and are baptized into His death, we have been raised from death to life by the Father for the glory of God. Because of this, we now walk in a newness of life. But this newness often exposes how sinful we are. This is not to condemn us but to allow us to understand our dependence on Christ. Apart from Him, there is no hope, no help. Puritan writer Thomas Brooks said, "There is no more miserable man than one who has the Spirit of God who makes room for sin in his life."[16] The opposite of this is: "Therefore, if anyone is in Christ, he is a new creation. The old has passed away; behold, the new has come" (2 Cor. 5:17).

SPIRITUAL UNION WITH CHRIST

For if we have been united with him in a death like his, we shall certainly be united with him in a resurrection like his. We know that our old self was crucified with him in order that the body of sin might be brought to nothing, so that we would no longer be enslaved to sin (vv. 5-6).

This does not mean that we will never sin in the Christian life. It says that while we still sin, our heart desires to please and obey God. It is about uprooting an old tree and planting a new one in its place. It is not about mostly good people trying hard to do better but about dead things being raised to life. Everyone mourns the consequences of sin, but the difference between a lost and saved person is that the believer does not merely hate the consequences of sin but hates the sin itself. We live our lives unto God, so we want to please Him. When we do fall into sin, we mourn our sin, repent of it, and pray for the power to overcome it. That is why Jesus said, "'Blessed are those who mourn, for they shall be comforted'" (Matt. 5:4).

If Christ saves us, He will sanctify and change us and make us like Him. He will ultimately perfect us and glorify us. We will eventually have a new body with no clinging fishhook of sin still in our flesh or no old memories of sin.

As Christians, we have been saved, are being saved, and will be saved. What does this mean? The best way to describe this is to illustrate a man drowning in an ocean. The waves come over his head; but suddenly, someone pulls up in a speedboat, grabs him, pulls him into the boat, and, at that moment, he is saved. He is being saved the entire time that boat races toward the shore. And when the vessel finally reaches dry land, he is ultimately saved.

When we are reborn in Christ, we are saved; and the entire time we live in the world, we are being saved. Ultimately, one day, we will make it to a place where we are saved and safe in Christ forever. However, we must realize salvation is about what Christ has done, not us. Christ saves and sanctifies us, and it will be Christ who will glorify us. Our only job is submission and living a life of faith toward God because we have a union with Christ spiritually. Philippians 1:6 says, "And I am sure of this, that he who began a good work in you will bring it to completion at the day of Jesus Christ."

If we truly have surrendered our lives to Christ, He will sustain us to the end. But we must ask ourselves, are we unified with Christ? Is our life hidden in Christ? This is why Paul says, "Examine yourselves, to see whether you are in the faith. Test yourselves. Or do you not realize this about yourselves, that Jesus Christ is in you?—unless indeed you fail to meet the test!" (2 Cor.13:5). True examination leads to repentance and salvation. The examination also builds our faith in Christ. We cannot have faith in ourselves and God at the same time. There has to be a gradual dying and a mutual growth. Sometimes, God will send trials of refining fire because He wants our dependence solely on Him.

SET FREE FROM SIN

For one who has died has been set free from sin. Now if we have died with Christ, we believe that we will also live with him (vv. 7-8).

Jesus told His disciples, "'For whoever desires to save his life will lose it, but whoever loses his life for my sake will find it'" (Matt. 16:25). A believer who has a new life and a new heart has new affections and desires. Because of this, their life will not look the same as it was before their salvation. This does not mean we will live a perfect life but have been set free from sin. We are set free. God gives us a new heart, but we must renew our minds. The old is gone; the new has come; and until we grab hold of that and become renewed by God's Word, we will not live free from sin.

THE VICTORIOUS LIFE

We know that Christ, being raised from the dead, will never die again; death no longer has dominion over him. For the death he died he died to sin, once for all, but the life he lives he lives to God (vv. 9-10).

The reason why Christ took on flesh was to live a perfect life so that He could be the perfect sacrifice for sin once and for all. There are no more sacrifices. No one else has to pay the price for sin. There is nothing left to be done. Jesus said on the cross, "'It is finished'" (John 19:30). He died and rose again, and now we must live in it. We have to live dead to sin. But just because we have been saved does not mean there is no work to do. As Christians, we have to renew our minds. Scripture says, "Do not be conformed to this world, but be transformed by the renewal of your mind, that by testing you may discern what is the will of God, what is good and acceptable and perfect" (Rom. 12:2). Our old nature has to die. Our salvation does not come from works, but there is discipline in the Christian life. It is about dying to self, dying to sin so that we can live a victorious life in Christ.

A VICTORIOUS LIFE

So you also must consider yourselves dead to sin and alive to God in Christ Jesus (v. 11).

We must live dead to sin, but we also must live our lives unto God in Christ. Our regenerate predisposition is toward obeying Christ. The true believer is living unto God because he has seen who God is, which has changed him. He is not living just for the things God can remedy in his life. He lives, realizing that his life belongs to Him. A lifetime of good deeds apart from Christ will find us bankrupt before God. Our desire should be to live our lives dependent on Christ as we live in Christ.

We all struggle with sin when we try to live toward Christ. But we have to come to the point of understanding that our goodness will never be good enough. We can take solace in how Paul looked at himself, knowing he needed a Savior:

> For I do not understand my own actions. For I do not do what I want, but I do the very thing I hate. Now if I do what I do not want, I agree with the law, that it is good. So now it is no longer I who do it, but sin that dwells within me. For I know that nothing good dwells in me, that is, in my flesh. For I have the desire to do what is right, but not the ability to carry it out. For I do not do the good I want, but the evil I do not want is what I keep on doing. Now if I do what I do not want, it is no longer I who do it, but sin that dwells within me (Rom. 7:15-20).

BATTLING SIN

Let not sin therefore reign in your mortal body, to make you obey its passions (v. 12).

Although we are saved and set free from the penalty of our sins, we still have to battle the lingering effects of sin; and at some point, we have to get serious about holiness toward God if we want to walk in freedom. We must separate ourselves from the world. Scripture says, "'Therefore go out from their midst, and be separate from them, says the Lord, and touch no unclean thing; then I will welcome you, and I will be a father to you, and you shall be sons and daughters to me, says the Lord Almighty'" (2 Cor. 6:17-18).

FREEDOM THROUGH GRACE

Do not present your members to sin as instruments for unrighteousness, but present yourselves to God as those who have been brought from death to life, and your members to God as instruments for righteousness. For sin will have no dominion over you, since you are not under law but under grace (vv. 13-14).

Christianity is not about works; it is about nature. It is about the old nature we were born into; and now, as Christians, our new nature is being made alive in Christ. If we believe that we were scheduled for destruction; but Christ, in His love, intervened and took our penalty upon himself—mocked, whipped, and beaten on that cross. So then, how should we live for Him? This is the reality that we must live in. We live dead to sin and dead to self, not to earn God's love but because God's love was poured out for us on the back of a jagged, wooden, blood-stained cross. The evidence of God's love is all around us, and our only rightful response is to live our life in worship, submission, and surrender to Him. And by this, we will live victorious in Him.

13

FREED FROM THE SLAVERY OF SIN

ROMANS 6:15-23

What then? Are we to sin because we are not under law but under grace? By no means! Do you not know that if you present yourselves to anyone as obedient slaves, you are slaves of the one whom you obey, either of sin, which leads to death, or of obedience, which leads to righteousness? But thanks be to God, that you who were once slaves of sin have become obedient from the heart to the standard of teaching to which you were committed, and, having been set free from sin, have become slaves of righteousness. I am speaking in human terms, because of your natural limitations. For just as you once presented your members as slaves to impurity and to lawlessness leading to more lawlessness, so now present your members as slaves to righteousness leading to sanctification.

For when you were slaves of sin, you were free in regard to righteousness. But what fruit were you getting at that time from the things of which you are now ashamed? For the end of those things is death. But now that you have been set free from sin and have become slaves of God, the fruit you get leads to sanctification and its end, eternal life. For the wages of sin is death, but the free gift of God is eternal life in Christ Jesus our Lord.

CHRISTIANITY IS NOT A WORKS-BASED religion; it is an evidence-based. A good tree will bear good fruit, and the first fruit or evidence of regeneration in the life of every Christian is the fruit of repentance. When

John the Baptist saw many Pharisees and Sadducees come out to witness people getting baptized as they repented of their sins, he said to them, "'You brood of vipers! Who warned you to flee from the wrath to come? Bear fruit in keeping with repentance. And do not presume to say to yourselves, *We have Abraham as our father*, for I tell you, God is able from these stones to raise up children for Abraham. Even now the axe is laid to the root of the trees. Every tree therefore that does not bear good fruit is cut down and thrown into the fire" (Matt. 3:7-10).

Paul is dealing with the same religious system as John the Baptist—people who think because they are born in the line of Abraham and are ethnic Jews, they are fine as long as they are living according to the law. This is why Jesus says, "'Woe to you, scribes and Pharisees, hypocrites! For you clean the outside of the cup and the plate, but inside they are full of greed and self-indulgence. You blind Pharisee! First clean the inside of the cup and the plate, that the outside also may be clean'" (Matt. 23:25-26). Jesus is saying that anyone who looks inside will see that their goodness is not good enough when compared to the standard of perfection that God gave us and the law.

The problem with the Jews and Pharisees in the first century was that many of them believed they were living up to the standard of the law. Paul was one of those Jews. He thought he was living up to a righteous standard; and maybe externally, he was. In Philippians, he described himself: "If anyone else thinks he has reason for confidence in the flesh, I have more: circumcised on the eighth day, of the people of Israel, of the tribe of Benjamin, a Hebrew of Hebrews; as to the law, a Pharisee; as to zeal, a persecutor of the church; as to righteousness under the law, blameless" (Phil. 3:4-6). Paul did the things he was supposed to do and was even above his peers, but what happened? In verse seven, he says, "But whatever gain I had, I counted as loss for the sake of Christ." No one can live up to God's standard, and nothing compares to the surpassing worth of knowing Christ. When he saw Who God was, he realized that his goodness was not good enough.

We are meant to be drawn to despair by looking to the law and God's holiness, a despair that brings us to our need for Christ and our need for salvation. It is only through the grace of God that we are saved. But the grace of God is only for those who repent, for those who see God for Who He is— holy, unapproachable, unknowable. Those who see sin for what it is: grievous and death-producing. Then, in light of those two things, we see God's grace as a beautiful, precious, unearned gift. So, in the first half of chapter six, Paul deals with the question: does the message of grace cause sin to abound? Now, beginning in verse fifteen, he addresses the other side of this question.

THE DIAGNOSIS AND THE CURE

What then? Are we to sin because we are not under law but under grace? By no means! (v. 15).

Many people get confused about the relationship between the law of God and the grace of God. Jesus clarified that He did not come to abolish the law but to fulfill it. However, He also made it clear that no one could be saved under the law. So, how do we reconcile these two things? There is a straightforward way to think about it. The law of God diagnoses the problem, and the gospel of grace is the cure for the problem. The problem with legalists is that they believe somehow that they can find acceptance from God based on the things they do.

One sin caused all of humanity to be spun into a perpetual original sin. So what is the solution? There is no solution in ourselves. This is why the rich, young ruler sadly walked away when Jesus told him to sell all he had and follow Him. The man thought he was living out the law. "When the disciples heard this, they were astonished, saying, 'Who then can be saved?'" (Matt. 19:25). The disciples thought if this good and respected Jewish man who has done all the right things cannot be saved, then what hope is there for any of us? Jesus responds, "'With man this is impossible, but with God all things are possible'" (Matt. 19:26).

Man, in and of himself, could not save himself. An important truth to understand is that if we could save ourselves, then Jesus would have died for nothing. If it was possible for the best among us to do right and to be approved by God, then Jesus came for no reason. But Jesus came because all mankind was dead in sin and trespass. We were hopeless and helpless. Christianity is about bringing the good news that brings life. It is not what we do; it is what Christ has done. The gospel is to look at what God has done and believe by faith. It is about being reborn in Christ and having a new nature.

How can a sinful man be in communion with a holy God? If you do not understand the importance of this question, you probably do not know God because coming into contact with Who God is brings fear. The Bible says, "The fear of the LORD is the beginning of wisdom, and the knowledge of the Holy One is insight" (Prov. 9:10). If we see God for Who He is, we will be overwhelmed with His holiness, like the prophet Isaiah: "'Holy, holy, holy is the LORD of hosts; the whole earth is full of his glory'" (Isa. 6:3). When Isaiah came in contact with God, he said, "'Woe is me! For I am lost; for I am a man of unclean lips, and I dwell in the midst of a people of unclean lips; for my eyes have seen the King, the LORD of hosts!'" (Isa. 6:5). Isaiah saw God for Who He is, and then a burning coal touched his lips. This was a symbolic representation of the ritual cleansing in the temple but also as a foreshadowing of the ultimate cleansing of our souls found in the finished work of Christ, Who took our burden and shame. Christ bore our sins and drank the cup of God's wrath so that we would not have to.

In the gospel, we do not receive the due wages of our sin under the law because Christ took our punishment. He paid for our guilt with His innocence. We are free from the penalty of death under the law because Christ took our punishment; and because of this, we are free, not only from the judicial consequences of our sin but also from the slavery of sin itself. As we conform to Christ's image, we become more like Christ. This does not mean we can live a sinless, perfect life. Faith is not about finding perfection in ourselves. It means that those who have been reborn in Christ are being conformed to the image of Christ through the washing of His Word and the power of His Spirit living in us. Ultimately, one day, by God's grace, we will be glorified with Him forever.

JUSTIFICATION AND SANCTIFICATION

Do you not know that if you present yourselves to anyone as obedient slaves,

you are slaves of the one whom you obey, either of sin, which leads to death,

or of obedience, which leads to righteousness? (v. 16).

Here, Paul presents a general axiom in anticipation of the accusation that the gospel will cause sin to abound. An axiom is a self-apparent truth. Paul uses this axiom to explain that obedience is evidence of allegiance.

Today, there is a problem with how many people present the gospel. They make it seem like we are asking Jesus into our hearts by saying a magic prayer without considering the qualifications or cost. Yes, the gospel is a gift accessible to us, but it is not free. It was secured through the cross of Christ. He paid a price that we could not pay. Christ paid the debt. He paid the judicial consequence of our sins, and Jesus was the only One able to pay our debt. No Scripture in the Bible tells us to ask Jesus into our hearts. It tells us to abandon our lives—our will, our way—that we might follow Jesus. True regeneration is about having the desire to follow Jesus and leave our lives of sin behind. It is also about having the power to do it, not perfectly but genuinely and more and more as we grow in sanctification.

Many Christians confuse the doctrines of justification and sanctification. Those with a legalistic mindset believe they are at various stages of being saved based on their performance. The truth about Christianity is that we are saved through grace alone, by faith alone, and in Christ alone. We are not on probation when we are reborn in Christ. We are justified before God based on what Christ did for us on the cross. Justification is instant and permanent, and our works cannot make it more secure or undo it. Some people get confused and ask, "Does this mean I can say a prayer, say I am a Christian and that I am saved, but then do whatever I want?" No, if we are truly saved before God, our new nature will want to walk with God, please God, be convicted by sin, and hunger and thirst to be right with God.

We could spend hours discussing our battle with sin and doing right and wrong. But the question is not, can someone lose their salvation? If someone is living in unrepentant sin with no stain of conviction on their conscience, the question is whether they were ever truly a Christian. This is why Paul says to the Corinthians, "Examine yourselves, to see whether you are in the faith" (2 Cor. 13:5). Self-examination is not just part of the early Christian life but part of the entire Christian life. This is encouragement for those of us in Christ because even in our failure and sin, Christ has a hold of us; and nothing can snatch us from His hand.

Justification is something Christ secured for us on the cross. If we are reborn into Christ, we are justified before God. Sanctification is this gradual, over-the-course-of-our-lives conforming to the image of Christ. It is not sinless perfection but growing and being refined by fire. Both Christians and non-Christians sin; but the difference is that once we are reborn in Christ, the sin we once loved, we now hate. When I was saved from a life of addiction, as a new convert, I remember falling into sin many times. I often questioned if I was really in Christ. But I was sad not just because of the consequences of my sin but because I was sinning. This is the difference between a believer and a non-believer. Everyone mourns the consequences of their sins, but the believer mourns sin itself. Scripture says, "'Blessed are those who mourn, for they shall be comforted'" (Matt. 5:4).

SLAVES TO RIGHTEOUSNESS

Justification happens at conversion; and sanctification is laying down our sins by the power of the Holy Spirit, as the Spirit of God conforms us to the image of Christ. Paul is conveying that we need to stop living like we are under slavery to sin and strive toward God. In Romans 8, Paul points out that if the Spirit of God lives in us, we will testify that we belong to God. We will cry out, "Abba Father!"

There will be moments of darkness in the Christian life when no words of man will be able to comfort you. In these moments, we need a testimony from the Spirit Himself that we belong to God. Whether we are burying a loved one, dealing with a vile sin, or experiencing a tragedy, we need to find our assurance in God. In dark times, we need to know who we are in Christ and that we belong to Him. The truly converted person wants to obey God. We are not sinless as Christians, but we do hate the sin we once loved because we are now devoted slaves to righteousness. We are devoted slaves to Christ. Some Bible translations shy away from translating the Greek word *doulos* into the English word "slave" because it has a negative connotation. Yet we are slaves to sin; but if we are sanctified and justified in Christ, then we are devoted slaves to Christ.

We cannot be a slave to two masters. We can be self-deceived about who we follow, but the Bible clarifies that we cannot serve two masters. Jesus said, "'No one can serve two masters, for either he will hate the one and love the other, or he will be devoted to the one and despise the other. You cannot serve God and money'" (Matt. 6:24, NIV). In this passage, Jesus is talking about money; but this truth can be applied to everything in the Christian life. We cannot serve God and serve the world. We cannot live for God and live for ourselves. This is why Jesus said, "If anyone would come after me, let him deny himself and take up his cross and follow me. For whoever would save his life will lose it, but whoever loses his life for my sake will find it" (Matt. 16:24-25).

This can be illustrated by a man holding onto the tails of two different horses at the same time. He can hold on to both tails for a moment; but eventually, these powerful stallions will want to go in different directions. Once this happens, the man will have to let go of one of the tails and be dragged by the other because if he continues to try and hold onto both, he will be torn apart. In other words, there is no middle ground; and you cannot serve two masters. Jesus' words in Matthew 16:24 refer to a narrow path to Christianity. It is not about reciting a prayer we do not mean to a God we are not interested in following. It is about seeing the eternal value of Christ and abandoning our lives for the glory of God as He remakes us from the inside out. It is putting our faith in Christ above all else.

HEART OBEDIENCE

But thanks be to God, that you who were once slaves of sin have become obedient from the heart to the standard of teaching to which you were committed, and, having been set free from sin, have become slaves of righteousness (vv. 17-18).

We cannot call Him Savior if we do not call Him Lord. Paul is not speaking merely about outward righteousness that his audience would have been accustomed to hearing. This is why in verse seventeen, he talks about obedience from the heart. Obedience does not save, but it is the fruit or evidence that we are saved. True faith in the Son of God is evidenced by how we react to His Word and what His Word produces in our lives.

Many people today believe that they can have salvation in Christ while denying the words of God. But you cannot; it is a contradiction. We are slaves to the master we follow and obey. To reject the Word of God is to reject Christ Himself. This does not mean we must have a robust theological understanding of the Word of God to be a Christian. The thief on the cross saw the value of Christ and put his faith in Him. Jesus told him, "'Today you will be with me in paradise'" (Luke 23:43). But if that man had come off the cross, I suspect his life would have been different, just like all the faithful followers of Jesus. They were not perfect but different—ever-changing and conforming to the image of Christ.

We must remember that the Spirit of God is conforming us to the image of Christ. But if we read His sacred, holy, inerrant Word and say, "No, I don't believe that is a sin anymore. I don't accept that," then we are denying God Himself. How can we deny one part of God's Word and accept another part? Either we believe by faith that Christ is the Word made flesh and we devote our lives to the obedience of God, or we ask ourselves whether we are truly following Christ. Will there be seasons of falling short or even times of falling away? Yes, maybe, but examining our lives according to God's Word is important because the Spirit of God and the Word of God will conform us to the image of Christ. If someone is far away and belongs to God, He will draw them back.

The true Christian whose heart is reborn in Christ strives to live a life of obedience. Our faithfulness to Christ is evidenced in our commitment to the teaching of God's Word and the image of Christ given to us by the witness of the apostles and prophets. No one can completely comprehend God's Word, but Paul is conveying that those no longer enslaved to sin have become obedient from the heart to the standard of teaching they were committed to. We have dedicated our lives to God. We were water baptized in obedience, signifying to the world that our old life is now in the ground. We have risen to life with a new nature, new priorities, new values, new ambitions, and with one singular purpose—to glorify God in all we do.

We are saved through the work of Christ alone, not by works; but we are willing to be grateful slaves of Christ. Pastor John MacArthur says it this way: "The life-changing work of salvation is by God's power alone, but it does not work apart from man's will. God has no unwilling children in His family, no unwilling citizens in His kingdom."[17] We believe by faith, and our lives evidence our faith and regeneration.

Sometimes, that seed of faith is way below the surface. When I first gave my life to God, people looked at me, still questioning whether I was truly a Christian. But they did not know the wrestling that was taking place inside me. Eventually, a little sprout started to make its way to the surface. I was slowly being remade from the inside out by the power of the Holy Spirit as I strived to obey the teaching of God's Word.

Remember, we do not strive to be accepted by God. We strive to obey because we *know* we are accepted by God. We know by faith we are accepted by Him. Theologian Warren Wiersbe once said, "A great evidence of true salvation is found in a newfound reverence for the word of God and a deep desire to obey it."[18] When I see a true convert, I see someone who is awakened and desires to know God's Word. The most significant revelation God has given us of Himself in this world is the Word of God.

BORN AGAIN!

I am speaking in human terms, because of your natural limitations. For just as you once presented your members as slaves to impurity and to lawlessness leading to more lawlessness, so now present your members as slaves to righteousness leading to sanctification (v. 19).

Either you are a slave to sin, or you are a slave to righteousness. There is no other option. You are either dead in sin and trespass, or you are alive in Christ. In New Covenant theology, we often hear the true follower of Christ referred to as the "new man." Paul acknowledges that regeneration is something beyond what human explanations can wholly and truly define. However, he uses the example of a slave and a master because it makes a very clear point. Although Paul calls for us to strive for a life of obedience and holiness to God, he is not preaching that Christianity is merely a moral or ethical discipline we are working toward. Rather, it is a new nature that we are working from, working out, conditioning, and disciplining.

There can be no true sanctification without regeneration. In other words, we cannot conform to the image of Christ if we have not been reborn in Christ. Jesus told Nicodemus, the Pharisee, "'Truly, truly, I say to you, unless one is born again he cannot see the kingdom of God'" (John 3:3). Works righteousness under the law teaches that we obey so that God can accept us. However, true Christianity teaches that we obey because we are accepted by God. Paul is saying if we are reborn in Christ, then let us present our bodies, "our members," as devoted, obedient slaves to righteousness, leading to sanctification.

Just as lawlessness leads to more lawlessness and sin begets sin, we are to strive toward a new nature. We work to promote growth in Christ and listen to voices that encourage each other in the faith. We must surround ourselves with people who teach God's Word, which sanctifies us in the faith. We must attend church and not forsake the gathering of ourselves together—growing as students of God's Word.

Only a good tree can bear good fruit, and only those who have been reborn in Christ can be sanctified by the Holy Spirit and conformed to the very image of Christ. Paul writes in Romans 12:1-2, "I appeal to you therefore, brothers, by the mercies of God, to present your bodies as a living sacrifice, holy and acceptable to God, which is your spiritual worship. Do not be conformed to this world, but be transformed by the renewal of your mind, that by testing you may discern what is the will of God, what is good and acceptable and perfect."

The truly regenerated person *wants* to discern God's will to understand what is pleasing to God and what is not. Martyn Lloyd-Jones describes it this way: "As you go on living the righteous life and practicing it with all your might and energy and all your time and everything else, you will find that the process that went on before in which you went from bad to worse and became viler and viler is entirely reversed. You will become cleaner and cleaner and purer and purer and holier and holier and more and more conformed to the image of the Son of God."[19]

Sometimes, it may seem like our sanctification is in pause mode. There will be seasons of fighting through sin and overcoming the lust of the flesh and the pride of this life. But the true Christian has the desire to wrestle with these things. We cannot superimpose the idea of wrestling with these things on unregenerated people. They need the gospel of grace. However, for those of us in Christ, we must conform to the image of Christ so that we are no longer conformed to this world but transformed. The Bible says we have a new heart and must transform our debased way of thinking. Understand that being born in Christ is something undeniably supernatural. Christianity is about a resurrection. It is not about good people working hard to be ethical or moral.

EXEMPLIFY AND MAGNIFY

For when you were slaves of sin, you were free in regard to righteousness. But what fruit were you getting at that time from the things of which you are now ashamed? For the end of those things is death (vv. 20-21).

One of the great indicators of true regeneration is that we become aware of our sinfulness and the holiness of God. We see God as holy, perfect, unapproachable, and unknowable. We see ourselves in the light of God's perfection; and when we get close to the light, it exposes our imperfections. It exposes our insufficiency and our inability and shows us our need for God Himself. The character of God shows us we are not God; and from that place, we accept the grace of God. People who live by faith know that apart from God, they can do nothing to save themselves.

We should not devalue how grievous our sins were before God or even our sins now because to do so is to devalue God's holiness and His offense toward sin. It also devalues His immense grace and forgiveness that has been given to us. We minimize the value of the cross if we act like sin is not grievous to God. Many people in the church today do this in an attempt to reach the lost. But we need to exemplify and magnify the grievousness of sin and, at the same time, exemplify and magnify the grace by which God secured our salvation—by the offense of the cross and the necessity and exclusivity of Christ.

We should not live in shame and condemnation for sins we have repented of, but shame is a valid emotion. We should feel shame when we sin. Otherwise, we will have a cavalier attitude toward it. We should strive not to sin because sin causes hurt and damage and always has a cost. But when we do sin, we have an Advocate in Christ, Who is ready and willing to forgive us. It is the conviction of sin that exposes our need for God.

Christ's glory and grace are not magnified when we play down sin or the holy nature of God. Christ is magnified and greatly glorified when we acknowledge the holiness of God, the grievousness of sin, and the cross by which Christ reconciled us to a holy God. Understand that God is no less angry at sin. However, the difference is that Jesus came to save sinners. This is the message the world needs to hear. God took on flesh and walked among us, died a brutal death, and rose from the grave so that we could be reconciled to a holy God.

There is a difference between living in shame because of past sins and mourning our sins and repenting of them. There is a difference between being convicted of sin and living in condemnation. We *should* be convicted and ashamed of our past sins, but we should *not* live in condemnation over them. I no longer live in condemnation over the fact that I was a drug addict, a liar, and a criminal. That is the testimony and platform on which God has built my ministry. I now testify that I was lost, but now I am found; but we don't represent sin as something God condones. God hates sin! We preach about sin in a way that shows that it is reprehensible to God but that Jesus came to forgive and save repentant sinners.

SET FREE FROM SIN

But now that you have been set free from sin and have become slaves of God,
the fruit you get leads to sanctification and its end, eternal life. (vv. 22).

The fruit in our life is the evidence of our heart's condition. According to the Word of God, self-examination or putting the perfect standard of Scripture against our lives is a conditioning post. It is a discipline. Those of us who want to grow in Christ do so willingly. Self-examination is healthy in all areas of our lives but especially in our walk with God. As Christians, our sin will drive us to more dependence on the cross. This does not happen instantly. Sometimes, it is long and painful, but it is the work of the Spirit of God. But in the end, we are more convinced that Christ is saving and changing us by His Spirit and that Scripture is true.

PARDONED FROM DEATH AND FREED UNTO LIFE

For the wages of sin is death, but the free gift of God is eternal life in Christ Jesus our
Lord (v. 23).

Sin is a progressive disease that gets worse and always leads to death. The outcome of sin is always death—always! It disconnects us from the source of life. That is what happened to Adam and Eve. This has been humanity's problem since the beginning. But for those of us who are in Christ, the innocence of Christ on the cross paid the price. God in Christ endured our punishment by His death. Hebrews 7:17 says God is a "'priest forever'" because of the value of His indestructible life. Jesus said, "In the world, you will have tribulation. But take heart; I have overcome the world'" (John 16:33). If we are in Christ, we are connected to the Source of life. That Source of life will be evidenced in our desire, hunger, and thirst for righteousness that God promises He will satisfy.

Sin always leads to death. The wages of sin are death. What are wages? Like wages at the end of a week's work, they are something we are owed and deserve. The same is true of sin. We must see death as the consequence of our sin as something we deserve. That way, when we receive the grace of God, we see it as a gift. Sin leads to death, but Christ leads to life. This is a gift we do not deserve, and we can never earn. No Scripture sums this up better than in the book of Ephesians:

> And you were dead in the trespasses and sins in which you once walked, following the course of this world, following the prince of the power of the air, the spirit that is now at work in the sons of disobedience—among whom we all once lived in the passions of our flesh, carrying out the desires of the body and the mind, and were by nature children of wrath, like the rest of mankind. But God, being rich in mercy, because of the great love with which he loved us, even when we were dead in our trespasses, made us alive together with Christ—by grace you have been saved—and raised us up with him and seated us with him in the heavenly places in Christ Jesus, so that in the coming ages he might show the immeasurable riches of his grace in kindness toward us in Christ Jesus. For by grace you have been saved through faith. And this is not your own doing; it is the gift of God, not a result of works, so that no one may boast. For we are his workmanship, created in Christ Jesus for good works, which God prepared beforehand, that we should walk in them (Eph. 2:1-10).

Our works do not save us, but God has saved us so that we can do good works. The wages of sin lead to death; but for those of us who are in Christ, we have been freed from that penalty only because of God's great love for us. If we find ourselves saved in that love, Paul tells us nothing will be able to separate us from it. "For I am sure that neither death nor life, nor angels nor rulers, nor things present nor things to come, nor powers, nor height nor depth, nor anything else in all creation, will be able to separate us from the love of God in Christ Jesus our Lord" (Rom. 8:38-39). This is the cross, and this is why we are justified and how we are sanctified.

Salvation is about being pardoned from the penalty of our sins. It is about God's mercy and not being given what we deserve. God is so lavish that He did not just pardon us from the penalty and wages of our sins; He gave us grace, victory, and abundant life. This is the love of God in the gospel. It is not by works; it is "not by might, nor by power, but by my Spirit, says the LORD of hosts" (Zech. 4:6).

14
RELEASED FROM THE LAW

ROMANS 7:1-6

Or do you not know, brothers—for I am speaking to those who know the law—that the law is binding on a person only as long as he lives? For a married woman is bound by law to her husband while he lives, but if her husband dies she is released from the law of marriage. Accordingly, she will be called an adulteress if she lives with another man while her husband is alive. But if her husband dies, she is free from that law, and if she marries another man she is not an adulteress.

Likewise, my brothers, you also have died to the law through the body of Christ, so that you may belong to another, to him who has been raised from the dead, in order that we may bear fruit for God. For while we were living in the flesh, our sinful passions, aroused by the law, were at work in our members to bear fruit for death. But now we are released from the law, having died to that which held us captive, so that we serve in the new way of the Spirit and not in the old way of the written code.

I N THESE VERSES, IT IS important to understand the distinction that Paul is making regarding being released from the law. He is not minimizing the value or importance of God's law. He is merely trying to explain its function and purpose in the life of a covenant believer. The prophet Isaiah said, "The LORD was pleased, for his righteousness' sake, to magnify his law and make it glorious" (Isa. 42:21). God's law is beautiful, powerful, and perfect; and Paul is putting it in its proper place.

THE VALUE OF THE LAW

There is a popular false teacher named Andy Stanley who said that Christians should disconnect from the Old Testament and that we should ignore it. He is absolutely wrong; and although he is an unfaithful preacher who does not hold to biblical inerrancy, many confessed Christians listen to him. But even out of those who have enough discernment to avoid false teachers like Stanley, many still have trouble understanding the place of God's law in the life of a New Covenant believer. The Old Testament is just as inspired and important as the New Testament. All the Word of God is glorious, powerful, and breathed out by the Spirit. But although this is true, we must understand how the law and gospel work together to reveal the holy perfection of God and how, through the gospel, man might be reconciled to God.

> How can a young man keep his way pure? By guarding it according to your word. With my whole heart I seek you; let me not wander from your commandments! I have stored up your word in my heart, that I might not sin against you. Blessed are you, O LORD; teach me your statutes! With my lips I declare all the rules of your mouth. In the way of your testimonies I delight as much as in all riches. I will meditate on your precepts and fix my eyes on your ways. I will delight in your statutes; I will not forget your word (Psalm 119:9-16).

The prophet Isaiah says that God will show favor and compassion to those who "are humble and contrite . . . and [tremble] at [his] word" (Isa. 66:2). He is the Sovereign, Holy God of the universe. We are not to minimize the importance of God's Word—Old and New Testament—but we should view the Old Covenant in proper perspective. The law of God is perfect, but it cannot save us.

> Deal bountifully with your servant, that I may live and keep your word. Open my eyes, that I may behold wondrous things out of your law. I am a sojourner on the earth; hide not your commandments from me! My soul is consumed with longing for your rules at all times. You rebuke the insolent, accursed ones, who wander from your commandments. Take away from me scorn and contempt, for I have kept your testimonies. Even though princes sit plotting against me, your servant will meditate on your statutes. Your testimonies are my delight; they are my counselors (Psalm 119:17-24).

As Psalm 119 reveals, the very words of God in the Old Testament are wisdom and counsel. Paul even calls God's law our "schoolmaster" (Gal. 3:25), which keeps us from wrongdoing. Many people confuse the law because they do not understand that there are three branches of the Old Testament law. First, the moral law is made up of the commandments and promises that reflect the unchanging and perfect character of a holy God. The Ten Commandments are part of God's moral law. Second, the civil law is a set of laws that God put in place according to His moral law to help the Israelites live good lives. This made particular distinctions in the law—such as if you murdered someone in cold blood, there was one penalty, but if you accidentally killed someone, there was a lesser penalty. Our American judicial system was meant to mirror this, imperfect as it is. Third, the ceremonial law is the temple's sacrificial system and rituals that the book of Hebrews describes as shadows and placeholders meant to point us to Christ. The Jewish ceremonial law and the temple ordinances are unnecessary now because they have been completely fulfilled in the Person of Jesus.

It is beautiful to know that Christ fulfilled the law. We do not need sacrifices and temple ordinances. The book of Hebrews explains how Christ fulfilled the law completely. He lived a life of perfection; and God, through Christ, fulfilled the law—something no man can do. The sacrificial system is no longer necessary. Civil law was for the Jewish nation but still has much wisdom and value. But God's moral law will never pass away because this is the unchanging character of God. The moral law of God's holy perfection is something no man can live up to, and it is meant to expose our desperate need for Christ.

Earlier in Romans, Paul tells us that God's moral law brings us to despair. This teaching is exemplified when Jesus told the story of the Good Samaritan. The story begins with a Jewish lawyer approaching Jesus and asking, "'What shall I do to inherit eternal life?'" (Luke 10:25).

Jesus said, "'What is written in the law?'"

He responds that the law says, "*'You shall love the Lord your God with all your heart and with all your soul and with all your strength and with all your mind,* and *your neighbor as yourself'*" (Luke 10:27). But instead of pondering this, the lawyer skips past the gravity of the moral law and says, "'And who is my neighbor?'" (Luke 10:29). His response exposed that while he might know the law of God, it had not produced the fruit of repentance in his heart.

Then Jesus tells a compelling story of what it truly means to love your neighbor. The problem was that the lawyer asking the question believes he is living up to the law. But the truth is that no one in all of history has ever loved the Lord their God with all of their heart, mind, soul, and strength for all of their life; and no person has ever truly loved their neighbor as themselves, except for one, and that was Jesus. This is the sum of the law, and we cannot live up to it; but that does not mean we should discard the value of the law.

THE FULFILLED LAW

Some say we are no longer under the Ten Commandments and can live as we please because of grace. As Christian believers, I would ask them which commandments offend them—the part about coveting your neighbor's wife, murdering, or putting other gods before the one true God. We do not devalue the importance of the commandments; we elevate them by acknowledging that the Ten Commandments cannot save us. What saves us is living by faith in the life, death, and resurrection of Jesus Christ.

The law is perfect, but it cannot save us—not because the law is flawed but because we are. The law is God's holy perfection and is perfect; and for us to be reconciled to God, we need a supernatural intervention. An analogy of this is to imagine a valley in between two mountain ranges. This valley is hundreds of feet deep; and when it rains, it floods, causing everything in the valley to be submerged underwater. In the middle of the valley, there is a thousand-foot tower made out of marble that rises high above the flood waters of the valley. And at the top of that tower, there is a room. It is well-insulated, safe, climate-controlled, and comfortable. The elements of the storm cannot penetrate it, and it is high above the waters of the flood. It is filled with furniture, a bed, food, water, and everything a person would need to survive and be well taken care of.

There is nothing wrong with the tower; it is perfect. The only problem is that there is no way to get to the top of the tower on our own. It is made of flat, smooth marble and cannot be climbed. The safety of the room and the tower's engineering are perfect, but it cannot save us without an outside intervention. But there is an elevator. We will be saved if we enter the elevator before the flood. We cannot get to the room on top of the tower to be saved apart from the elevator; but in the elevator, we are saved.

In this analogy, the Elevator is Jesus. We cannot save ourselves, and we cannot fulfill the law. But in Christ, we are saved in God, and we can find peace and safety in Him. We have faith in the elevator, so we get in, and the elevator carries us to safety.

Romans 6 examines the concept of being freed from the law. We are no longer slaves to sin but slaves to righteousness because we are in Christ. In

Romans 7, Paul uses a legal example to explain that our freedom from the law comes from Christ's perfect life and brutal death on our behalf. The cross was a just and legal transaction in which Christ paid the penalty of our sin and took it on Himself so that we could be free. But for this to be applicable in our lives, we must die and be born again. This is the mysterious nature of spiritual regeneration. This is what it means to be a new man or a new woman in Christ.

Remember, Christianity is not the religion of mostly good people trying hard to do better. It is not a self-improvement project. It is a miracle of God. In the Gospel of John, Jesus explains this to Nicodemus:

> Now there was a man of the Pharisees named Nicodemus, a ruler of the Jews. This man came to Jesus by night and said to him, "Rabbi, we know that you are a teacher come from God, for no one can do these signs that you do unless God is with him." Jesus answered him, "Truly, truly, I say to you, unless one is born again he cannot see the kingdom of God." Nicodemus said to him, "How can a man be born when he is old? Can he enter a second time into his mother's womb and be born?" Jesus answered, "Truly, truly, I say to you, unless one is born of water and the Spirit, he cannot enter the kingdom of God. That which is born of the flesh is flesh, and that which is born of the Spirit is spirit. Do not marvel that I said to you, 'You must be born again.' The wind blows where it wishes, and you hear its sound, but you do not know where it comes from or where it goes. So it is with everyone who is born of the Spirit."

> Nicodemus said to him, "How can these things be?" Jesus answered him, "Are you the teacher of Israel and yet you do not understand these things? Truly, truly, I say to you, we speak of what we know, and bear witness to what we have seen, but you do not receive our testimony. If I have told you earthly things and you do not believe,

how can you believe if I tell you heavenly things? No one has ascended into heaven except he who descended from heaven, the Son of Man. And as Moses lifted up the serpent in the wilderness, so must the Son of Man be lifted up, that whoever believes in him may have eternal life (John 3:1-15).

We could spend the entire chapter unpacking that section from John, but here are a couple of important truths we must know to understand the work of salvation in the life of a believer. First, no man can see the kingdom of God unless he is born again. A supernatural regeneration happens to those who are truly in Christ. It is a spiritual rebirth that happens through the power of the Spirit of God, based on what Christ did on the cross. Jesus explains that salvation is mysterious, like the wind. The wind blows where it wants, and it does what it wants. You do not know where it comes from or where it is going, but you feel it and see the evidence of its existence as it moves the branches of the trees. The Greek word *pneuma* can be translated as either "wind" or "spirit," depending on the context. In John 3, Jesus talks about the Spirit, the third Person of the Trinity, and compares Him to the wind that blows through the trees.

God does what He pleases, and He indicates that we cannot understand the mysterious nature of the mechanics of spiritual rebirth. But we do not have to completely understand it to be the recipient of it. By faith, we believe we are reborn through the Spirit of God because of what Christ did for us in the gospel. He gives a very good explanation of what it costs and why it is necessary. We are sinners; that is why it is needed. "All have sinned and fall short of the glory of God" (Rom. 3:23). However, He makes it clear that this is accomplished through the payment of Christ on the cross. Remember, Christ is the only One Who lived a perfect life of moral perfection. He is the only One Who fulfilled the moral law, the civil law, and every part of the ceremonial law. Everything that happened in the Old Testament—the ordinances of the temple, the ceremonial prayers, the sacrifices, and all the types and shadows in the Old Testament—were merely placeholders that point us to Christ's fulfillment in the New Testament. He is the eternal, perfect, and all-sufficient Sacrifice.

THE NEW COVENANT

Or do you not know, brothers—for I am speaking to those who know the law—that the law is binding on a person only as long as he lives? (v. 1).

Jesus explained to Nicodemus the need for regeneration to enter the kingdom of Heaven. Remember, Christianity is not a renovation project of the old man; it is the birth of a new man. It is a new nature born in Christ, and that nature is not born under the damnation of the law. So Paul will explain that Jesus did not come to abolish the law but to fulfill it. When we are born again, we are no longer under the Old Covenant but instead under a New Covenant.

Paul once again gives an axiom or a self-evident truth that does not need to be explained because it is so evident. He provides an axiom to explain that the gospel is faithful to and consistent with the law of God and that the law points to and magnifies the supremacy and perfection of Christ. The law's magnification and elevation simultaneously magnify the gospel of grace. "Where sin increased, grace abounded all the more" (Rom. 5:20). Grace is always more evident as we magnify how vast and damning the law of God is to us. It also magnifies just how deep and wide the grace of God is and how beautiful and powerful it is.

The law of the flesh applies to all born after the fall. What does Paul say in Romans 6? All flesh is born under sin, and "the wages of sin is death" (Rom. 6:23). Everyone born is subject to die. The one thing that unites every person in humanity is that we will all one day die. As people get older, they often start questioning things, reviewing the landscape of their lives, and thinking about what they have accomplished and what they are leaving behind. What legacy will they leave for their grandchildren, or what mark have they made on the world? However, the looming fact is that death is coming, and this is something that touches all of us. But Christianity is not a wish for a better life in this life. Yes, being a Christian does have benefits and blessings in this life; but the truth is that we understand that in Christ, we will live forever through and with Him.

BOUND TO THE LAW

For a married woman is bound by law to her husband while he lives, but if her husband dies she is released from the law of marriage. Accordingly, she will be called an adulteress if she lives with another man while her husband is alive. But if her husband dies, she is free from that law, and if she marries another man she is not an adulteress (vv. 2-3).

The law—its decrees, promises, and punishments—are only binding as long as you are alive. This is a truth that could be understood both by Jews and Gentiles. This applies to the Romans, the Greeks, and even God's Mosaic Law. If a criminal dies, he is no longer bound to his sentence, no matter how numerous or grievous his acts are. The law is only binding on the living, so those living in the flesh are under the law of the flesh.

Paul gives a practical example that he hopes will explain his point. Under Mosaic Law, the Jews would have understood that a woman is free to remarry if her husband dies and she becomes a widow. This is why when two people marry, they say, "Till death do us part." It is a covenant or a commitment that two will be joined as one; but if one dies, the other is free to remarry. Paul uses marriage in Jewish law to explain the law's impact on the flesh.

Some Christians and preachers overcomplicate this section of scripture, but it is straightforward. We are only bound to a covenant if the person we are in covenant with is alive. In verse one, we see this apparent truth. In verses two and three, Paul gives an analogy to help explain this truth, and now, in verses four and five, he gives the analogy's practical application.

DEAD TO THE LAW

Likewise, my brothers, you also have died to the law through the body of Christ, so that you may belong to another, to him who has been raised from the dead, in order that we may bear fruit for God. For while we were living in the flesh, our sinful passions, aroused by the law, were at work in our members to bear fruit for death (vv. 4-5).

Paul is addressing the progressive, embedded, and original nature of sin in our members. Being a Christian is not about sinning less; it is about being reborn. I am not talking about cheap grace or the idea that because we are Christians, we can live and do as we please. No, the truly regenerated heart will be like the author of Psalm 119 when he wrote, "Consider how I love your precepts . . . I love your law" (Psalm 119:159, 163). The law that we used to live under, now we live outside of. We obey God not because we are trying to be accepted by Him but because we have been made like Him and are being sanctified and changed daily.

Christians and non-Christians alike sin, but the true believer hates the sin he once loved. The mortification of sin is a significant struggle every Christian must engage in because sin opposes our new nature in Christ. But we do not fight this battle alone; we fight it by the power of God's Spirit. And we fight knowing that through Him, we will be victorious.

We are born dead in sin and trespass; and as we live under the perfection of God's law, our guilt is compounded more and more every day. Here is the distinction that separates New Covenant Christianity and the idea of Christian moralism or any works-based religion in the world. The standard of God's holiness is unattainable because God Himself is unattainable. Only God Himself could fulfill and satisfy the righteous requirement of the law. How is God unattainable? We only have fellowship and communion with God because He chose to reveal Himself to us and intervene in our lives. We did not find God; He found us. God is unknowable and unattainable; but God, in His grace, came to us where we were. Only God, through the person of Christ, could fulfill and satisfy the righteous requirement of the law. To be saved, justified, sanctified, and ultimately glorified, we must die with Christ to be raised in Christ.

The problem with much of the positive preaching we hear today is that many will discuss the resurrection but not address the dying. Christianity is about dying so that we might be raised anew in Christ. There must come a point when giving up everything from our old life becomes our all-consuming passion because we now have a new purpose and direction that governs everything in our lives. If a person thinks that sounds harsh or legalistic, they do not see the beauty, supremacy, and worthiness of Jesus Christ. We have to raise Jesus high and proclaim the majesty of a God Who created the world with the power of His words. Yet because He loved us, He took on flesh and walked among us. This is the beauty of the gospel of Jesus Christ.

RELEASED FROM THE LAW

But now we are released from the law, having died to that which held us captive, so that we serve in the new way of the Spirit and not in the old way of the written code (v. 6).

We are saved by God and justified in our salvation because of what Christ did on the cross. Jesus traded His innocence for our guilt. To be free from the penalty of the law, which says "the wages of sin is death" (Rom. 3:23), we must die to self. So now we live and have life in a new nature. That is why Jesus tells us to deny ourselves. But in our justification, we are free from the penalty we are due under the law. To be saved is to be reborn in Christ and justified before God. This is biblical faith. This is why all the hymnwriters sing songs about the cross—the beauty of Christ's sacrifice and the blood of Jesus. He paid the debt He did not owe because we owed a debt that we could never pay and we needed Jesus to wash our sins away.

Paul has clearly laid out the fact that freedom from the law does not mean we are free to disobey the law and do what the law forbids. It means we are free from the law's penalty and the undeniable disposition to gratify our flesh.

This does not mean we will not have the desire to satisfy our flesh. Jesus tells us to deny our flesh. But we are saved because of what Christ did on the cross.

Those who are genuinely saved will bear fruit because of the mysterious work of the Spirit that brings life and liberty. I still sin; but when I do, it grieves me. And by God's grace, I feel conviction—not because I am afraid that I am not a Christian but because I love God and have the Spirit of God living inside of me. We can walk with a newness of life because we are in Christ. God poured the wrath, punishment, and curse on His Son, Who willingly took it because of His love for us.

Scripture says we are under a curse of death, a penalty of damnation, if we do not live up to the perfection of the law. "For all who rely on works of the law are under a curse; for it is written, 'Cursed be everyone who does not abide by all things written in the Book of the Law, and do them'" (Galatians 3:10). But it says, "Now it is evident that no one is justified before God by the law, for 'The righteous shall live by faith.' But the law is not of faith, rather 'The one who does them shall live by them'" (Gal. 3:11-12).

Paul lays out the problem, but then he gets to the solution in Galatians 3:13-14: "Christ redeemed us from the curse of the law by becoming a curse for us—for it is written, 'Cursed is everyone who is hanged on a tree'— so that in Christ Jesus the blessing of Abraham might come to the Gentiles, so that we might receive the promised Spirit through faith."

Christ became a curse so that we would be free from the rightful penalty of the curse on us. A curse passed on to us by our forefather Adam and a curse that we have compounded by our sin over a lifetime. Every person on earth has committed grievous sin in the sight of God, and all sin brings death. All sin is wicked. It is right to put sin into categories in a legal and just society. Some sins are more or less grievous. But in God's economy, all sin is grievous. All sin separates us from Him, and He hates all sin. If we minimize sin's grievousness, we minimize God's holiness. We also minimize the beauty, importance, and lavish nature of God's grace and Christ's sacrifice on the cross.

In the gospel, God not only takes away the penalty for trespassing the law; Hut he gives us a new heart that desires to obey the law of God. It is not about what we do but what Christ has done. We are reborn, saved, justified, sanctified, and glorified. In the death of Christ, we have been released from the law. In the resurrection of Christ, we have been given a new life in Him. We have died with Christ; and because of this, we have life through Christ. This is why Jesus said, "'If anyone would come after me, let him deny himself and take up his cross and follow me'" (Matt. 16:24). Jesus is not talking about a silver-plated cross bought in a Christian bookstore to show everyone that you are a Christian. "Follow me" is about picking up an instrument that brings death so that we might have life.

The beauty of the gospel is found in our complete inability to save ourselves and the fact that we do not deserve His grace. When we understand the righteous requirements of the law and how grievous our sin is in God's sight, we begin to scratch the surface of the boundless depths of God's love toward us.

15

THE LAW OF GOD AND THE SIN OF MAN

ROMANS 7:7-25

What then shall we say? That the law is sin? By no means! Yet if it had not been for the law, I would not have known sin. For I would not have known what it is to covet if the law had not said, "You shall not covet." But sin, seizing an opportunity through the commandment, produced in me all kinds of covetousness. For apart from the law, sin lies dead. I was once alive apart from the law, but when the commandment came, sin came alive and I died. The very commandment that promised life proved to be death to me. For sin, seizing an opportunity through the commandment, deceived me and through it killed me. So the law is holy, and the commandment is holy and righteous and good.

Did that which is good, then, bring death to me? By no means! It was sin, producing death in me through what is good, in order that sin might be shown to be sin, and through the commandment might become sinful beyond measure. For we know that the law is spiritual, but I am of the flesh, sold under sin. For I do not understand my own actions. For I do not do what I want, but I do the very thing I hate. Now if I do what I do not want, I agree with the law, that it is good. So now it is no longer I who do it, but sin that dwells within me. For I know that nothing good dwells in me, that is, in my flesh. For I have the desire to do what is right, but not the ability to carry it out. For I do not do the good I want, but the evil I do not want is what I keep on doing. Now if I do what I

do not want, it is no longer I who do it, but sin that dwells within me.

So I find it to be a law that when I want to do right, evil lies close at hand. For I delight

in the law of God, in my inner being, but I see in my members another law waging

war against the law of my mind and making me captive to the law of sin that dwells in

my members. Wretched man that I am! Who will deliver me from this body of death?

Thanks be to God through Jesus Christ our Lord! So then, I myself serve the law of God

with my mind, but with my flesh I serve the law of sin.

THIS CHAPTER WILL EXAMINE THE doctrine of sanctification in greater depth and the inward battle of sin in the life of a believer. We know we must wage war on our sins and strive to live dead to sin. We must treat sin with seriousness, but we often tend to do this from a place of trying to earn our salvation. Previously, we discussed how we are not trying to earn God's pleasure or approval but are justified before God based on Christ. We are justified, but we must draw a line of distinction and acknowledge that sin is evil and that our new nature hates it, and we must wage war against it. We fight against sin not to be saved but because we *are* saved and love God and are loved by God.

Pastors today rarely use language like striving, fighting, or warring against sin because they fear that people will think they are preaching "works righteousness" or legalism. However, we must preach this because the Word of God does. The Bible does not say we can do what we please because we are saved. No, it says those saved in Christ can live free from sin. This does not mean we are sinless, but we will sin less and less.

The false doctrine of works righteousness is about striving or working toward something to earn justification and salvation from the Lord. That is legalism. Our striving to put our sin to death has nothing to do with justification; it is the work of the Spirit in us as He sanctifies us. Some people teach works righteous, while others simply make a category error. Ephesians tells us that our salvation is of grace, not works, "so that no one may boast" (Eph. 2:8-9) but that those who are truly saved by God's grace will produce works as evidence of their spiritual regeneration.

People often wrestle with the question of losing one's salvation. In the modern church, we resist examining ourselves to see if we are truly in the faith. As a preacher, it is not my job to convince someone that they are saved; it is to preach the uncompromised Word of God under the anointing of the Holy Spirit. If we belong to God, His Word and Spirit living in us will testify that we belong to Him.

Often, preachers are so desperate to convince someone they are saved because they attend church or repeat a prayer at some point that we try to talk them out of the conviction of the Holy Spirit produced by biblical gospel preaching. Yet we should not take it for granted. If someone questions their salvation and feels God is doing a convicting work in their heart, the Bible is the source to guide them. Scripture says, "There is therefore now no condemnation for those who are in Christ Jesus" (Rom. 8:1). It also says, "The Spirit himself bears witness with our spirit that we are children of God" (Rom. 8:16).

Christianity is often reduced to religious moralism, the idea that being a Christian is about doing good works. Many people who live this legalistic life focus on their outward appearance but not on the inward nature of their hearts. This is not about giving someone a license to be immoral or do sinful things. But in salvation, the Spirit of God causes a new desire to rise up in us. It is a desire that wants to please God and begins to hate sin. Sometimes, brand new Christians or false converts ask, "Can I or can I not do something and still be a Christian?" It is about seeing how close to the line they can get and still claim to be a Christian. But the true believer in Christ asks, "What does the Bible say, and does this glorify God?" A genuine Christian wants to please and glorify God and desires to live a holy life, drawing others to Him.

We wage war against the sin of the flesh because we now hate the sin we once loved. As we wage this war for the glory of God, we do so from a place of victory. We do not strive to be accepted by God; we strive because God accepts us. We know that Jesus will never leave or forsake us (Heb. 13:5), and nothing can snatch us from His hand (John 10:28).

THE LAW'S DIAGNOSIS

What then shall we say? That the law is sin? By no means! Yet if it had not been for the law, I would not have known sin. For I would not have known what it is to covet if the law had not said, "You shall not covet" (v. 7).

Once again, Paul asks a question that he believes his critics are asking of him and immediately answers it. Paul asks, "Is the law sin because the law causes the sin in us to manifest and come to the surface and become known?" To phrase, this in a modern-day question: Is a Magnetic Resonance Imaging (MRI) machine the same thing as the cancer it is designed to detect? No, of course not, but cancer is not diagnosed without the MRI machine.

A person may feel unhealthy symptoms in their body, and there may be outward signs that something is wrong. Perhaps they adjust their diet, sleep patterns, or medications. If the physical symptoms persist, they realize the problem needs to be addressed by a doctor. The physician uses an MRI scan to pinpoint the part of the body causing pain and symptoms. After the MRI, the doctor confirms whether or not there is a malignant cancerous tumor. Now that the person knows the symptoms are from the cancer, it weighs on them. As the symptoms get worse, they will need a prognosis of the disease, and they will need to decide whether or not they will get treatment. The MRI machine is not the cancer, but it helps make a diagnosis.

In the same way, the law of God is that diagnosis; and the gospel of Jesus Christ is the cure. A person will still have the cancer, even if the cancerous tumor is undiagnosed without an MRI. With or without the diagnosis, the cancer will still spread and produce death if left untreated. As Paul previously mentioned, those in the law will die under the law; and those outside the law will die outside the law. We are all going to die because "the wages of sin is death" (Rom. 6:23). If left untreated, the cancer of sin is fatal 100 percent of the time.

The nineteenth-century theologian Charles Hodge wrote:

> The law, although it cannot secure either justification or sanctification of men, performs an essential part in the economy of salvation. It enlightens conscience and secures its verdict against a multitude of evils, which we should not have otherwise recognized as sins. It arouses sin, increasing its power and making it both in itself and in our consciousness, exceedingly sinful. It therefore produces that state of mind which is a necessary preparation for the reception of the gospel.[20]

Charles Haddon Spurgeon said it another way: "The law is the needle, and you cannot draw the silken thread of the gospel through a man's heart unless you first send the needle of the law through the center thereof, to make way for it."[21] We need the law of God to diagnose how sinful our sinfulness is and how holy God is. The law of God represents the very character of God.

When I was living in sinful rebellion as a young musician, chasing my dreams, getting drunk and high, and allowing addiction to take hold of my life, I realized that I needed to get off drugs. I was not having success in my life, and I prayed, "God, if you will help me overcome addiction and my self-destructive habits, then I will be a good, healthy, functioning person." I thought if I could just overcome addiction, then I would be a better person.

But once I became a Christian, I was brought to despair because I realized through the Word of God that I had sins in my life that I was not previously aware were sins. As God's truth shined in my heart, root problems were brought to light. I began to realize that not only was I a drug addict, I was also a liar, angry, selfish, and living for myself in every possible way. Even some of my good deeds and good intentions had little caveats of a personal agenda attached. I began to see the truth of who I really was.

The closer we get to a holy God, the less encouraged or good we feel about ourselves. As the prophet Isaiah described, "'Woe is me! For I am lost; for I am a man of unclean lips, and I dwell in the midst of a people of unclean lips; for my eyes have seen the King, the Lord of hosts!'" (Isa. 6:5). It is not that God is making us feel bad about ourselves. But the juxtaposition between the holiness of a perfect, Sovereign, glorious, and loving God and us—fallen, wretched sinners—is dramatic. It is striking! So, while we understand that we are justified before God, we look at ourselves and realize that we are sinful. Sin is wired into our members, hands, minds, and hearts. Many, if not most of us, have spent much of our lives growing, nurturing, and building that sin. The law of God does not make us more sinful; it exposes and alerts us to our sins.

GROUND ZERO OF THE SIN BATTLE

But sin, seizing an opportunity through the commandment, produced in me all kinds of covetousness. For apart from the law, sin lies dead. I was once alive apart from the law, but when the commandment came, sin came alive and I died. The very commandment that promised life proved to be death to me. For sin, seizing an opportunity through the commandment, deceived me and through it killed me (vv. 8-11).

Sin leads to more sin. It is progressive; it grows in power, and the law exposes and exacerbates it. This shows us we are desperate and just how needy we are for Christ. Paul means this when he says, "And put no confidence in the flesh" (Phil. 3:3). There is nothing to be confident in about our flesh. One of the most popular mantras in the modern-day evangelical church is "Follow your heart, or God wants you to follow your dreams." But the law of God in Jeremiah says, "The heart is deceitful above all things, and desperately sick; who can understand it?" (Jer. 17:9). Do you know Who does know it? God. This magnifies the love and grace of God and the gospel. As we come to grips with Who God is and compare our life to the light of God's law, it magnifies God's love and grace immensely. God is not saying to follow our hearts; He wants to give us new hearts. He wants to take away that "heart of stone" and give us "a heart of flesh" (Ezek. 36:26). God knows your heart and intentions even better than you do—the good, the bad, the really bad, and the ugly—and despite this, He loves us, died for us, saved us, and holds us in the palm of His hand.

The real battle of sin is not just with the devil or the fallen world. Often, psychoanalytical jargon gets meshed in with the church, and it usually takes a predominant seat in the order of how we prioritize truth. We try to use the Bible to support it, but the truth is our environment is not the reason why we are sinful. It may help magnify and nurture that sin, but we are sinful because it is in our members. We were born into sin, original sin—the total depravity of humanity. Yet the greatest deception of mankind is that we are mostly good people. However, the Bible says no one is good, not even one (Rom. 3:10). Ground zero of this sin battle is in the heart and mind. We wage war against our own flesh. Understand this is an unwinnable war *apart* from Christ's saving and regenerating power. We should have no confidence in the flesh. This is why Paul wrote, "For we are the circumcision, who worship by the Spirit of God and glory in Christ Jesus and put no confidence in the flesh" (Phil. 3:3).

Apostle Paul, like the rest of us, was once under the delusion of this great deception. He thought that because he was outwardly keeping the law and doing all the right things, he was living a pleasing life to God. This is the deception of the law. But when we truly understand the commandments of God in the Old Testament, we see that the promised blessings are unobtainable apart from the gospel. We can still benefit from the proverbial wisdom of God's promises, even if we are not in Christ. If we manage our money correctly or treat people well, we will probably live a better life. But the ultimate promise is that if we live in obedience, we will have favor with God. The only problem is no one can perfectly keep the law. If we think we are living up to the law of God, we are deceived, just like the apostle Paul once was.

Living under the law apart from Christ can only produce despair and death. Paul is saying that the promises of the law deceived him because he believed they were attainable through keeping the law. The promises of the law are good but unattainable apart from Christ. Paul was very deceived. If anyone could have been saved by keeping the law, it would have been him. Paul fleshes this out in great detail in Philippians 3:

> Though I myself have reason for confidence in the flesh also. If anyone else thinks he has reason for confidence in the flesh, I have more: circumcised on the eighth day, of the people of Israel, of the tribe of Benjamin, a Hebrew of Hebrews; as to the law, a Pharisee; as to zeal, a persecutor of the church; as to righteousness under the law, blameless. But whatever gain I had, I counted as loss for the sake of Christ. Indeed, I count everything as loss because of the surpassing worth of knowing Christ Jesus my Lord. For his sake I have suffered the loss of all things and count them as rubbish, in order that I may gain Christ and be found in him, not having a righteousness of my own that comes from the law, but that which comes through faith in Christ, the righteousness from God that depends on faith—that I may know him and the power of his resurrection, and may share his sufferings, becoming like him in his death, that by any means possible I may attain the resurrection from the dead (Phil. 3:4-11).

Paul was a righteous law keeper: a Pharisee of Pharisees, Jew of Jews, Hebrew of Hebrews. He was from the prestigious tribe of Benjamin, keeping all the outward appearances of the law. But when he met Christ and saw Him as the image of the invisible God, He was struck with the understanding that he was a wretched sinner and that everything else in his life was rubbish compared to Christ. Christ is the fulfillment of the law. We could not fulfill or keep it, but Christ did on our behalf.

THE HOLY LAW

So the law is holy, and the commandment is holy and righteous and good. Did that
which is good, then, bring death to me? By no means! It was sin, producing death in
me through what is good, in order that sin might be shown to be sin, and through the
commandment might become sinful beyond measure (vv. 12-13).

If we go back to my original analogy, the question is, did the MRI bring cancer? No, but it exposed it; and if we view the cancerous cells in the MRI scan, we will see their progression. It gets worse and worse until it causes death.

As humans, we sometimes want to find a remedy besides Christ crucified. Some people in the church preach a therapeutic version of Christianity—a few steps to being a better person, a better husband, wife, businessman, or whatever you desire to focus on—cleaning the outside of the cup with no real thought to the dead bones inside. Some try and follow Jewish calendars and participate in the festival observances because they believe it is the key to receiving a special blessing from God instead of realizing it was all meant to point us to Christ. It is rubbish, utter rubbish! The cancer is getting worse, and it is going to kill us no matter how we look on the outside. Sin grows and grows and produces death. We can try to make personal changes in our lives, but it will not cut out the sin.

Jesus is the only Way to God! There is no way to come to the Father except through Him. This is the message of the foolishness of the cross—the power of the blood of Jesus Christ that washes away our sins. "'Behold! The Lamb of God, who takes away the sin of the world!'" (John 1:29). There is no other cure for sin in our flesh that brings death. It will bring death, no matter what. Our only hope for a new life is in the Author and the Creator of Life—only in Jesus Christ.

The law is holy because God is holy. It is perfect because God is perfect. The law shows us that the problem is not God but us. We are subject to the law of God and the severe consequences that come along with transgressing it.

Paul says this is not only because of our outward actions but also because of what is in our hearts and minds. Jesus taught that we should be as concerned about the root of sin as the fruit it produces. This is why in Matthew 5, Jesus said, "You feel good about yourself because you do not cheat on your wife. But have you ever looked at a woman with lust? You may not have murdered someone, but have you been angry with your brother?"

Jesus is just as concerned about the root as He is about the fruit. The fruit is just the evidence of what is in our hearts. So often, we hear people try to justify their open and unrepentant sinful lifestyles by saying, "Yes, I am living my life this way, but God knows my heart." God does know our hearts; He knows everything that is in our hearts and minds, and that should terrify us. The law of God shows us that our hearts are wicked and that our good works or good intentions are not enough, but that is why Christ came to earth. In a culture that tries to make sin seem less and less sinful, we must preach that sin is grievous, wicked, and offensive to God. Yet Jesus came to save sinners. We are subject to the perfect law of God in our thoughts, deeds, and intentions.

THE BELIEVER'S BATTLE

For we know that the law is spiritual, but I am of the flesh, sold under sin. For I do not understand my own actions. For I do not do what I want, but I do the very thing I hate. Now if I do what I do not want, I agree with the law, that it is good. So now it is no longer I who do it, but sin that dwells within me. For I know that nothing good dwells in me, that is, in my flesh. For I have the desire to do what is right, but not the ability to carry it out. For I do not do the good I want, but the evil I do not want is what I keep on doing. Now if I do what I do not want, it is no longer I who do it, but sin that dwells within me (vv. 14-20).

Here is a sneak peek at Paul's overall message. He is pointing out that apart from Christ, there is no good in us. All good things come from God, and Paul wants us to come to this conclusion so that we do not rely on even the things that seem good about our flesh and our humanity. He wants us to entrust our whole lives to the unchanging, eternal, all-powerful truth of God's Word.

Some argue that Paul is writing about his life before Christ in these verses, but I don't believe that is true. He is referring to the two natures that are at war within us. There were not two natures at war in us before we were reborn in Christ. Before Christ, we were deceived to believe that our goodness is good enough or that it could be with some hard work and self-improvement; but it is all rubbish and loss. No, Paul is talking about the idea of sinful members that are cursed to death, being at war with a new nature living inside of us. A new man, a new woman with new desires, new passions, and a new heart. God gives us a new heart in salvation, and Paul calls us not to conform to the patterns of the world or our flesh but to the patterns given through the Word of God. "Do not be conformed to this world, but be transformed by the renewal of your mind, that by testing you may discern what is the will of God, what is good and acceptable and perfect" (Rom. 12:2).

The knowledge of the law arouses the sin in us, but it is not until we are spiritually reborn that we are actually at odds with our flesh. Do not confuse a desire for self-betterment as the same as being at odds with a sinful nature. Everyone wants to have a better life. Everyone wants answers for depression, addiction, or our purpose in life. That is why there is a trillion-dollar self-improvement industry. However, the truth is nothing in this world can satisfy the hunger of our souls—only Jesus. And while we know this to some extent when we first become Christians, we often do not perceive the depth and fullness of it. A new nature rises up that shows us how sinful sin is and how holy God is, and that causes us to rely on Christ more and more. Yet when we fall into besetting sin, it is not meant to drive us back to despair or to sin more. It should drive us to cling to Christ—faith in Christ's salvation through Christ alone—all for the glory of God.

Everyone hates the consequences of sin and living in a fallen world. Non-Christians work to eradicate any discomfort that sin brings into their lives. But only the spiritually reborn person hates and mourns sin. Paul says, "For godly grief produces a repentance that leads to salvation without regret, whereas worldly grief produces death" (2 Cor. 7:10). Worldly grief is being sorry for the wrong caused or the suffering or pain experienced by a sinful person. But godly grief is grieving over sin itself. This is the mechanism of repentance that draws men to salvation. Like Paul says, "I want to be different, but it is hard. I need You, Jesus!"

The law of God is essential not just to draw us to salvation. It also reveals to us God's holiness in an ever-increasing way. We examine our lives according to His righteous life, which produces obedience and, more importantly, an ever-increasing dependence on Christ. The more we look at how holy God is and how unlike Him we are, the more dependence we will put in Christ and live by faith. Then, we will find victory from our sins. Remember, before Christ, Paul thought he had it all figured out. He was a Pharisee. He kept the law and the ceremonies, but he could not eradicate what was in his heart. One day, on the road to Damascus, he met the Savior—the image of the invisible God, the God of Abraham, Isaac, and Jacob—and Paul was radically changed!

PAUL'S FIRST LAMENTATION OVER SIN

For we know that the law is spiritual, but I am of the flesh, sold under sin. For I do not understand my own actions. For I do not do what I want, but I do the very thing I hate. Now if I do what I do not want, I agree with the law, that it is good. So now it is no longer I who do it, but sin that dwells within me (vv. 14-17).

Paul then makes four laments over this battle with sin. He explains why he wrestled with sin. If the great apostle Paul, the apostle John, and even the prophet Isaiah—the man with "unclean lips" in the presence of a holy God (Isa. 6:5)—wrestled with sin, this should bring us comfort. Our battle with sin is not uncommon to man. It includes all of us, and when we point the law of God at our hearts, we begin to see it all the more clearly.

Paul's first lament gives us the condition: the law is spiritual, but Paul is a fleshly person who is born into and sold into the death of sin. We do not have a choice in this matter; everyone born in our world is born into sin. The second part is the evidence: he knows right from wrong but cannot seem to do what is right. Paul struggles to control his mind and bear the fruit of self-control. He is not saying this to make us feel hopeless but to help us understand we are hopeless outside of Christ. He then moves on to the source of the problem: The sin dwelling in him is the source of the problem that brings on the condition that he cannot live a perfect life according to the law of God.

PAUL'S SECOND LAMENTATION OVER SIN

For I know that nothing good dwells in me, that is, in my flesh. For I have the desire to do what is right, but not the ability to carry it out. For I do not do the good I want, but the evil I do not want is what I keep on doing. Now if I do what I do not want, it is no longer I who do it, but sin that dwells within me (vv. 18-20).

The second lament follows the same order. Paul lays out the condition in the first part of verse eighteen: there is nothing good in him. He dwells in the flesh. Then he moves on to the problem evidenced by that fact that he wants to do right but is unable to do so: (vv. 18b-19). Once again, Paul tells us the source of the problem: this sin that dwells in us is the source of the problem. It is not a socioeconomic situation, our family, nor where we were born that is the source. The problem is the sin that dwells in our members. As soon as we understand this, we will rightly apply the cure of Christ and His glorious gospel. He is our only Hope. Jesus came to save sinners, of whom Paul says he is chief (1 Tim. 1:15). Paul says when we examine our hearts and intentions according to the Word of God, we come away realizing we need Jesus.

PAUL'S THIRD LAMENTATION OVER SIN

So I find it to be a law that when I want to do right, evil lies close at hand. For I delight in the law of God, in my inner being, but I see in my members another law waging war against the law of my mind and making me captive to the law of sin that dwells in my members (vv. 21-23).

Paul gives us the condition with the third lament. The condition is that when he wants to do right, he seems to fail even more. All who leave sin unchecked are on a downward trajectory to death. It is inevitable. The devil does not care if he deceives a person on their way to Hell with addiction or if he does it with prosperity in this life. We are all subject to death, and the second death comes from sin unless we are reborn and connected to the Source of life. Then Paul moves on to the evidence of the problem: Paul knows that in his innermost being, through the Spirit of God, he delights in the law of the Lord. But looking at his flesh, he sees another power at work. The power of sin makes us captive to the law of sin that dwells in our members. When Paul says, "Sin that dwells in my members," this is the depravity of man, the sin we are born into. We did not become sinners the first time we did something wrong. We were born dead in sin and trespass. Our situation was hopeless from the start, apart from Christ.

PAUL'S FOURTH LAMENTATION OVER SIN

Wretched man that I am! Who will deliver me from this body of death? (v. 24).

Then Paul gives his fourth and final lament without evidence, condition, or source. He yells out a final mourning over his sin (v. 24). The law of God should drive us to this question. Every person needs to come to a place in their life where success, relationships, money, drugs, sex, or chasing a dream will not satisfy them. Paul said he got to a place where he cried out, "Oh, wretched man of death! Who will deliver me from the body of sin and death?" This is what good preaching should do. It should take us to repentance, where we say, "'What must I do to be saved?'" (Acts 16:30). We have to give the diagnosis for the cure to be paramount and for people to see the need. We have to put people in the diagnosis machine of the law of God, the holiness of God, and the sinfulness of man.

THE VICTORIOUS LIFE IN CHRIST

Thanks be to God through Jesus Christ our Lord! So then, I myself serve the law of God with my mind, but with my flesh I serve the law of sin (v. 25).

Like Paul, we now live with transplanted, reborn hearts with new affections and passions. We conform to the image of Christ as we read, study, and apply the Word of God in our lives. Our minds are no longer conformed to the patterns of this world. We are no longer slaves to the desires of our hearts but have new hearts and new passions. Paul is saying while the heart and mind are changed, we will still have to wage war against our flesh. Sometimes, we will experience victory, but it will not come by catering to our flesh.

Many people refuse to mortify and wage war on their sins because they believe striving to kill their sins is "legalistic." But those who truly value and understand and value their blood-bought justification will go to any lengths to kill their sin because of their love for the God who saved them. This is why Paul says, "Work out your own salvation with fear and trembling" (Phil. 2:12). We love Jesus and want to be like Him; and we should strive to live out an example that shows we want to give Jesus to our children, families, neighbors, and the whole world.

We do not mourn and repent our sins only at the beginning of our Christian walk; it is a part of our daily Christian life. It is the work of sanctification as the Spirit of God refines us and conforms us to the image of Christ, our Savior and Lord. There is a staggering difference between our sinful nature, which we are born into, and our new nature, which is birthed in us in regeneration. We mortify, resist, and strive against our sins—not to stay saved, not to earn salvation, but because we have the very Spirit of God living in us. Paul laments his sin because he loves Christ and wants to live for Christ because he has been reborn in Christ; and through Christ, God breathed life into the law, which Paul strived to keep in His life as a Jewish Pharisee. Now, the same law which brought him to despair has become to him the law of liberty through Christ. "Wretched man that I am, who will save me from this body of death?" In Romans 8, Paul will answer this question and explain the power and freedom that comes with life in the Spirit through the gospel of Jesus Christ.

Those who take the diagnosis seriously and tremble at the law of God will cling to the gospel of Jesus Christ. Although we struggle with sin, we struggle from a place of victory, knowing the battle is won and our salvation is secure because it is of the Lord! He initiated and secured salvation on the cross. He justifies and sanctifies those He has saved and promises a crown of righteousness for all who persevere to the end.

16
ROMANS 1-7 REVIEW

U P TO THIS POINT, THE book of Romans has laid out fallen humanity's
hopeless and desperate nature outside God's intervention through
Christ's death and resurrection. The two most under-preached parts of the
gospel are the holiness of God and the grievousness of sin. This is why Paul
spends so much of the first seven chapters of Romans laying this out for us.
Grace is not important if it is not saving us from something. If we do not
understand how dire our situation is, then we do not know how beautiful
and precious God's amazing grace is in the gospel. In Romans, Paul has taken
great aims to elevate the holiness of God and repeatedly addresses how
grievous, wicked, and despised sin is by God.

For God to be perfectly loving, He must also be perfectly just. Perfect
justice demands the righteous punishment of sin. This is often difficult to
understand because we are born into sin and trespass. Our hearts and our
minds are crooked, and we are children of wrath by nature (Rom. 1:18). We
are born into sin and under a curse that we have no way of overcoming other
than the Divine intervention of God Himself. That is why the true Christian
is eternally grateful for what Christ did on the cross. We never tire of hearing
about the cross of Christ preached because it is why we have life, not death. It
is not something we outgrow in Christianity. Paul said, "But we preach Christ
crucified, a stumbling block to Jews and folly to Gentiles" (I Cor. 1:23). It is
the cross of Jesus Christ that saved us; and for us to understand what a great

salvation we have, we must realize how desperate our situation was and how grievous, wicked, and offensive sin is to a holy and just God.

King David talks about his sin when he says, "Behold, I was brought forth in iniquity, and in sin did my mother conceive me" (Psalm 51:5). Even before the New Testament, King David understood that he was a sinful man born into sin and had a compulsion in his heart to sin. This was a man God called "a man after his heart own heart" (1 Sam. 13:14). However, David understood that apart from God, he had wicked tendencies, plans, and schemes. In David's life, those schemes were played out when he committed adultery, impregnating a woman, and covered up his sin by having the woman's husband killed. In Psalm 51, David acknowledges that he is utterly sinful apart from God.

When the prophet Isaiah came into the presence of a holy God, it says, "The train of his robe filled the temple" (Isa. 6:1). Isaiah responded, "'Woe is me! For I am lost; for I am a man of unclean lips, and I dwell in the midst of a people of unclean lips; for my eyes have seen the King, the Lord of hosts!'" (Isa. 6:5). He was rightly contrasting himself to a holy God, Who, in His presence, was made aware that he was filled with sin and iniquity. Christianity is about men and women who are dead in sin and trespass and who have been raised to life in Christ. Once that life is raised, nothing can take it away. Those who are in Christ are being saved not only from the consequences of our sin but from the wrath of God Himself.

Many people talk about being saved; but if asked what they are saved from, they get tongue-tied and do not know how to answer. But we are saved from the righteous, rightful wrath of God that is being stored up for humanity. Romans 3:23 says, "For all have sinned and fall short of the glory of God." The Bible is a book of grace and salvation, but it is also a book of condemnation and judgment. If we deny this, we undermine the greatness of grace and salvation. But for those who belong to Christ, we are no longer subject to that condemnation because Christ has saved us into the eternal family of God. In Ephesians, Paul says, "And you were dead in the trespasses and sins in which you once walked, following the course of this world, following the prince of the power of the air, the spirit that is now at work in the sons of disobedience—among whom we all once lived in the passions of our flesh, carrying out the desires of the flesh and the mind, and were by nature children of wrath, like the rest of mankind" (Eph. 2:1-3). This mirrors when he says, "'None is righteous, no, not one'" (Rom. 3:10).

We are also under the power of Satan. This is strong terminology to use, but there are only two groups of people: those inside Christ who belong to God and everyone else who are under the demonic control of Satan. Now, one might say, "But I know people who are not Christians, and they are good people." I am not arguing that point. I, too, have friends who do not believe in Christ and who are some of the friendliest and most generous people I know. But that does not matter because if they are not in Christ, they are a part of the kingdom of darkness. The apostle John addresses this:

> Whoever makes a practice of sinning is of the devil, for the devil has been sinning from the beginning. The reason the Son of God appeared was to destroy the works of the devil. No one born of God makes a practice of sinning, for God's seed abides in him; and he cannot keep on sinning, because he has been born of God. By this it is evident who are the children of God, and who are the children of the devil: whoever does not practice righteousness is not of God, nor is the one who does not love his brother (1 John 3:8-10).

John is not saying that Christians will be sinless. We know from Romans 7 that Christians will wrestle with the sin born into our members. The difference is that we have a new nature inside of us that wants to keep the law of God and live in obedience to please God. Our works are not saving us, but they are now the evidence that the Spirit of God lives in us.

Furthermore, we are under God's judgment, not only because we cannot keep the law but also because those who resist and turn their back on Christ will be condemning themselves by that as well. This is outlined in the book of Hebrews:

> For if we go on sinning deliberately after receiving the knowledge of the truth, there no longer remains a sacrifice for sins, but a fearful expectation of judgment, and a fury of fire that will consume the adversaries. Anyone who has set aside the law of Moses dies without mercy on the evidence of two or three witnesses. How much worse punishment, do you think, will be deserved by the one who has trampled underfoot the Son of God, and has profaned the blood of the covenant by which he was sanctified, and has outraged the Spirit of grace? (Heb. 10:26-29).

The writer of Hebrews tells us that if we trample or dismiss the grace of Christ, then there is no other way of escape. "Jesus said . . . 'I am the way, and the truth, and the life. No one comes to the Father except through me" (John 14:6).

Finally, we are also cursed, as Paul tells us in Galatians *"For all who rely on works of the law are under a curse*; for it is written, 'Cursed be everyone who does not abide by all things written in the Book of the Law, and do them.' Now it is evident that no one is justified before God by the law, for 'The righteous shall live by faith'" (Gal. 3:10-11, emphasis added). This is saving faith—knowing we stand justified before God exclusively because of what Christ did on the cross. No one can boast. We cannot earn God's salvation or love.

Yet what makes grace so beautiful? It is a gift God gave to undeserving people. It is an unmerited favor, which means we did nothing to deserve it. However, the Bible says our rightful wage for our lives is death because the wages of sin is death.

Remember, in Romans 1, Paul explains that condemnation and wrath are being stored up for humanity. Not only will there be a final judgment, but groups of people in societies will also be under judgment because we cannot live up to the law but mainly because we do not acknowledge or worship God and treat Him as holy. Because of this, God will condemn us in the end but also turn our minds over to wicked and debaucherous things. Our minds will be darkened, and we will begin to have unnatural affections.

> For the wrath of God is revealed from heaven against all ungodliness and unrighteousness of men, who by their unrighteousness suppress the truth. For what can be known about God is plain to them, because God has shown it to them. For his invisible attributes, namely, his eternal power and divine nature, have been clearly perceived, ever since the creation of the world, in the things that have been made. So they are without excuse. For although they knew God, they did not honor him as God or give thanks to him, but they became futile in their thinking, and their foolish hearts were darkened. Claiming to be wise, they became fools, and exchanged the glory of the immortal God for images resembling mortal man and birds and animals and creeping things. Therefore God gave them up in the lusts of their hearts to impurity, to the dishonoring of their bodies among themselves, because they exchanged the truth about God for a lie and worshiped and served the creature rather than the Creator, who is blessed forever! Amen (Rom. 1:18-25).

The Bible says that those who seek God will find Him. Yet many want the things God can provide but do not want God. Many want a Savior but do not want to call Him Lord. Jesus is Lord; and God is worthy of our praise, worship, and honor. God breathed life into our lungs because we were created to bring glory to God. That is the purpose of our creation—not to live well and prosper, not to have our best life now, but to do all things for the glory of God. Our careers, raising children, food, and hobbies should be an expression of honor, thanksgiving, and glory to God.

But we do not want to give glory to God, so the Bible says we pretend like there is no God. Even worse, we make ourselves gods or worship animals, nature, or other things. Those things do not ask anything of us. God demands our allegiance. The gospel is not some invitation. It is an ultimatum—"follow

Me!" However, if we follow our will to be lord of our lives, we will follow that to our ultimate destruction.

RECAP OF ROMANS 1-7:

- Paul tells us we are under God's judgment.
- Paul elaborates on the righteousness of God's judgment.
- Paul explains God's righteousness and shows that compared to Him, no one is righteous on their own merit or works. He conveys that no one is good, not even one. However, Paul also tells us there is a way to be righteous, but only by putting faith in Christ alone.
- Paul explains that even Abraham, the Jewish patriarch, was justified by faith and not by works. God's promise to Abraham that the world would be blessed through his seed was fulfilled in the gospel of Jesus Christ.
- Paul conveys that the only way to find peace with God is through faith in the atoning work of Christ on the cross. He explains that all born after Adam were born into sin and death. Sin came into the world through one man, but also sin would be eradicated from the world through one Man—Jesus.
- Paul tells us that we have been released in Christ from the law's curse; and because of this, we should live dead to sin because we have new life in Christ.
- Paul explains that although we have been released from the law because we are technically dead to it, we must fight against the sin in our members. We are not fighting so that we will be justified before God; we are justified on the basis of our faith in Christ. We are saved by grace alone, through faith alone, in Christ alone, according to the Scripture alone—and it is all the glory of God alone.

17

FULLY ALIVE IN CHRIST

ROMANS 8:1–11

There is therefore now no condemnation for those who are in Christ Jesus. For the law of the Spirit of life has set you free in Christ Jesus from the law of sin and death. For God has done what the law, weakened by the flesh, could not do. By sending his own Son in the likeness of sinful flesh and for sin, he condemned sin in the flesh, in order that the righteous requirement of the law might be fulfilled in us, who walk not according to the flesh but according to the Spirit. For those who live according to the flesh set their minds on the things of the flesh, but those who live according to the Spirit set their minds on the things of the Spirit. For to set the mind on the flesh is death, but to set the mind on the Spirit is life and peace. For the mind that is set on the flesh is hostile to God, for it does not submit to God's law; indeed, it cannot. Those who are in the flesh cannot please God.

You, however, are not in the flesh but in the Spirit, if in fact the Spirit of God dwells in you. Anyone who does not have the Spirit of Christ does not belong to him. But if Christ is in you, although the body is dead because of sin, the Spirit is life because of righteousness. If the Spirit of him who raised Jesus from the dead dwells in you, he who raised Christ Jesus from the dead will also give life to your mortal bodies through his Spirit who dwells in you.

W E HAVE ARRIVED AT WHAT many call the most significant chapter in the Bible. All Scripture is equally important because it is all breathed out and inspired by God from Genesis to Revelation. However, there is something very special about Romans 8 because it gives us a hopeful glimpse and understanding of what salvation in Christ means to the believer. The great theologian Warren Wiersbe said that Romans 8 is like a bright light at the end of a very dark tunnel. Pastor John Piper referred to it as a mountaintop for Christian living and the Christian life.

At the end of Romans 7, Paul makes four laments about the desperate nature of the sin that he cannot seem to squelch out completely. Even as a Christian, he makes a final lament and cries out, "'Wretched man that I am! Who will deliver me from this body of death?'" (Rom. 7:24). The entire book of Romans has led up to the question of who will deliver us. The whole Bible before Christ also asks who will deliver us? Who will save us—not just out of Egypt or out of a bad situation or momentary pain in our life? Who will save our souls? Paul answers his own question in Romans 7:25: "Thanks be to God through Jesus Christ our Lord! So then, I myself serve the law of God with my mind, but with my flesh, I serve the law of sin."

The question leading into Romans 8 is meant to magnify Paul's statement in verse one. Until this point, Paul has belabored the hopelessness of humanity and the despair of understanding that the law cannot save us because no one is good. All humanity deserves the righteous wrath and judgment of God. But back in Romans 5:8, Paul tells us that "God shows His love for us in that while we were still sinners, Christ died for us" so that we could be "in Christ" and so Christ could be in us. So what should those who are saved into Christ accept regarding the wrath and condemnation of God? And here we come to the light at the end of a long and dark tunnel Warren Wiersbe speaks of.

SAFE IN CHRIST

There is therefore now no condemnation for those who are in Christ Jesus (v. 1).

Here is the greatest news in history—no condemnation exists for those in Christ. Paul spends seven chapters laying out the contextual foundation for understanding the greatness, necessity, and power of the gospel of Jesus Christ. He has repeatedly shown us that we cannot work our way out of our sins. We cannot try our way to God. Our good deeds are not good enough. We were hopeless and helpless; and Paul is saying that if we are in Christ and the Spirit of God is living in us, He is saving, has saved, and will save us. There is no condemnation for us, and that is the best news in the history of the world.

Paul spends seven chapters explaining why everyone—both Jews and Greeks—are subject to the curse and condemnation of God. Then he says that if we are in Christ, we are not subject to death that comes from sin because Jesus took our punishment. That is why Paul says, "For I am not ashamed of the gospel, for it is the power of God for salvation to everyone who believes, for the Jew first and also for the Greek" (Rom. 1:16). He makes sure this includes everyone because all have been rejected, all were born into sin, and all were estranged from God. There is only one exclusive passageway to salvation, and His beautiful and precious name is Jesus.

Paul's usage of the word condemnation in Greek means to be condemned to death. In the original language, this means condemned to die, that there is a death sentence looming over you just waiting to be carried out. Paul is now saying there is no longer a Divine judgment over us. However, if this is true, the inverse is also true. While those in Christ are not subject to condemnation, we must honestly and lovingly address that all outside Christ are subject to judgment and condemnation.

Paul uses the phrase "in Christ" repeatedly in the epistles. For those in Christ, there is no condemnation; the fruit of the Spirit will be displayed, and no righteous judgment is reserved. Being in Christ is a picture of being protected or in safety. This is why, in Christianity, we refer to those reborn in Christ as saved.

The best Old Testament illustration of this is in Genesis in the story of Noah's ark. God tells Noah to build an ark because His righteous wrath is being stored up for wicked humanity. The book of Hebrews later reveals that Noah was a preacher of righteousness. He was preaching a message of salvation and judgment, which we know are two concepts that cannot be divorced from each other. We are being saved from God and His righteous wrath, which is the picture revealed in Noah's ark. God's wrath was being stored up.

First came the warning, and Noah preached God's righteousness, followed by the preparation, where Noah spent many years preparing the ark according to God's specifications. Then, God's condemnation and judgment came in the form of a rainstorm that would flood the entire earth and destroy everyone in the world except for those in the ark. Noah and his family were safe inside the ark; the door was shut, and the wrath of God rained down on humanity. Then God killed every person who was not inside the boat.

This is a picture of the gospel and our world today. As we build our lives on the Word of God and live in obedience to what He has spoken, the world mocks and mistreats us. But there is a way of escape, and that place is in Christ. When we lay down our lives and surrender them to Christ, repent of our sins, and put our trust in Christ by faith, we are safe in Him. Those who put their faith in Him will be saved because of Christ's perfect life, death on the cross, and resurrection.

The understanding of being "in Christ" is further understood by looking at a concept known in theology as the hypostatic union. This phrase refers to the theological truth that Jesus is fully Divine and fully Man. He was not God pretending to be a Man. He was not 50 percent God and 50 percent man. He is 100 percent God and 100 percent Man. This can be a difficult concept to understand, but it is essential to rightly understand Jesus' role as our Savior and Great High Priest. The apostle John warned against false teachers who teach that Jesus is not God, as well as those who believe He is not fully man. His humanity fulfilled the law and paid the price for our sins. "For Christ also suffered once for sins, the righteous for the unrighteous, that he might bring us to God, being put to death in the flesh but made alive in the spirit" (1 Peter 3:18). He had to die as a Man to pay the penalty for the sins of man. He paid a human price that we should have paid.

Christ also became a Curse in the flesh as Paul wrote to the church in Galatia:

> For all who rely on works of the law are under a curse; for it is written, "Cursed be everyone who does not abide by all things written in the Book of the Law, and do them." Now it is evident that no one is justified before God by the law, for "The righteous shall live by faith." But the law is not of faith, rather "The one who does them shall live by them." *Christ redeemed us from the curse of the law by becoming a curse for us*—for it is written, "Cursed is everyone who is hanged on a tree"— so that in Christ Jesus the blessing of Abraham might come to the Gentiles, so that we might reccive the promised Spirit through faith (Gal. 3:10-14, emphasis added).

The book of Deuteronomy says that anyone who is hung on a tree is cursed (Deut. 21:23).

It was a despicable and undignified way to die. This is why the Romans crucified Jews—because it was the most disgraceful way for Jews to die—naked, beaten, and hung out for everyone to see as they slowly suffocated over the course of several days. So Jesus became a Curse for you and me in the flesh. But the good news is that in Christ Jesus, we might receive the blessing of Abraham as the heir of God. The evidence of that is the Spirit of God living in us.

And since He is also Divinely God, He had the power and the right to lay down His life and raise it up again. Jesus said, "'For this reason the Father loves me, because I lay down my life that I may take it up again. No one takes it from me, but I lay it down of my own accord. I have authority to lay it down, and I have authority to take it up again. This charge I have received from my Father'" (John 10:17-18).

He is not some suffering Messiah Who was crucified and is still dead in the ground somewhere. He is not merely some moral example of love. He is God, and He proved that He had mastery over the thing that every human dreads—death. Jesus says if we are in Him, we, too, will have life. "This becomes even more evident when another priest arises in the likeness of Melchizedek, who has become a priest, not on the basis of a legal requirement concerning bodily descent, but by the power of an indestructible life" (Heb. 7:15-16). Jesus became a Priest forever by the power of His indestructible life and proved that He has power over death because He is the Source of life.

THE GREAT EXCHANGE

For the law of the Spirit of life has set you free in Christ Jesus from the law of sin and death. For God has done what the law, weakened by the flesh, could not do. By sending his own Son in the likeness of sinful flesh and for sin, he condemned sin in the flesh, in order that the righteous requirement of the law might be fulfilled in us, who walk not according to the flesh but according to the Spirit (v. 2-4).

Christ died as a perfect Man; and because of what He did, we are now free to obey God. We are also free from the consequences of the curse because Christ became the Curse for us. It is critical to understand that in the gospel, God is saving us from God. Jesus bore our sins and drank the cup of God's wrath that was being stored up for us. This is what we call "the great exchange." Jesus exchanged His perfection—His perfect, law-keeping, life and innocence—for our guilt.

In verse four, we are not righteous because we walk according to the Spirit; we walk according to the Spirit as evidence that we are in Christ and His Spirit is living in us. He has regenerated us and is sanctifying us. Our desire to please and obey God is evidence that the Spirit of God is living in us. In Galatians 5:22, the fruit of the Spirit is not a moral list or chores we do as Christians. It is the evidence that Christ is living in us. In regeneration, we are filled with the love of God; because of that, we have joy in our salvation and our lives. It is a joy that nothing in this world can give us, and nothing can take away. Because of this, we also have "peace . . . which surpasses all understanding" (Phil. 4:7). The chaos and trials of this life cannot steal our joy because we are at peace with God. A life transformed by God's love, filled with supernatural joy and an unbreakable peace will produce kindness, patience, goodness, gentleness, and self-control (Gal. 5:22-23). We are not perfect, but we are genuine and being sanctified and conformed to Christ's image in an ever-increasing way.

We are safely rooted in Christ, and Jesus perfectly explained this in the Gospel of John:

> "I am the true vine, and my Father is the vinedresser. Every branch in me that does not bear fruit he takes away, and every branch that does bear fruit he prunes, that it may bear more fruit. Already you are clean because of the word that I have spoken to you. Abide in me, and I in you. As the branch cannot bear fruit by itself, unless it abides in the vine, neither can you, unless you abide in me. I am the vine; you are the branches. Whoever abides in me and I in him, he it is that bears much fruit, for apart from me you can do nothing. If anyone does not abide in me, he is thrown away like a branch and withers; and the branches are gathered, thrown into the fire, and burned. If you abide in me, and my words abide in you, ask whatever you wish, and it will be done for you. By this my Father is glorified, that you bear much fruit and so prove to be my disciples. As the Father has

loved me, so have I loved you. Abide in my love. If you keep my commandments, you will abide in my love, just as I have kept my Father's commandments and abide in his love. These things I have spoken to you, that my joy may be in you, and that your joy may be full (John 15:1-11).

Jesus is saying that if we are in Christ, not only are we free of condemnation but we will also bear fruit. Our hearts will be transformed, and our lives will be changed. We are not changing our lives to please God; God is changing our lives because we are in Christ, and His Spirit is in us. When your heart is changed, your desires change; and because of this, your life is changed.

CONNECTED TO THE VINE

For those who live according to the flesh set their minds on the things of the flesh, but those who live according to the Spirit set their minds on the things of the Spirit. For to set the mind on the flesh is death, but to set the mind on the Spirit is life and peace. For the mind that is set on the flesh is hostile to God, for it does not submit to God's law; indeed, it cannot. Those who are in the flesh cannot please God (vv. 5-8).

Paul reiterates that there are people who live in and according to their fallen flesh, and their end is death. The best works of an unregenerated person do not please God. We cannot please God unless the Spirit of God lives in us. This is the imputed righteousness of Christ. We live from the abundance of the Spirit of God living in us. If we are connected to the vine, we will bear fruit. God will fill us with His love, joy, and peace; and we will be patient, kind, good, faithful, gentle, and self-controlled. These are not works we do to please God; they are the evidence that we are in Christ. We are connected to the Vine, and nothing can snatch us from His hand.

Although we cannot perfectly keep God's law, those who are reborn in Christ are submitted to it because they have the imputed righteousness of Christ. They have a new nature that can please God. This does not mean a born-again Christian does not sin. Paul explains in Romans 7 that we will battle our fallen, sinful flesh. But the ongoing battle is evidence that while we are still in our fallen flesh, there is a new nature inside us that hates sin and wants to keep the law, obey God, and please Him.

LIVING IN THE SPIRIT

You, however, are not in the flesh but in the Spirit, if in fact the Spirit of God dwells in you. Anyone who does not have the Spirit of Christ does not belong to him (v. 9).

Paul discusses the positive side of living in the Spirit but then gives the gospel caveat of *if* we are in Christ. Charles Spurgeon referred to preaching the full and true gospel as a way of always dividing the room, helping those in Christ find security in Him and helping them to see that salvation and all of the Bible's promises to God's children are for them. However, we lovingly make it very clear that these promises are only for those who are in Christ. And we explain that God has also promised those who reject Christ that they will receive their well-deserved judgment and condemnation.

The most important question to ask is, are you in Christ? Here, Paul is talking about being in the flesh. This section of Scripture is not talking about when Christians fall short because they are still growing in sanctification. The phrase "in the flesh" here refers to being outside of Christ's regeneration and salvation. If the Spirit dwells in us, we are not in the flesh. We are free of condemnation and spiritual damnation. Remember, Jesus is Lord and our great High Priest forever on the virtue of His indestructible life. If we are in Christ, that indestructible life is inside us, saving and changing us.

Christians often accidentally misuse this Scripture. When they fall short or do something that is not Christ-honoring, they might say, "Sorry, I was walking in the flesh." Or when they feel like they are walking in love and obedience, they might say, "I am walking in the Spirit." This is not a horrible error, and I understand what people mean when they say this. But the term "walking" in Greek is not referring to a moment of falling short or being victorious; it is referring to a pattern of life. If you are walking according to the Spirit, that means you are a reborn Christian; and if you are walking according to the flesh, it means that you are still dead in sin and trespass. This will become undeniably clear as we look at Romans 8:12-17 in the next chapter.

ETERNAL LIFE IN CHRIST

But if Christ is in you, although the body is dead because of sin, the Spirit is life because of righteousness. If the Spirit of him who raised Jesus from the dead dwells in you, he who raised Christ Jesus from the dead will also give life to your mortal bodies through his Spirit who dwells in you (vv. 10-11).

We are promised eternal life in the gospel of Jesus Christ. Yet there will be evidence of the Spirit living in us in this life. There is no such thing as truly confessing faith but never bearing fruit. There is no such thing as people who are in Christ but who do not follow Christ. The salvation mantra, which many today call "the sinner's prayer," will not save a person merely because they were persuaded to recite some words. What saves us is the understanding that God is good and we are not. But we will be saved if we are attached to the Vine that is Christ by faith. The confession of our mouths that Jesus is Lord is just the fruit and evidence of what we truly believe in our hearts. Those connected to Christ, Who is the Vine of Life, will bear fruit. Jesus said, "So, every healthy tree bears good fruit, but the diseased tree bears bad fruit. A healthy tree cannot bear bad fruit, nor can a diseased tree bear good fruit. Every tree that does not bear good fruit is cut down and thrown into the fire. Thus you will recognize them by their fruits" (Matt. 7:17-20).

LIVING OUT A GENUINE FAITH

The truly regenerated person may fall, get stuck, and have doubting moments; but he is not turning his back on God. He cannot live as a prodigal forever because "he who began a good work in [him] will bring it to completion (Phil. 1:6). Salvation is Christ saving us, continuing to save us through our whole lives, and ultimately saving us to the end.

"The wages of sin is death" (Rom. 6:23); and any branch that is not connected to life will be gathered up and thrown into the lake, which burns with sulfur and fire. This is the truth; and there is no more important question to ask your children, family, friends, and loved ones than, "Do you know what it means to be in Christ?" Jesus "'came to seek and save the lost'" (Luke 19:10). According to the Scripture, there is nothing wrong with examining and ensuring the evidence is inside us. Paul said, "Examine yourselves, to see whether you are in the faith. Test yourselves. Or do you not realize this about yourselves, that Jesus Christ is in you?—unless indeed you fail to meet the test!" (2 Cor. 13:5). What is the test? It is genuine faith.

A Christian named Richard Wurmbrand lived in Romania under the socialist-communist regime. The Romanian authorities began to beat and imprison Christians brutally. Many leaders were told to recant their faith publicly, or they would be thrown in prison. Many did recant, but Wurmbrand would not. He continued to preach the gospel and stand for Christ. He was thrown in prison, where he was tortured and beaten. On several occasions, the prison authorities told him that if he recanted his faith, they would let him go home to his family. He refused and served a total of fourteen years in prison.

Eventually, he was released and founded The Voice of the Martyrs, a missions organization that has taken the gospel to all parts of the world. Richard Wurmbrand preached worldwide and wrote many books, one titled *Tortured for Christ,* which recounted his time in prison. One day, a reporter asked him to recall his greatest accomplishment; and he responded, "It is being counted worthy to suffer for fourteen years in prison for the name of Christ." In that interview, the reporter asked him, "How did this not break your faith?" He replied with one of the most powerful truths I have ever heard: "A faith that can be destroyed by suffering is not faith."[22]

For those whose faith is genuinely in Christ, nothing can break that faith. There is no more important question to ask than are you in Christ? Are you safe in the ark? God's righteous wrath and judgment are coming, and there is only one way of escape. It is by putting the entirety of our faith and our hope in Christ alone. We cannot call Him Savior if we do not call Him Lord. If the Spirit Who raised Jesus from the dead lives in us, we are no longer subject to condemnation. We are not only pardoned from the consequences of our sins; we become the sons and daughters of God with all of the rights, benefits, and responsibilities that come along with that. This is good news.

This is the gospel! We do not surrender our lives to Christ just to avoid judgment. We follow Him because we love Him and understand that He first loved us (1 John 4:19). He laid His life down for us because His love for us was great as was His dedication to save us.

18
THE SPIRIT OF ADOPTION

ROMANS 8:12-17

So then, brothers, we are debtors, not to the flesh, to live according to the flesh. For if you live according to the flesh you will die, but if by the Spirit you put to death the deeds of the body, you will live. For all who are led by the Spirit of God are sons of God. For you did not receive the spirit of slavery to fall back into fear, but you have received the Spirit of adoption as sons, by whom we cry, "Abba! Father!" The Spirit himself bears witness with our spirit that we are children of God, and if children, then heirs—heirs of God and fellow heirs with Christ, provided we suffer with him in order that we may also be glorified with him.

A BEAUTIFUL AND EXCITING EXPLANATION of who we are to God the Father is contained in these few verses. It is amazing news that should bring us great certainty in the Christian life. In the last chapter, we arrived at the mountaintop of spiritual regeneration. Paul addresses how we cannot save ourselves. It reminds me of an old hymn with the lyrics: "He paid a debt He did not owe / I owed a debt I could not pay."[23] There is no way to exaggerate the chasm that is between God and sinful men.

This is why the beauty of the cross is so powerful. Christ, who knew no sin, became sin for us. The Son of God became a curse for us (Gal. 3:13)—not just so that we would not face the consequences of our sins but that we might be children of the very God we were once living in rebellion to. This is the good news of the gospel. Through the cross of Christ, we are no longer under God's righteous wrath and condemnation. We were dead to sin and now have a reborn nature. We were the hopeless dead with no way to help ourselves, but now we are brought to eternal life in Christ.

In the beginning of Romans 8, Paul makes it very clear that the Spirit indwells those who have been reborn in Christ. They will be less and less characterized by worldly and fleshly concerns and more and more by the things of God. A Christian's great concern is obeying God and living a life that is pleasing to Him—not to earn our salvation but because we have been saved by faith in Christ alone. Paul states clearly that those who do not have the indwelling rebirth of the Spirit of God living in them are not in Christ. We are either in Christ or out of Christ. But those in Christ will never be able to be snatched from the hand of God. This is often controversial, but the Bible screams this truth all throughout the Scripture. It is not a question of whether one can lose their salvation but whether they were ever truly saved. Paul makes this clear in another passage:

> For the love of Christ controls us, because we have concluded this: that one has died for all, therefore all have died; and he died for all, that those who live might no longer live for themselves but for him who for their sake died and was raised. From now on, therefore, we regard no one according to the flesh. Even though we once regarded Christ according to the flesh, we regard him thus no longer. Therefore, if anyone is in Christ, he is a new creation. The old has passed away; behold, the new has come (2 Cor. 5:14-17).

Paul is saying that those who do not have the indwelling, saving, regenerating, and sanctifying power of God will look at Christ through fleshly, dead eyes. In our American culture, many think they are saved because they recited a salvation prayer, although that profession does not bear any fruit in their lives. Similarly, there was a time when Paul regarded Christ in a fleshly way through his natural dead eyes. But one day, he met Christ; and everything changed. He was reborn. He went from death to life and lived in worship and service to Christ for the rest of his life, and this is true of every person who has been saved. A good tree *will* bear fruit. It is not a question of whether or not we have done enough because the answer is we could never do enough. But does the regenerating power—the same Spirit that raised Christ from the dead—live in us? And Paul shares some really good news about how we can be sure of this.

DEBTORS NOT TO THE FLESH

So then, brothers, we are debtors, not to the flesh, to live according to the flesh (v. 12).

Paul follows up from the previous verses, expressing that we are reborn, saved in Christ, free from the judgment of the law and the wages of sin because Jesus died for us. We now have the desire and the power to overcome sin. Those who have truly been reborn into Christ are justified and sanctified through the Spirit of God, as they are transformed and conformed to the image of Christ. We are now able to fight and overcome sin. Paul says, "Flee from sexual immorality" (1 Cor. 6:18). There are action steps in the Bible to help us flee sin because it is dangerous, and Paul outlines how to defeat sin and grow in Christ. We are no longer indebted to sin anymore.

If we have indeed been reborn in Christ, we are saved. There is not a tally of bad deeds on one side of the column; and there is no tally of good deeds on the other, which we hope ultimately outnumbers the bad. It is not about being good or whether we have done enough to make up for past sins. That is not how it works. If we have committed one sin against the law, we have broken the entire law. The law is based on God's sinless perfection and holiness and is meant to draw us to Christ.

Paul later explains that the Spirit of God will give assurance of our salvation because not only is the Word of God alive and active but also is the Spirit of Christ living in us. We will not be dominated by sin anymore. This is what it means to be born again. It is a new life. Remember what Paul said: "But if Christ is in you, although the body is dead because of sin, the Spirit is life because of righteousness. If the Spirit of him who raised Jesus from the dead dwells in you, he who raised Christ Jesus from the dead will also give life to your mortal bodies through his Spirit who dwells in you" (Rom. 8:10-11). In an ever-increasing way, God is transforming us. The good news is that through the Spirit of God, we have the desire and ability to overcome sin.

God is alive and active. His Word is alive and active. His Spirit is alive and active. If the Spirit of God resides in a person's life, His life and His power live in them. All things of the flesh will die, including those who walk according to the flesh. They will suffer death and the second death, separated from God for all eternity. However, those in Christ will die once in this body, but God promises us that He will raise us up on that last day and glorify our bodies. We will be like Christ and will be co-heirs with Him forever. This is the will of God, for the glory of God; and we are merely grateful benefactors of this glorious and beautiful truth.

PROCLAIMING HOPE FOR THE LOST

Understand that when Paul talks about walking according to the flesh, he is talking about the unregenerate, not the struggling Christian. When Paul uses the term "living" and "walking in the flesh," he is not referring to a fleshly decision or a mistake but to a pattern of life. He references those who are estranged and separated from God's eternal love and power in salvation. Hebrews 11:6 states, "And without faith it is impossible to please him." This Scripture is often taken out of context to mean we please God by really believing for something we want. However, this verse is actually about saving faith, not our wants or hopes.

Hebrews mentions two groups of people: "We are not of those who shrink back and are destroyed, but of those who have faith and preserve their souls" (Heb. 10:39). By faith, we are justified before God on the basis of Christ; and God will keep the promises He has made to us in His precious Word. That is the faith Hebrews mentions. It is deep, real, eternal, and un-divorceable from the gospel.

Our faith is not in something; it is in Some*one*. He is the Rock of Ages, the Chief Cornerstone; and those who put their faith in Him "'will not be put to shame'" (Rom. 10:11). "Those who are in the flesh cannot please God" (Rom. 8:8). The word "cannot" means there is no desire or ability to please God because one is not of God. We cannot please God until regeneration or spiritual rebirth takes place. People often say we have to give hope to the lost; but honestly, the only hope we have for the lost is the gospel. There is no hope for the lost outside of Christ, and all things outside of Christ are subject to judgment. Yet "if any man is in Christ, he is a new creation" (2 Cor. 5:17), and there is no coming condemnation looming over them.

We cannot condition lost people to want to please God. It is a heart thing. We proclaim the truth of God's Word because we belong to God and we are His messengers and servants. We plant and water, knowing that only God can till the soil of a heart and make things grow. This is why the seeker-sensitive church that crafts a message not to offend people is utter garbage. It denies the power of God's Word through the Spirit of God. It is not my job as a preacher to decide which parts of the Word someone needs to hear. I am to be an obedient, humble servant and plant seed as written in the Scripture and pray. God does the work of salvation; and when He saves, He saves to the uttermost (Heb. 7:25).

BENEFACTORS OF GOD'S LOVE

In obedience, we boldly proclaim the whole council of God for the sake of His holy name without compromise, and we pray and believe that God will change people's hearts. Preaching a compromised message that avoids topics people do not want to hear because we believe it will reach people is foolish and arrogant. If we think we have a way to reach people that is more relevant than the words of the almighty, eternal, omniscient, omnipresent, all-powerful, sovereign God of the universe, it shows that we do not have saving faith in God's Word. We preach the Word of God by the power of the Spirit of God, and we pray that God will change people's hearts.

The prophet Ezekiel wrote:

> The word of the LORD came to me: "Son of man, when the house of Israel lived in their own land, they defiled it by their ways and their deeds. Their ways before me were like the uncleanness of a woman in her menstrual impurity. So I poured out my wrath upon them for the blood that they had shed in the land, for the idols with which they had defiled it. I scattered them among the nations, and they were dispersed through the countries. In accordance with their ways and their deeds I judged them. But when they came to the nations, wherever they came, they profaned my holy name, in that people said of them, 'These are the people of the LORD, and yet they had to go out of his land.' But I had concern for my holy name, which the house of Israel had profaned among the nations to which they came (Ezek. 36:16-21).

God will judge the sinner for the sake of His holy name. We do not like to hear this in modern Christianity, but God is for God. He will protect and preserve His holy name. Even when we are faithless, Paul says, "God is faithful" (1 Cor. 1:9). He will not go back on His promises. He will not profane His own name. God will judge the sinner for the sake of His holy name, but

God will also save those who repent for the same reason because He promised He would in His Word. The love of God is that God is for God, and we are the benefactors of that truth. He saved us because He is good and for the sake of His holy name to make a remnant of people for His Son. Perhaps this does not make one feel special, but it is the God we serve.

Ezekiel continues with his prophecy to God's people:

> "Therefore say to the house of Israel, Thus says the Lord God: It is not for your sake, O house of Israel, that I am about to act, but for the sake of my holy name, which you have profaned among the nations to which you came. And I will vindicate the holiness of my great name, which has been profaned among the nations, and which you have profaned among them. And the nations will know that I am the LORD, declares the Lord GOD, when through you I vindicate my holiness before their eyes. I will take you from the nations and gather you from all the countries and bring you into your own land. I will sprinkle clean water on you, and you shall be clean from all your uncleannesses, and from all your idols I will cleanse you. And I will give you a *new heart*, and a *new spirit* I will put within you. And I will remove the heart of stone from your flesh and give you a *heart of flesh.* And I will put my Spirit within you, and cause you to walk in my statutes and be careful to obey my rules. You shall dwell in the land that I gave to your fathers, and you shall be my people, and I will be your God (Ezek. 36:22-28, emphasis added).

We must attach ourselves to the truth of God's love and the truth of His Word. We cannot have an emotional misunderstanding of Who God is based on our flawed human understanding of love. It is not because we are unique or talented in the sense that God needs something from us. All we are and have rightly belongs to God, anyway. Our surrender to Him is not a grand gesture but, in fact, simply giving Him what is already His. We are made in God's image; because of this, we are all unique, special, and beautiful. But we have profaned God. We have lived to gratify our fleshly desires, and we have lived as if God would not judge us according to His holy standard.

The fact that God would save us is not something we deserve but a lavish display of His goodness, mercy, and grace. Understand that grace has nothing to do with our works, deeds, abilities, talents, or potential. It is solely based on a love that we cannot humanly comprehend. It is complete charity. The King James Bible often translates the Greek word *agape* into charity rather than love because God gives us a love we cannot earn or return on any significant level. The true love we have comes from His Spirit living in us. We cannot rightly love God outside of regeneration. This beautiful and powerful truth should govern how we view God's love.

THE SURETY OF OUR SALVATION

Make no mistake: God will be glorified in our salvation or our destruction. Scripture says, "The LORD says to my Lord, 'Sit at my right hand, until I make your enemies your footstool'" (Psalm 110:1). All those outside of Christ are a part of the kingdom of darkness and will be subject to God's wrath, judgment, and eternal condemnation. They will be made as a footstool for the Son of God to rest His feet upon, surely crushing the head of the serpent (Gen. 3:15). The only way not to be a part of that footstool is to be *in* the body of Christ.

There is so much depression in our world because we have been taught to find the answer inside of ourselves, and this is why therapeutic/self-help type Christianity is so very popular. The mirror is the last place we need to look for hope and power when we are in trouble. Despite what much popular teaching tells us today, the answer is not inside of you. In our darkest place, we should cling to what is real and true—Christ our Rock. This should bring surety for those who are in Christ. We only need to look into the mirror to find the problem, not the solution—to take responsibility for our sins as we repent and cast our hope on Christ. Paul points to God's desire to save repentant sinners in the following Scriptures:

- "The saying is trustworthy and deserving of full acceptance, that Christ Jesus came into the world to save sinners, of whom I am the foremost" (1 Tim. 1:15).
- "For 'everyone who calls on the name of the Lord will be saved'" (Rom. 10:13).
- "And I am sure of this, that he who began a good work in you will bring it to completion at the day of Jesus Christ"(Phil. 1:6).

By faith, we call upon the all-powerful, saving name of Jesus for salvation. We repent of our sins and surrender our lives to Him. Regeneration is the work of God; justification was accomplished by Christ; sanctification is the work of the Spirit; and final salvation and ultimate glorification are promised and accomplished by God. It is for His glory, His namesake, and our benefit. This is grace. It is scandalous to the legalist; it is offensive to those rejecting God; it seems unfair to those blind to their own sin; and it looks like foolishness to the academic. But God came down and took on flesh to save wretched sinners who call upon His name by faith. This is the power and the work of the gospel.

The book of Revelation says we will cry out, "'Worthy is the Lamb who was slain . . . To him who sits on the throne and to the Lamb be blessing and honor and glory and might forever and ever!'" (Rev. 5:12-13). We will sing about the cross and the Lamb that was slain for all eternity. To the world, this is scandalous; it is foolishness. Paul said, "For Christ did not send me to baptize but to preach the gospel, and not with words of eloquent wisdom, lest the cross of Christ be emptied of its power. For the word of the cross is folly to those who are perishing, but to us who are being saved it is the power of God" (1 Cor. 1:17-18).

Salvation is of God; it is not by works lest no man should boast (Eph. 2:8-9). If the Spirit of God lives in us, we will fight sin. We will hate sin; and to a measure, we will overcome it in this life. But ultimately, we will overcome sin, death, Hell, and the grave because Jesus overcame them for us. It is not in our own power but through the Spirit of God's power that regenerates us. In His power, "'we live and move and have our being'" (Acts 17:28).

LED BY THE SPIRIT

For if you live according to the flesh you will die, but if by the Spirit you put to death the deeds of the body, you will live (v. 13).

The Puritan writer, John Owen, famously said, "Be killing sin, or sin will be killing you."[24] This does not mean we are working toward being saved; it means Spirit-indwelt believers are Spirit-led. There is a sharp juxtaposition between the flesh and the Spirit, light and darkness, and death and life. It is staggering! Only those the Spirit truly indwells are working to put their sin to death. We cannot convince non-saved people to try to do better or live more moral lives because God's law does not guide them and the Spirit of God does not lead them.

Sometimes, if there is evidence that our loved ones are striving to become better, we think maybe they are getting closer to God. This thinking is wrong. The Spirit cannot lead a person until they allow the Spirit to lead them to repentance. They must see God for Who He is and their sin for what it is. We cannot expect lost people to live like Christians. However, for those in Christ, there will be a sharp juxtaposition between light and dark, flesh and spirit, death and life.

A somewhat crude example of this is a viewing at a funeral service. A deceased loved one in the casket looks much different than they did when they were alive. They are just a shell of who they were, and we hardly recognize them. There is no comparison because the life inside of them is gone. There is no confusing life with death. Similarly, there is a staggering difference and evidence between those living in and outside of Christ.

Paul is not warning us about losing our salvation; he is describing the characteristics of someone truly alive. He is urging true Christians who are alive in Christ to cooperate with the vinedresser (John 15:1-6). We must let Him cut out the dead branches, or the sin we are attached to will limit our growth. This is why trees are pruned. Dead branches are cut away, so the tree might grow back stronger, better, and full of life. Paul is urging us to battle sin so that we might bear much fruit. This analogy is true regarding pruning and cutting the dead branches off the life of a believer so that he might grow back stronger and fuller of life. But this is also true of the Church. The dead and broken branches will be pruned and cast into the fire so that the true vine might grow stronger and full of life.

SONS OF GOD

For all who are led by the Spirit of God are sons of God (v. 14).

Paul reiterates that those who are genuinely reborn in Christ are being led by the Spirit of God. Once, while teaching a crowd, Jesus said, "I am the good shepherd. I know my own and my own know me, just as the Father knows me and I know the Father; and I lay down my life for the sheep. And I have other sheep that are not of this fold. I must bring them also, and they will listen to my voice. So there will be one flock, one shepherd'" (John 10:14-16).

Jesus is talking to Jews here, but He is also referring to the gathering of the Gentiles. There is one Savior, one Shepherd, one Spirit, and one God. He leads us even when we fall. He leaves the ninety-nine to save the one. Jesus is talking about those who belong to Him. He runs to the prodigal son. Jesus never leaves or forsakes us if we are His sheep—His sons and daughters. The only question that matters is are we in Christ? If we are, He will lead, guide, keep, reprove, correct, and love us. We are not just His creation but also His adopted sons and daughters.

While it is true that the Spirit leads us and we are secure in Christ, this does not mean we cannot be led astray. We can make life difficult by being disobedient and stubborn sheep. We can pull against His yoke and make life very difficult for ourselves. We can toy with sin and ride the line. When we go our own way as believers, God often sends an outward conviction from Christian friends and people we know. But there is another voice of conviction, correction, and reproof besides the external one. When faithful people correct, reprove, or encourage us, those words will also be verified by the Spirit of God living inside us.

THE SPIRIT OF ADOPTION

For you did not receive the spirit of slavery to fall back into fear, but you have received the Spirit of adoption as sons, by whom we cry, "Abba! Father!" (v. 15).

Proverbs 9:10 says, "The fear of the LORD is the beginning of wisdom, and the knowledge of the Holy One is insight." The fear of the Lord being the beginning of wisdom brings us the knowledge of our need for the Holy One, Who is Christ. Paul explains that as Christians, we are no longer slaves motivated by fear. We already know there is no condemnation for those who are in Christ (Rom. 8:1). When we were living as slaves to sin, our lives in the flesh were lived under the looming promise of judgment, which caused us to live in fear. There is evidence of this today as people hoard money and do dishonest things out of fear. The deeper we live in sin, the deeper we live in fear. But Paul is saying through Christ, we are no longer motivated by fear. We know and fear the Lord and have been saved by the unmerited grace of God. Those who love and fear the Lord need not fear anything else in this life because we live knowing there is no longer a looming fear of judgment.

The apostle John wrote about the perfect love of God that transforms us:

By this we know that we abide in him and he in us, because he has given us of his Spirit. And we have seen and testify that the Father has sent his Son to be the Savior of the world. Whoever confesses that Jesus is the Son of God, God abides in him, and he in God. So we have come to know and to believe the love that God has for us. God is love, and whoever abides in love abides in God, and God abides in him. By this is love perfected with us, so that we may have confidence for the day of judgment, because as he is so also are we in this world. There is no fear in love, but perfect love casts out fear. For fear has to do with punishment, and whoever fears has not been perfected in love. We love because he first loved us. (1 John 4:13-19).

We cannot truly know and understand love unless we have God's love. Galatians 5 teaches us that this is the fruit of the Spirit. Understand that worldly, human, emotional, and temporal love does not cast out fear. Only the perfect, saving, agape love of God does. Perfect love is the cross. The Bible says, "Greater love has no one than this, that someone lay down his life for his friends" (John 15:13). The Good Shepherd laid His life down for us; because of that, the Spirit of God lives in us. Even in our darkest moments, when everything seems to be going wrong, the Spirit of God will testify that we belong to Him. It is not human love that will comfort us but the love of God our Father that will never fail us. God is Love, and this is the love of God in the gospel.

Because of Christ's work on the cross, God is our Father. *Abba* is a Hebrew word for a personal translation of the word "father." It is similar to the English word "Daddy" that a small child would call his father. The Bible refers to God as our "Abba." He is our God; we can come to Him like helpless children whose hope is in Him alone for all things. When Paul says we "have received the Spirit of adoption," he does not use a little "s" like the spirit of friendship or the spirit of peace. It is the "Spirit of adoption" with a capital S. It is a title personified. It is something that the Spirit of God is, and here He is called the Spirit of adoption. One of the functions of the Spirit of God is testifying internally to us that what the Bible says about His children is true:

- "He predestined us for adoption to himself as sons through Jesus Christ, according to the purpose of his will" (Eph. 1:5).
- "But to all who did receive him, who believed in his name, he gave the right to become children of God" (John 1:12).
- "For in Christ Jesus you are all sons of God, through faith" (Gal. 3:26).
- "And not only the creation, but we ourselves, who have the first fruits of the Spirit, groan inwardly as we wait eagerly for adoption as sons, the redemption of our bodies" (Rom. 8:23).

TRUE HEIRS OF GOD

The Spirit himself bears witness with our spirit that we are children of God,
and if children, then heirs—heirs of God and fellow heirs with Christ,
provided we suffer with him in order that we may also be glorified with him (v. 16-17).

We are sealed by Him, and we live by faith in the promises of God's Word that we will inherit everything God has promised His children. However, there is an element of waiting where we are in a sort of holding pattern as the Spirit of God lives in us. God has made a promise to us; but we groan inwardly, eagerly awaiting the final step of our adoption. Christ has accomplished it, and we are living toward it by faith. Christ is saving us throughout this life, and this temporary waiting period will one day end. We are positionally sons and daughters now because the price has been paid and we are sealed with an unbreakable seal. But this will be fully realized once we are transformed in the blink of an eye and receive our glorified bodies on the final day. We will be heirs with Christ in His reward. He made a way for us to be His spiritual brothers and sisters as we worship Him forever as Lord. He will always be Lord and King, and we will worship Him for eternity.

Will it be Heaven if when we arrive we find there are no more tears, no more fear, no more pain, streets of gold, and everything we ever wanted, but there is no Jesus? The answer is no. For where Christ is, we long to be. He is Love, Joy, and Peace. Until then, we inwardly and eagerly grow in anticipation of His coming. He is the Treasure hidden in a field. He is the King of Glory. It is Christ and Christ alone.

When we present the glorious gospel to people, it is not a step toward a better life because you will be free of problems, trials, and troubles externally. It is the promise of a better life internally because we are filled with God's love, are at peace with Him, and understand our future is secure. There are Christians all around the world suffering and dying for the sake of Christ. We are fellow heirs with Christ, provided we suffer with Him so that we may also be glorified with Him. Christianity is about resurrection; but first and foremost, it is about death.

Come and die! We die to a life of sin and surrender to our great Savior and King. If we try to be the lord of our life, waging in rebellion against God, it is fearful and painful. Jesus said, "'Come to me, all who labor and are heavy laden . . . For my yoke is easy, and my burden is light'" (Matt. 11:28-30). All those things of the world that we thought revolved around us, we lay them down at Jesus's feet. We lay down our sin, the illusion we are in control, and our fear; and we take on the yoke and burden of Christ. To make it to the end, we need the inward witness of God's Word that we belong to Christ. It is not self-assurance, self-love, or worldly assurance but the love of God and His unending, eternal, all-powerful assurance. True heirs of God will be able to suffer with Christ and for Christ because they know they will be glorified with Him. It is "'not by might, nor by power, but by my Spirit, says the LORD of hosts'" (Zech. 4:6).

The "perfect love" of God that "casts out fear" (1 John 4:18) and saves us from condemnation and judgment permeates our lives. Through that love, we have joy in our salvation. No amount of pain, suffering, or tragedy can take it away. We will also have peace that passes all human understanding because Christ's presence in our lives is peace. People do not greatly glorify in Christ when they see we have an easy life and great blessings. People see Christ in us most clearly when we suffer and stand firm for the glory of God, when it is apparent that we are living for a future city "whose designer and builder is God" (Heb. 11:10) and that we believe we are co-heirs with that same Savior. Amen.

19

PRESENT SUFFERING, FUTURE GLORY

ROMANS 8:18-30

For I consider that the sufferings of this present time are not worth comparing with

the glory that is to be revealed to us. For the creation waits with eager longing for the

revealing of the sons of God. For the creation was subjected to futility, not willingly, but

because of him who subjected it, in hope that the creation itself will be set free from its

bondage to corruption and obtain the freedom of the glory of the children of God. For we

know that the whole creation has been groaning together in the pains of childbirth until

now. And not only the creation, but we ourselves, who have the firstfruits of the Spirit,

groan inwardly as we wait eagerly for adoption as sons, the redemption of our bodies. For

in this hope we were saved. Now hope that is seen is not hope. For who hopes for what he

sees? But if we hope for what we do not see, we wait for it with patience.

Likewise the Spirit helps us in our weakness. For we do not know what to pray for as

we ought, but the Spirit himself intercedes for us with groanings too deep for words.

And he who searches hearts knows what is the mind of the Spirit, because the Spirit

intercedes for the saints according to the will of God. And we know that for those who

love God all things work together for good, for those who are called according to his

purpose. For those whom he foreknew he also predestined to be conformed to the image

of his Son, in order that he might be the firstborn among many brothers. And those

whom he predestined he also called, and those whom he called he also justified, and
those whom he justified he also glorified.

PAUL PREVIOUSLY EXPLAINED THE GLORIOUS reality of being in
Christ and how we are now adopted as sons and daughters into the family
of God; and because of this, we can call God our Father. He also reminds us
that through His Spirit we are being conformed to the very image of Christ
Himself. These truths are beautiful and powerful realities for the believer. It
is because of these powerful and present truths that we can bear up under
any and every present suffering that we are currently enduring.

The evidence that we are children of God is that the same Spirit that
raised Christ from the dead now lives in us. The Spirit bears witness with our
spirit that we are children of God. This is the internal verification and seal of
the Spirit of God, marking us for the day of salvation. Jesus spoke about the
Spirit of God living in us in John's Gospel:

> "If you love me, you will keep my commandments. And I will ask
> the Father, and he will give you another Helper, to be with you
> forever, even the Spirit of truth, whom the world cannot receive,
> because it neither sees him nor knows him. You know him, for
> he dwells with you and will be in you. I will not leave you as
> orphans; I will come to you. Yet a little while and the world will
> see me no more, but you will see me. Because I live, you also will
> live. In that day you will know that I am in my Father, and you
> in me, and I in you (John 14:15-20).

To the same degree that God and the Father are in eternal unity and
fellowship, Christ, through His death and resurrection, has made us
partakers in this same unity. Scripture says that reborn believers are brought
into spiritual unity with God. This was God's intended purpose from the

beginning. We bear the very mark and seal of the Spirit, which is the assurance that we belong to Him. Paul explains this to the church in Ephesus:

> In him we have obtained an inheritance, having been predestined according to the purpose of him who works all things according to the counsel of his will, so that we who were the first to hope in Christ might be to the praise of his glory. In him you also, when you heard the word of truth, the gospel of your salvation, and believed in him, were sealed with the promised Holy Spirit, who is the guarantee of our inheritance until we acquire possession of it, to the praise of his glory (Eph. 1:11-14).

While living in this fallen world, there is a time of waiting before we are glorified in our resurrected bodies. This is why we must have hope and faith in the promises of God. It is a blessed and promised hope and a faith that cannot be broken or thwarted by this world. We are sealed as a promise of God for the day of salvation. We have been imprinted with a marking that says, "This one is mine!" The Spirit of God is alive, active, and living in us, encouraging and leading us into all truth—convicting us of sin and conforming us into the image of Christ. But the reality of this is not completely fulfilled until the day we take our last breath. Paul acknowledged this: "For now we see in a mirror dimly, but then face to face" (1 Cor. 13:12).

It is foolish to pretend that the reality of kingdom-come is fully realized. The kingdom of God has come, but the kingdom of God is still coming. In the church today, there are kingdom-now people with an over-realized eschatology who believe we can walk to the same degree that we will someday. Understand that there is the imparting and power of the Spirit, but we still have the temptation to sin and make mistakes. We are still in the process of being conformed to the image of Christ. We have a blessed hope because we believe that no matter our circumstances or shortcomings, we have a promise, a seal that ensures we belong to God. This will be fully realized on the day of salvation.

TEMPORARY SUFFERING THAT PRODUCES ETERNAL

For I consider that the sufferings of this present time are not worth comparing with the glory that is to be revealed to us (v. 18).

To these first-century Christians, Paul conveys that their present suffering and fiery trials are not even worth comparing to this blessed hope we have in Christ and the future glory that will be revealed to them. He wants them to understand that its beauty and value are incomparable to what they are currently going through. We are sealed with the Spirit of God for salvation, but this reality is not fully realized in this life. This is why we must live by faith. God is the Guarantor of the promise so that we can live confidently in it. This is what it means to be sealed.

It is like cattle that are branded; so in the end, when everything is sorted out, it is clear that you belong to God. A seal represents a promise that will be enforced. In our case, the seal of God's Spirit on us is His proof of purchase. However, we live in a fallen world; and even as Christians, we will not be free from pain and suffering. Paul often addressed this reality of the Christian life: "The Spirit himself bears witness with our spirit that we are children of God, and if children, then heirs—heirs of God and fellow heirs with Christ, provided we suffer with him in order that we may also be glorified with him" (Rom. 8:16-17). This life has trial, persecution, and suffering, but Jesus said, "'Take heart! I have overcome the world'" (John 16:33).

Paul was writing to people who were undergoing great suffering and persecution for following Christ. While most of us will never endure the same level of physical persecution, we all experience pain, suffering, affliction, and persecution. If we identify with Christ and are truly in Him and He in us, we will have seasons of suffering and trial; and we will experience persecution on some level. "Indeed, all who desire to live a godly life in Christ Jesus will be persecuted" (2 Tim. 3:12).

Paul's encouragement in this verse is not that we will never endure trial or suffering but that any affliction or suffering we endure is "not worth comparing" or considering next to the glorious treasure of being in Christ and the future "glory that is to be revealed to us" (Rom. 8:18). It is like comparing a teardrop of pain that falls into an ocean of joy and grace; it is swallowed up and lost immediately and forever, never to be found again or remembered. The glory of God is revealed in us and to us. On that final day, there will be no more tears, no more pain; and we will be consumed with God's love and unspeakable joy. Scripture says, "'What no eye has seen, nor ear heard, nor the heart of man imagined, what God has prepared for those who love him'" (1 Cor. 2:9).

As Christians, we experience joy and freedom to some degree in this life as we bear the fruit and evidence of the Spirit of God living in us. But walking in victory does not mean that we will never experience any trials in this life. Walking with Jesus is knowing He will walk through every painful trial and suffering with us. He will never leave us; and we are to hold fast to our faith in cancer, financial hardship, divorce, the loss of a loved one, chaos, temptation, and persecution. God did not promise world peace; He promised that the Spirit of God would give us an internal "peace . . . which surpasses all understanding" (Phil. 4:7).

Taking God at His word means we walk by faith, knowing His word never fails. There will be times when this concept may be shaken; but for the true believer, there is an internal assurance that comes from the Spirit of God. It leads us to the truth that we belong to Him, and nothing can snatch us from His hand. We must hold fast to our faith; it is worth it!

Paul's message to the first-century Christians he wrote to was true then and is still true for us today. Our present suffering is not worth comparing to the eternal treasure of Christ. Anything compared to Him is meaningless by comparison. No good thing is better than Him; and no pain, suffering, or tragedy is worth comparing to Him. He truly is worth the loss of all things and the endurance of all pain. Paul also encouraged the Christians at Philippi with this truth:

> But whatever gain I had, I counted as loss for the sake of Christ. Indeed, I count everything as loss because of the surpassing worth of knowing Christ Jesus my Lord. For his sake I have suffered the loss of all things and count them as rubbish, in order that I may gain Christ and be found in him, not having a righteousness of my own that comes from the law, but that which comes through faith in Christ, the righteousness from God that depends on faith— that I may know him and the power of his resurrection, and may share his sufferings, becoming like him in his death, that by any means possible I may attain the resurrection from the dead (Phil. 3:7-11).

There is nothing in this life comparable to Christ. There is no loss too great for the expense of being counted with Christ, not even the cost of our own lives. Peter encouraged a group of Christians he wrote to, saying, "Resist him, firm in your faith, knowing that the same kinds of suffering are being experienced by your brotherhood throughout the world" (1 Peter 5:9). Suffering and trials are not odd or unique, for this world is filled with suffering. The world; our own flesh; and our adversary, the devil, fight against us. All true Christians will endure suffering. Peter also said, "Beloved, do not be surprised at the fiery trial when it comes upon you to test you, as though something strange were happening to you" (1 Peter 4:12).

We should not be surprised by suffering. Jesus told us in His Word that it is coming. He suffered at every turn. This does not mean that life is only suffering or even that suffering in and of itself is noble. But there will be seasons of internal and external pain as we live in this fallen world. Do not be surprised when the trial comes, as if something strange is happening. It's coming, no doubt about it. Peter continues this thought in verse thirteen:

"But rejoice insofar as you share Christ's sufferings, that you may also rejoice and be glad when his glory is revealed" (1 Peter 4:13). Every person born of woman will suffer at some time in this life. The difference is that the non-believer suffers for nothing, but those in Christ suffer *for* something. When we suffer for Christ, we suffer with Christ; and it's not for nothing. Dear believer, know this: not one drop of that suffering will be in vain.

THE CHILDREN OF GOD

For the creation waits with eager longing for the revealing of the sons of God (v. 19).

This personification of creation is poetic language meant to magnify how all things will forever belong to God as Christ reconciles all things to Himself. Paul expresses how creation yearns for the sons of God to be revealed—those of us who, from before the earth's foundation, have been predestined to be God's children, those He foreknew would belong to Him in all eternity; their names are written in the Lamb's Book of Life. We should not only be humbled and honored but overjoyed to be a part of the revelation and magnification of the ultimate supremacy of Christ.

Today, we live in a world where Christ is often considered a good teacher or a sage prophet, while others mock and scoff at the mention of Him or deny His existence altogether. Some say that He existed but did not resurrect from the dead. Even if they do not know it, all of creation awaits the true revelation of Christ and for those who belong to Him to be revealed. And while it's true that many deny Christ, many others profess to follow Him; but they blaspheme Him with their words or with their lives. Sometimes, it is difficult to distinguish the weeds from the plants or the wheat from the tares. However, true believers of Christ, who are exclusively surrendered to glorifying God with their entire lives, are being revealed as the true children of God.

No greater test reveals who truly belongs to Christ than joyful participation in suffering for the sake of Christ's name. This is why Jesus said, "'For whoever is ashamed of me and of my words, of him will the Son of Man be ashamed when he comes in his glory and the glory of the Father and of the holy angels'" (Luke 9:26). Jesus uses the word "ashamed," meaning that a person will have no place in the kingdom of God. Just as Jesus said in Scripture, "'And then will I declare to them, *I never knew you; depart from me, you workers of lawlessness'*" (Matt. 7:23). We stand firm for Christ because we believe He is King, and we are surrendered to His Lordship. When we minister to people, we cannot dance around the truth or be reluctant to declare and exalt Christ as King. Jesus is Lord; the Bible is His Word; and "every tongue [will] confess that Jesus Christ is Lord" (Phil. 2:11).

CREATION RESTORED

For the creation was subjected to futility, not willingly, but because of him who subjected it, in hope that the creation itself will be set free from its bondage to corruption and obtain the freedom of the glory of the children of God (vv. 20-21).

Nature's destiny is linked to that of humankind. Man was given dominion over all creation. When man fell, creation also fell under a curse. In the same way, Paul is poetically saying that creation is anxiously anticipating the freedom of the glory of the children of God. The restoration of all things is ultimately linked to man's redemption. The cross was not some afterthought to try and salvage humanity. It was always God's plan to magnify the glory of His Son through the redemption of His people. All things in creation—good and bad throughout history—are merely a backdrop to magnify the glory of Christ our Lord.

THE GROAN OF CREATION

For we know that the whole creation has been groaning together in the pains of childbirth until now. And not only the creation, but we ourselves, who have the firstfruits of the Spirit, groan inwardly as we wait eagerly for adoption as sons, the redemption of our bodies (vv. 22-23).

The groan of creation has slowly grown stronger and more violent, like the contractions of a pregnant woman. They get stronger and more frequent; and Paul says this friction grows closer and closer, like childbirth, while we wait in joyful expectation of the beauty that will soon be revealed. Because the Spirit of God has opened our eyes, we are aware of the sin, decay, and destruction all around us. Like Paul, we long to be free of this wretched body of death and for the reconciliation of all things. We long for the end of suffering, not primarily because of the relief it will bring but because of what we anxiously await to happen after. We long for true justice, reconciliation, and the restoration of all things that can come only through the One Who subjected creation to futility in the first place. The time is coming when creation will be renewed, but not only creation. Our mortal bodies will be completely free of death, decay, and every stain of sin:

- "'Come now, let us reason together, says the LORD: though your sins are like scarlet, they shall be as white as snow; though they are red like crimson, they shall become like wool'" (Isa. 1:18).
- So is it with the resurrection of the dead. What is sown is perishable; what is raised is imperishable. It is sown in dishonor; it is raised in glory. It is sown in weakness; it is raised in power. It is sown a natural body; it is raised a spiritual body. If there is a natural body, there is also a spiritual body (1 Cor. 15:42).

The same spirit that raised Christ from the dead lives in us and is currently conforming us to the image of Christ. It is making us victorious, leading us into all truth, convicting us of sin, and glorifying the presence and glory of Christ in our lives. Ultimately, all the things that entangle us will be cut from us, and we will be raised in power and glory forever and ever. Amen.

OUR BLESSED HOPE

For in this hope we were saved. Now hope that is seen is not hope. For who hopes for what he sees? But if we hope for what we do not see, we wait for it with patience (vv. 24-25).

This is the problem with believing we can draw people to God through external means. Only the Spirit of God can draw people to Himself, and He does this through many means but primarily through the proclamation of His Word. God is Sovereign; He heals, performs miracles, and is alive and active among us. But He does those things because He is good. Jesus tells the parable of a man named Lazarus who goes to Heaven and a rich man who goes to Hell. The rich man laments over his life in Hell and cries out to Abraham, *"'Then I beg you, father, to send him [Lazarus] to my father's house—for I have five brothers—so that he may warn them, lest they also come into this place of torment'"* (Luke 16:27-28). Abraham responded, *"'They have Moses and the Prophets; let them hear them.* And he said, *No, father Abraham, but if someone goes to them from the dead, they will repent.* He said to him, *If they do not hear Moses and the Prophets, neither will they be convinced if someone should rise from the dead'"* (Luke 16:29-31). Understand that we have more than the Law and the Prophets; we have the gospel. In this parable, Jesus says that the Word of God is sufficient all on its own.

We put our faith in God and His promises to us in His Word. He is our blessed hope. We do not use words like faith and hope the way the world does. Our hope is a blessed hope that has a guarantee from God Himself. We take God at His Word. Paul says if you have to see it, then it is not hope. Hebrews 11:6 says, "And without faith it is impossible to please him, for whoever would draw near to God must believe that he exists and that he rewards those who seek him." Paul also said, "For I am not ashamed of the gospel, for it is the power of God for salvation to everyone who believes, to the Jew first and also to the Greek. For in it the righteousness of God is revealed from faith for faith, as it is written, 'The righteous shall live by faith'" (Rom. 1:16-17). That faith is in the Word of God. We take God at His Word, no matter what our eyes see or the world says. God's Word is unbreakable, and it is the anchor and the rock we stand on in this life. Paul also stated:

> Remember Jesus Christ, risen from the dead, the offspring of David, as preached in my gospel, for which I am suffering, bound with chains as a criminal. But the word of God is not bound! Therefore I endure everything for the sake of the elect, that they also may obtain the salvation that is in Christ Jesus with eternal glory. The saying is trustworthy, for: If we have died with him, we will also live with him; if we endure, we will also reign with him; if we deny him, he also will deny us; if we are faithless, he remains faithful—for he cannot deny himself (2 Timothy 2:8-13).

THE SPIRIT'S HELP

Likewise the Spirit helps us in our weakness. For we do not know what to pray for as we ought, but the Spirit himself intercedes for us with groanings too deep for words (v. 26).

We wait with patience, but that patience is a fruit of the Spirit because the Spirit of God helps us in our weakness. The Spirit helps us in our weakness to temptation, the weakness of our mortal bodies, or weakness to stand firm in our faith. When we groan, so does the Spirit, "with groanings too deep for words." When we cry out and do not know how to pray, the Spirit of God intercedes on our behalf.

THE INTERCESSION OF THE SPIRIT

And he who searches hearts knows what is the mind of the Spirit, because the Spirit intercedes for the saints according to the will of God (v. 27).

This statement might seem redundant or even unnecessary. Paul is saying that the mind of the Spirit that intercedes for us is the same mind and will of God. God the Father, God the Son, and God the Spirit are three distinct Persons—one God with one eternal and united will. Paul reminds us that the Spirit intercedes for us because He has good plans for us. It is the same will of the same God Who is in Heaven and Who created the earth, the same God Who took on flesh and died on our behalf. That Spirit is interceding for us. That Spirit is working through us and helping us when we are in a dark place of despair. When we do not have the words to pray or do not know what to do, the Spirit Who lives in us intercedes for us.

God searches the heart, and He knows who we are. He is not confused about who we are because of what we show on the outside and the periphery of our lives. He searches the heart and knows the internal truth of man, even more so than we do about ourselves. God knows the good and the bad. He knows our intentions, even when we are deceived about our own thoughts and intentions. One of the greatest deceptions of men is believing that we know our hearts better than God does. King David asked God to reveal his heart and to open his eyes to the deceptions in his life, and the New and Old Testament Scripture reiterates this point:

- "Every way of a man is right in his own eyes, but the LORD weighs the heart" (Heb. 21:2).
- "But the Lord said to Samuel, 'Do not look on his appearance or on the height of his stature, because I have rejected him. For the LORD sees not as man sees: man looks on the outward appearance, but the LORD looks on the heart'" (1 Sam. 16:7).
- "The heart is deceitful above all things, and desperately sick; who can understand it? "I the LORD search the heart and test the mind, to give every man according to his ways, according to the fruit of his deeds" (Jer. 17:9-10).

ALL THINGS FOR HIS PURPOSE

And we know that for those who love God all things work together for good,

for those who are called according to his purpose (v. 28).

This is our faith: we trust God for our salvation and that He is in control of all things. He works all things together for our good, acting on our behalf, fighting our battles, and interceding for us. This is why we meekly trust God. "'Blessed are the meek, for they shall inherit the earth'" (Matt. 5:5). Who will inherit the earth? The sons and daughters of God, whom He has adopted through the gospel and to whom He will give the earth as a gift. It is not because we are smart or strong but because we meekly trust God. And God will shame the rest of creation when He gives the meek the earth because we put our trust in the Lord. We put our trust in God; and not only do we trust Him in His promises, but we also trust Him in His goodness.

This is not referring to human love but to God's sacrificial, give-everything-up kind of love—the love Christ demonstrated on the cross when we had nothing to offer Him and He gave us everything. The Bible refers to those who love God when Jesus said, "'If you love me, you will keep my commandments'" (John 14:15). Paul is speaking of the effectual calling unto salvation. We trust in the true sovereignty of God. We are the called, the saved, the elect, the adopted sons and daughters, and no matter what it looks like through our fleshly eyes, we hold fast to the promise that God is working all things together for our good.

Based on God's promise, Paul confidently says *we know* God is working all things together for good. Not we think, not we hope, but we *know*! There is great security in our salvation and in the phrase "all things." This is a comprehensive and all-encompassing statement. All things: the good, bad, ugly, and messy. For those in Christ, God is working, has worked, and will work all things together for their good. This does not mean there will be no suffering, but our present suffering is not worth comparing to the good God has promised us in glorification.

THE IMAGE OF HIS SON

For those whom he foreknew he also predestined to be conformed to the image of his Son, in order that he might be the firstborn among many brothers. And those whom he predestined he also called, and those whom he called he also justified, and those whom he justified he also glorified (vv. 29-30).

These final verses are known in theology as the golden chain of salvation. In the life of the believer, the purpose of salvation is to be conformed to the image of Christ. He is the Firstborn of many brethren. Christ is eternal, but He died for us in His human nature so we could live through Him eternally. Paul writes that those who are justified in salvation will also be glorified. Scripture says, "And I am sure of this, that he who began a good work in you will bring it to completion at the day of Jesus Christ" (Phil. 1:6).

There has never been a person who was truly saved, justified before God, and reborn in the Spirit who was unjustified or "unborn" later. Yes, Scripture mentions falling away or backsliding, but this is about people who were never truly justified by faith. If they are, God will draw them back. If we are true believers and take God at His Word, He will give us security to help us endure every trial in this life. Many find this doctrine contentious and question whether believing this requires a person to live for God. But understand that a good tree will bear good fruit. Those who truly believe in God, having made a confession of faith, will be sanctified and ultimately will be glorified. It is no surprise to God who belongs to Him in eternity because He knew this before the foundations of the world. God knows the beginning from the end. He is sovereign. These names are written in the Lamb's Book of Life; they will never be blotted out, and God will save them.

It is impossible to be justified before God through Christ and later become unjustified. When God saves, He saves to the uttermost (Heb. 7:25). If you have been justified, you will be glorified. If a person is living in open, unrepentant sin, the question is not whether they lost their salvation but whether they were ever really saved.

Paul is trying to assure the believers in Rome because they were experiencing a fiery trial. They were living in a wicked society. Today, we might not be experiencing the same level of persecution as the early church, but we are living in a wicked world. It is not a popular message to tell people that Jesus is the only Way to God and all those outside of Christ will suffer condemnation and loss. This is why most preachers do not preach the true gospel of Jesus Christ. The true gospel magnifies the holiness of God, the grievousness of sin, and the chasm caused by sin. The present sufferings we experience today "are not worth comparing with the glory that is to be revealed to us" (Rom. 8:18) and in us.

20

THE UNFAILING POWER OF THE LOVE OF GOD

ROMANS 8:31-39

What then shall we say to these things? If God is for us, who can be against us? He who did not spare his own Son but gave him up for us all, how will he not also with him graciously give us all things? Who shall bring any charge against God's elect? It is God who justifies. Who is to condemn? Christ Jesus is the one who died—more than that, who was raised—who is at the right hand of God, who indeed is interceding for us. Who shall separate us from the love of Christ? Shall tribulation, or distress, or persecution, or famine, or nakedness, or danger, or sword? As it is written,

"For your sake we are being killed all the day long; we are regarded as sheep to be slaughtered."

No, in all these things we are more than conquerors through him who loved us. For I am sure that neither death nor life, nor angels nor rulers, nor things present nor things to come, nor powers, nor height nor depth, nor anything else in all creation, will be able to separate us from the love of God in Christ Jesus our Lord.

THERE IS NO GREATER OR more important theological concept than the love of God. However, it is a concept often distorted and confused in today's culture and from many church pulpits. We often speak incorrectly about who the children of God are or who are the benefactors of God's unfailing love. God loves all and has shown His love to the world by sending His Son to be a sacrifice for our sins, but here in Romans 8, Paul refers to a love specifically aimed at those who call upon the name of the Lord and are saved.

As we conclude this chapter, we will see a picture of God's love toward regenerate believers, not all of humanity. We know this is true because Scripture says nothing will be able to separate us from the love of God we have in Christ Jesus our Lord. However, this is not true for those who ultimately reject the gospel. Sadly, they will be separated from the eternal love of God because they have rejected the one and only Son of God. Scripture says, "'Then he will say to those on his left, *Depart from me, you cursed, into the eternal fire prepared for the devil and his angels*'" (Matt. 25:41).

Many people do not like to hear the phrases "eternal Hell" or "fire and brimstone." Some pastors refuse to preach about Hell or do so in a flowery way which almost makes it seem like it is unlikely many people are going there. I do not preach about it because I am a Hell-fire preacher but because it is a grave reality that some will be separated from the love of God and will be subject to His righteous wrath and condemnation for all eternity. They will be with the devil and his angels in eternal separation and damnation. There is no joy in saying this; but for those who reject Christ, there will be no seat at His Father's table or the wedding feast of the Lamb. The only way to be a part of the family of God is by being the bride of the Bridegroom as we marry into the family and are adopted as children into the kingdom of God. You cannot reject Christ and be a part of God's kingdom.

We see the loving character of God toward the world in Scripture. The most famous verses in the Bible that tell us that God loves the world are in the Gospel of John: "'For God so loved the world, that he gave his only Son, that whoever believes in him should not perish but have eternal life. For God did not send his Son into the world to condemn the world, but in order that the world might be saved through him'" (John 3:16-17).

Those who do not believe in Christ for their salvation will not benefit from the love of Christ that was poured out for us on the cross. However, those who do respond because of regeneration will come to the light. If you keep reading John's Gospel in chapter eight, it says that Jesus is the Light of the world; and in 1 John, it says, in Him, there is no darkness at all or shadow of turning. "And this is the judgment: the light has come into the world, and people loved the darkness rather than the light because their works were evil. For everyone who does wicked things hates the light and does not come to the light, lest his works should be exposed" (John 3:19-20).

Those who benefit from the loving salvation of Jesus Christ see God for Who He is and see themselves for who they are. We come to the light, expose ourselves, confess our sins, repent, and hold fast by faith to the saving power of the cross. Those who reject Him will have no place in the kingdom of God. This is not a joyful message but an important one nonetheless. If we discuss who benefits from God's eternal, unbreakable love, we must acknowledge those who do not. John 3:18 says, "Whoever believes in him is not condemned, but whoever does not believe is condemned already, because he has not believed in the name of the only Son of God."

The book of Romans addresses that all of us are subject to condemnation. "All have sinned and fall short of the glory of God" (Rom. 3:23). Yet for those of us who are in Christ, there is no longer condemnation for us (Rom. 8:1) because we have been saved through the saving power of Jesus Christ.

> "And this is the judgment: the light has come into the world, and people loved the darkness rather than the light because their works were evil. For everyone who does wicked things hates the light and does not come to the light, lest his works should be exposed. But whoever does what is true comes to the light, so that it may be clearly seen that his works have been carried out in God" (John 3:19-21).

The world is divided into two groups of people. It is not based on money, skin color, or geographical location. It is based on the fact that all of us are in darkness but that a group of people, a remnant, will be saved by faith in Christ and come into the light, which becomes life for them. They are grafted into the Vine that is Christ; and they will have eternal, abundant life in Him forever.

Paul begins Romans 8 with the message that there is condemnation for those outside of Christ who reject God. But those in Christ are not subject to wrath or condemnation. He goes on to say that we are God's children, adopted into the very family of God, "by whom we cry, 'Abba! Father!'" (Rom. 8:15). Paul spends several verses explaining that nothing will snatch us from His hand. We can hold fast to His love that will keep us forever. Charles Spurgeon said, "Nothing binds me to my Lord like a strong belief in His changeless love."[25] Paul writes about this as he painstakingly explains the gospel to those who benefit from it and those who will not. To those who have truly surrendered their life to the Lordship of Christ, Paul reveals the beautiful depths of the love of God.

The unchangeable, unbreakable, all-powerful, never-ending, never-failing love of God is reserved for those who are in Christ. For those who have been spiritually reborn and are now children of God by adoption through the work of Christ on the cross and His precious blood. The precious blood of the Lamb of God takes away the sin of the world. However, this saving love of God is not unconditional. Some like to sing songs or preach that God's love is unconditional and He loves all creation in the same way. If His love were unconditional in that sense, then no one would be in Hell. It is conditional, and there is a critical condition to be part of God's personalized, saving love. It is believing in Christ, His Son, as the exclusive means of salvation, clinging to Christ.

CONVICTION VERSUS ASSURANCE

What then shall we say to these things? If God is for us, who can be against us? (v. 31).

The last verses of Romans 8 are in the form of a hymn or song where Paul summarizes the unbreakable security of the believer. When pondering all the trials and present sufferings of this fallen world and the external and internal struggle against sin, how can we be sure that those in Christ will be victorious in the end? Remember, Paul is talking to people enduring persecution who are being thrown in jail or killed for the gospel of Christ. What do we say to all these things? Paul says, "If God is for us, then who can be against us?"

Today, this Scripture is taken out of context to make people feel encouraged without including what Paul wrote in the first seven chapters. He clearly defined that God is for some and against others. Many do not like to hear this truth, but all of us were rebel sinners against God. Those in Christ have laid down the crown of our authority. We recognize that we are not the king of our lives. God has created us, and we throw ourselves at the mercy of the King. God is for you if you are in Him. Unless we repent and surrender to Christ, we are God's enemies. Ephesians 2 says we were all once enemies of God; but because God is rich in mercy, He gave us saving grace.

The Bible promises that those who approach God with a contrite heart will be extended mercy and God's saving grace. We cannot read the end of Romans 8 without understanding that Paul is making clear that only those in Christ have escaped God's righteous wrath and condemnation. Charles Spurgeon addressed the importance of inserting the gospel into every message because the gospel divides the congregation. We have to make sure we are talking to the right group of people. We must make sure it is clear when we are addressing those outside of the fellowship with Christ and when we are addressing those in the fellowship with Christ. It is conviction to the lost sinner and assurance to those who are truly in Christ.

The good news of the gospel can be compared to this illustration. A husband and wife were in their house when suddenly, two criminals broke through their door. They tied up the couple and robbed them. Realizing that the man and woman had seen their faces, the two criminals realized they would have to kill them after they were finished robbing them. The couple was panicked with fear, but what the husband did not know was that his wife had hit the panic button on their alarm system before the two men subdued them. Suddenly, the sound of a police siren could be heard faintly off in the distance. At first, it was not clear if it was headed for them or not; but the sound kept growing louder and louder. Eventually, it became clear that the police were about to be at the house. To the couple who were being robbed, the sound of the police sirens right outside their house was the sound of help, hope, and salvation. But this same exact siren sounded like judgment and condemnation to the robbers.

This is like the gospel; how we respond to it decides how it sounds to us. If someone comes to the light, exposing their deeds and throwing themselves upon Christ's mercy to be saved, the gospel is a message of help, hope, and salvation. But to the person who rejects Christ and wants to retain the illusion that they have lordship of their own life, the gospel does not sound like good news; it sounds like judgment and condemnation. And it should sound that way because it is. This is the full gospel of Jesus Christ. First Corinthians 1:18 says, "For the word of the cross is folly to those who are perishing, but to us who are being saved it is the power of God."

This is also what 2 Corinthians talks about; but instead of referring to the gospel of Christ as a sound, it refers to it as a smell:

> But thanks be to God, who in Christ always leads us in triumphal procession, and through us spreads the fragrance of the knowledge of him everywhere. For we are the aroma of Christ to God among those who are being saved and among those who are perishing, to one a fragrance from death to death, to the other a fragrance from life to life. Who is sufficient for these things? For we are not, like so many, peddlers of God's word, but as men of sincerity, as commissioned by God, in the sight of God we speak in Christ (2 Cor. 2:14-17).

For those being saved, it is an aroma from life to life. We are reborn and saved from being dead in sin and trespass in this life and will have eternal life. For those not being saved, the aroma of Christ is from death to death, which means that they remain dead in their sin and trespasses in this life and will be condemned to the second death for all eternity.

In 2 Corinthians 2:17, Paul says, "For we are not, like so many, peddlers of God's word, but as men of sincerity, as commissioned by God, in the sight of God we speak in Christ." The Greek word *kapēleuontes*, which we translate into "peddling" or "peddlers," literally means "to dilute." In Paul's day, people called "peddlers" would take a vile of medication; and to make a profit, they would dilute the medication so that they could turn one vile into three or four. The medicine faintly had the right taste and smell but was ineffective in helping the person taking it because it was diluted.

Paul is comparing people who dilute the gospel and message of Christ to these peddlers. What they say sounds faintly right; but because the message is diluted, it has no power to save. We must preach the love and judgment of God, the grace and the wrath of God, the kindness and severity of God. We must never dilute the message of Christ because when we do, we rob it of its power. We preach the truth of God in love; but we must always remember that the truth is love, and the truth is the only thing that can set us free (John 8:32).

THE GOSPEL IMPERATIVE

All born into sin are born under God's curse, so all stand condemned. Only because of Christ can we become the saved children of God. This is why we glorify and magnify Christ, our Savior King. It is only through Him, not through good works or because we have potential, talent, or anything else. It is because, as wretched, rebel sinners, we threw ourselves on the mercy of Christ. And He promises He will not reject those who come to Him with a contrite and humble heart.

We cannot love the darkness of this world and the things of this world if we are a child of God. John wrote about this to the first-century Christians: "Do not love the world or the things in the world. If anyone loves the world, the love of the Father is not in him. For all that is in the world—the desires of the flesh and the desires of the eyes and pride of life—is not from the Father but is from the world. And the world is passing away along with its desires, but whoever does the will of God abides forever" (1 John 2:15-17).

John says whoever does the will of God abides in Christ—in the family of God—not part-time, not for a little while, but forever! People who have embraced the true transforming love of God are changed by it. The person who has the love of God in their heart begins to hate the sin of this world and the sin still residing in their members. This is why we crucify our flesh and lay down our lives. This is the new man living inside of us. So, the only pertinent question regarding salvation is: Are you in Christ?

The gospel imperative is the most meaningful and important qualification in Christianity because it is the factor on which everything else hinges. God has promised, "There is therefore now no condemnation for those who are in Christ Jesus" (Rom. 8:1). Salvation is not about working to be better; it is committing our lives to Christ. It is being reborn in Christ, and God is changing us throughout our lives. He is changing, keeping, and sustaining us. Pastor John MacArthur comments regarding Paul's question in verse thirty-one: "The obvious implication is that if anyone were able to rob us of salvation they would have to be greater than God Himself, because He is both the giver and sustainer of salvation. To Christians, Paul is asking, in effect, 'Who would conceivably take away our no-condemnation status?' Is there anyone stronger than God, the Creator of everything and everyone who exists?"[26]

The only person to fear in this life is the Lord. Scripture tells us:

- "The Lord is my light and my salvation; whom shall I fear? The LORD is the stronghold of my life; of whom shall I be afraid?" (Psalm 27:1).
- "The fear of the LORD is the beginning of wisdom, and the knowledge of the Holy One is insight" (Prov. 9:10).

THE UNBREAKABLE PROMISE

He who did not spare his own Son but gave him up for us all, how will he not also with
him graciously give us all things? (v. 32).

Having established that God is all-powerful and sovereign and that no one but Him could accomplish and make our salvation possible, it stands to reason that no one but Him could take it away; and Paul answers here why God will not. The idea God would allow the death of His son to be for nothing is absurd. It is also impossible because the sacrifice of God in Christ is tied to the promise of God that He made to Abraham. God made a promise to His people in the Old and New Testaments. He revealed how He would fulfill it through His promise in the person of Christ. If God went back on His word, He would not be God. Paul is saying that God would not forsake us in salvation because it is tied to a promise that He made to us.

The promise of the word of the Lord is unbreakable, unchangeable; and it will not return void. Our faith is in the Word of the Lord. God spoke to Noah. He believed Him; and because of his faith in the word of God, he built an ark. God spoke to Abraham. He believed; and because of this, he dwelled in tents waiting on the Promised Land. The pattern of the Bible is that God speaks; and we believe it, and we believe it by faith.

Today, we are still taking God at His word from His Word. It was always God's plan to save us through the cross, to magnify His Son, and to save a people as an inheritance for Him. Knowing the grandeur and the ultimate eternal nature of this plan should help us find security in God's sovereignty and saving power. Our faith rests on God, who created the world and sent His Son. He knows the end from the beginning and is working all things together to accomplish this purpose. "And we know that for those who love God all things work together for good, for those who are called according to his purpose" (Rom. 8:28).

In a very well-known passage of Scripture, Isaiah prophesied about the will of God for Jesus, His Son:

Who has believed what he has heard from us? And to whom has the arm of the LORD been revealed? For he grew up before him like a young plant, and like a root out of dry ground; he had no form or majesty that we should look at him, and no beauty that we should desire him. He was despised and rejected by men, a man of sorrows and acquainted with grief; and as one from whom men hide their faces he was despised, and we esteemed him not.

Surely he has borne our griefs and carried our sorrows; yet we esteemed him stricken, smitten by God, and afflicted. But he was pierced for our transgressions; he was crushed for our iniquities; upon him was the chastisement that brought us peace, and with his wounds we are healed. All we like sheep have gone astray; we have turned—every one—to his own way; and the LORD has laid on him the iniquity of us all.

He was oppressed, and he was afflicted, yet he opened not his mouth; like a lamb that is led to the slaughter, and like a sheep that before its shearers is silent, so he opened not his mouth. By oppression and judgment he was taken away; and as for his generation, who considered that he was cut off out of the land of the living, stricken for the transgression of my people? And they made his grave with the wicked and with a rich man in his death, although he had done no violence, and there was no deceit in his mouth.

Yet it was the will of the LORD to crush him; he has put him to grief; when his soul makes an offering for guilt, he shall see his offspring; he shall prolong his days; the will of the LORD shall prosper in his hand. Out of the anguish of his soul he shall see and be satisfied; by his knowledge shall the righteous one, my servant, make many to be accounted righteous, and he shall bear their iniquities. Therefore I will divide him a portion with the many, and he shall divide the spoil with the strong, because he poured out his soul to death and was numbered with the transgressors; yet he bore the sin of many, and makes intercession for the transgressors (Isa. 53:1-12).

It was always the will of God for Christ to take on flesh for the glory of God—to save a people unto Himself. It was God's will to crush Him as He took our sins, pain, and shame upon Himself. God willingly took on our grief so that we could be free of those things to some degree now but completely in eternity as we dwell in fellowship with Him forever. Through the love of God in Christ, we are forgiven for our rebellion and sin and made children of God. To reject this is to deny the love of God.

Although we are saved by faith, it is ludicrous to think that we are the ones sustaining our salvation. It devalues the sacrifice of Christ and the power of God; and it reduces the Christian faith to every other works-based religion in the world, like Islam, Jehovah's Witness, Mormonism, and Roman Catholicism. It is the false idea of a new and wicked revelation that by working hard to change our own lives, God accepts us. I am not against self-help or self-improvement, but we cannot self-help our way to salvation. We are lost, desperate, and hopeless. However, if we truly see Who Christ is and what He has done for us, there is no possible way that it cannot transform our lives. God is the Author and Orchestrator of salvation. Christ secured our salvation on the cross, and we are justified before God based solely on that. And if we are justified through Christ, He is sustaining our salvation through the sanctification of His Spirit and the washing of His Word. We repent of our sins by faith and believe and confess that Jesus is Lord and by faith are saved. Salvation is a free gift of God that will transform our lives forever.

GOD'S BEAUTIFUL REVELATION

Who shall bring any charge against God's elect? It is God who justifies. Who is to condemn? Christ Jesus is the one who died—more than that, who was raised—who is at the right hand of God, who indeed is interceding for us (vv. 33-34).

Paul and the entire weight of the Old Testament have clearly shown that God is sovereign and He will judge the living and the dead. But Paul says that the only One with the ultimate power and authority to judge us, if we are in Christ, has pardoned and accepted us. If the Judge is on our side, who can condemn us? Who can rob us of our salvation or separate us from God? The only Person Who has that authority is Christ—the same Christ Who took on flesh to die for us, the same Christ Who rose from the dead and is now interceding for us at the right hand of the throne of God. Paul points out how preposterous it is to think that Christ went to those great lengths for us only to discard us at some point. Understand that if we have believed in Him by faith, Christ is fighting for us. He is interceding on our behalf; and if His Spirit lives in us, He is saving us until the very end.

Who can condemn us if we are living in Christ? This is a beautiful and powerful revelation. For if we are at peace with God, what does it matter what anyone else thinks? If we are at peace with God, what can anyone in this world do to us? It is only God who can judge the hearts of men. The only true Judge is Christ. So, other than Him, who can condemn us? The answer is no one, for only Christ can condemn us. And if we are in Christ, "there is therefore now no condemnation" because of Him who loved us (Rom. 8:1).

THE PERFECT SACRIFICE

Who shall separate us from the love of Christ? Shall tribulation, or distress, or persecution, or famine, or nakedness, or danger, or sword? As it is written, "For your sake we are being killed all the day long; we are regarded as sheep to be slaughtered" (vv. 35-36).

This is one of the major themes in the book of Hebrews. God, our Judge, guaranteed our salvation by becoming the perfect Sacrifice. Only Christ could have accomplished what He did on the cross. Christ, the Judge, came to earth and became the perfect Sacrifice for our sins—the Prophet, the Priest, and the King of our lives, a Priest Whose heart desires to bring us close to God so that we might fellowship with Him. The reason that Jesus was so harsh with the scribes, Pharisees, and priests of the first century was that they were the very people who were supposed to draw the people to God. Instead, they kept them from God, using their power and authority for condemnation rather than drawing people to repentance.

Paul is following up after everything he has written, asking, "Who shall separate us from the love of Christ?" The saving power of Christ and the redemptive love of Christ are universally joined. They are inseparable. If we have God's saving love, we have God's saving salvation. This is what he means by the love of Christ. But understand, we cannot call Christ our Savior if we do not call Him sovereign Lord. This is not a quippy statement. The truth is we cannot benefit from the saving power of Christ if He is not the Lord of our lives. The two things are not mutually exclusive. We cannot have one without the other. We cannot have the saving love of Christ living in us and not be transformed. We cannot be saved and not make it to the end. Those who are saved by the love of Christ are saved until the end. Scripture says, "Now before the Feast of the Passover, when Jesus knew that his hour had come to depart out of this world to the Father, having loved his own who were in the world, he loved them to the end" (John 13:1).

At first glance, it might seem that this means Jesus loved His disciples until He died. But Scripture does not refer to that end. We know this because later in John, Jesus is not only talking to His disciples but also to all disciples who would believe in Him—those who had not seen Him yet still believed. John explains this in further detail:

> Beloved, let us love one another, for love is from God, and whoever loves has been born of God and knows God. Anyone who does not love does not know God, because God is love. In this the love of God was made manifest among us, that God sent his only Son into the world, so that we might live through

him. In this is love, not that we have loved God but that he loved us and sent his Son to be the propitiation for our sins. Beloved, if God so loved us, we also ought to love one another. No one has ever seen God; if we love one another, God abides in us and his love is perfected in us.

By this we know that we abide in him and he in us, because he has given us of his Spirit. And we have seen and testify that the Father has sent his Son to be the Savior of the world. Whoever confesses that Jesus is the Son of God, God abides in him, and he in God. So we have come to know and to believe the love that God has for us. God is love, and whoever abides in love abides in God, and God abides in him. By this is love perfected with us, so that we may have confidence for the day of judgment, because as he is so also are we in this world. There is no fear in love, but perfect love casts out fear. For fear has to do with punishment, and whoever fears has not been perfected in love. We love because he first loved us. If anyone says, "I love God," and hates his brother, he is a liar; for he who does not love his brother whom he has seen cannot love God whom he has not seen. And this commandment we have from him: whoever loves God must also love his brother (1 John 4: 7-21).

Those who have the saving love of God have confidence that they will not be judged in the end because there is no looming condemnation or fear of judgment anymore. Many false converts or misguided preachers try to pick and choose the word "love" and apply it to a worldly or fleshly view of love. This is about a transformative, saving love. It cannot be separated from the gospel because God's "perfect love casts out fear." We are being saved unto God. It casts out fear of judgment and fear of this world. In this context, John is saying that those saved by the love of God are not afraid of what is coming at the end of their lives.

MORE THAN CONQUERORS

Who shall separate us from the love of Christ? Shall tribulation, or distress,
or persecution, or famine, or nakedness, or danger, or sword? (v. 35)

Now Paul gives a practical application to what the Christians faced in his day. He writes about the all-encompassing saving love of God; but then he personalizes it by mentioning tribulation, distress, and persecution. Yet the love of God transcends this because the world is not our home. This applies to all Christians at all times throughout history. Do we let distress, tribulation, or persecution separate us from the saving love of God? How about when people curse or mistreat us? Jesus addressed this by saying, "'Blessed are you when others revile you and persecute you and utter all kinds of evil against you falsely on my account. Rejoice and be glad, for your reward is great in heaven, for so they persecuted the prophets who were before you'" (Matt. 5:11-12).

We are knit into the same legacy and saving power that Isaiah prophesied about and that Abraham was grafted into. We are grafted into that same living Vine. Understand that persecution is evidence that we belong to God. Distress, famine, nakedness, danger, the sword—everything up to and even in death—nothing can separate us from the all-powerful, never-failing love of God. When Paul says, "Love never ends" (1 Cor. 13:8), he talks about this kind of love—a love that never fails to save those who have called upon the name of the Lord. Paul's list is not exhaustive but covers most things, from life to death. It cuts to the heart of the truth that Christ is worth laying our lives down for, an incomparable Treasure.

To have the love of Christ living in us is to have the eternal, abundant life of Christ dwelling in us. These two things are inseparable. The love of God and the life of Christ are joined together in His saints forever. The glory of the gospel is not merely about being saved from damnation; it is that we are eternally joined to Christ. This is the problem with much modern-day preaching that makes Christ a lottery ticket to get the things we want in life, like money, security, or success. This is utter garbage. Christ is King! Christ is the Treasure of the gospel! When we present the gospel to people, we are to present to them Christ and Him crucified; we know nothing among them except Christ alone. In verse thirty-six, Paul quotes from Psalm 44, a song of lament:

> All this has come upon us, though we have not forgotten you, and we have not been false to your covenant. Our heart has not turned back, nor have our steps departed from your way; yet you have broken us in the place of jackals and covered us with the shadow of death. If we had forgotten the name of our God or spread out our hands to a foreign god, would not God discover this? For he knows the secrets of the heart. Yet for your sake we are killed all the day long; we are regarded as sheep to be slaughtered.

> Awake! Why are you sleeping, O Lord? Rouse yourself! Do not reject us forever! Why do you hide your face? Why do you forget our affliction and oppression? For our soul is bowed down to the dust; our belly clings to the ground. Rise up; come to our help! Redeem us for the sake of your steadfast love! (Psalm 44:17-26).

This psalm is about people who have suffered but have not denied God. They are lamenting, "God, for Your sake, we are being killed. For Your sake, we are being mistreated. It is not for our sake but for the sake of Your holy name." The author of this psalm is asking God to redeem them not because of anything they have done but by appealing to His steadfast love. He is saying, "God, rise up and help us. We are hopeless without You." Christ is the Answer to that prayer. Christ came for the sake of His name and because of His steadfast love. And He did not subject us to the shame and misery of our sin; instead, He took the shame, punishment, and pain we deserved. He took it upon Himself. "Christ redeemed us from the curse of the law by becoming a curse for us" (Gal. 3:13).

The world looks at the true believer's salvation the same way they look at the Savior, the same way the unrepentant thief on the cross looked at Him, saying, "'Are you not the Christ? Save yourself and us!'" (Luke 23:39). But Jesus came to die and to be a Sacrifice on our behalf. And those of us who are saved by the love of God are now living to show that love to a lost and dying world. Now, if Christ is our God, why does it seem like He has forsaken us at times? Paul answers, reminding us that nakedness, danger, sword, persecution, lack, ridicule, being marginalized by society, being mistreated, or even being killed are not evidence that we are not in God. It very well might be the evidence that we are in Him because we are being treated like Him, as written in Isaiah 53.

MORE THAN CONQUERORS

No, in all these things we are more than conquerors through him who loved us (v. 37).

The love of God in the gospel is unfailing, unending, incomparable, transformative, and supernatural. Paul is reassuring those dealing with all sorts of trials and persecution that they are more than conquerors because of God's unfailing love. And nothing will separate us from the love of God that we have in Christ Jesus our Lord if He truly is the Lord of our life. Paul is saying that if Christ is the Lord of our life, we never have to doubt that He is our Savior.

In all the trials Paul mentions in verses thirty-five and thirty-six, he says we are more than conquers. Oh, how we wish it said, "No, and *from* all of these things, we are more than conquerors through Him who loved us." But it doesn't; it says, "No, in *all* these things, we are more than conquerors through Him who loved us." In the trial, in the suffering, in this momentary affliction, we are more than conquers because none of these things will ever separate us from the love of God and our promised eternity with Christ Jesus our Lord. This is why Paul says in Romans 8:18, "For I consider that the sufferings of this present time are not worth comparing with the glory that is to be revealed to us." "In all of these things, we are more than conquerors," and anything we suffer in this life is light and momentary when compared to four gospel truths that are revealed to us in Romans 8:

1. We have been freed from eternal condemnation (Rom. 8:1-2).
2. We are God's children forever through adoption (Rom. 8:14-17).
3. Our suffering is working in us as an everlasting glory (Rom. 8:28-29).
4. Nothing can "separate us from the love of God" (Rom. 8:31-39).

Not only can we endure the trials, afflictions, and suffering of this life because of what God has promised in the future; but we must also understand that it is not at all pointless or meaningless because it is producing something in us, something necessary, something good—namely, the very image of Christ. Paul tells us in 2 Corinthians 4:16-18, "So we do not lose heart. Though our outer self is wasting away, our inner self is being renewed day by day. For this light momentary affliction is preparing for us an eternal weight of glory beyond all comparison, as we look not to the things that are seen but to the things that are unseen. For the things that are seen are transient, but the things that are unseen are eternal."

AN INSEPARABLE LOVE

For I am sure that neither death nor life, nor angels nor rulers, nor things present nor things to come, nor powers, nor height nor depth, nor anything else in all creation, will be able to separate us from the love of God in Christ Jesus our Lord (vv. 38-39).

Paul sums up the chapter with a final encompassing affirmation. The first phrase "I am sure" is translated in the New American Standard Bible as "I am convinced" (v. 38). Faith is being convinced beyond anything else that we stand justified before God on the basis of our faith in Christ alone. God will keep His promises He has made to us in His Word—that absolutely nothing "will be able to separate us from the love of God in Christ Jesus our Lord." This is the doctrine of eternal security; and if one does not believe in it, then explain Paul's words in Romans 8. What will "separate us from the love of God"? Is it danger, sword, or persecution? Is it you? No, God is sovereign, and Christ is King; and those who are in Christ will be saved to the end. Faith is being convinced of that truth in a way that is verified by our lives.

Paul was not convinced because he considered himself a good person or because he did great things for the kingdom of God. How does Paul introduce himself in the epistles? He calls himself an apostle, a messenger; but often, he calls himself a slave or servant of Christ. He wants people to know that he is a slave and a son of Christ because that is *all* that matters. Paul is less concerned about telling people who he is and more concerned with sharing with them *Whose* he is. Are we convinced to the point that our faith is what matters most in our lives? Do we have faith in God that, because of Christ, absolutely nothing can separate us from a love that saves us into the eternal family of God?

The portrait of every true Christian life is a love that is so life-changing and transformative that all other loves pale by comparison to it: your spouse, your children, your hopes, your dreams, your career, even your own life. He is worthy of all honor and praise. We did not love Christ first—He first loved us to the point of death! "While we were still sinners, Christ died for us" (Rom. 5:8). Our saving faith is in His atoning work on the cross. Because we believe this in our hearts, we declare Him as Lord with our mouths, repenting from our sins and following Him as disciples and slaves who positionally have become sons, daughters, and co-heirs with Him in His inheritance. The love of God in salvation is undeniable, unbreakable, and eternal. It never fails, and it will never pass away. If we come to Christ humbly in repentance, He will not reject us.

Those who truly perceive His love, who have found forgiveness and salvation in His love, who are being sanctified and transformed through

His love, and whose confidence and security rest alone in His love will live their lives unashamed of the gospel because they know that it alone brings salvation for all who believe; first for the Jew, but by His grace and thankfully for me, also the Gentile. Soli Deo Gloria!

ABOUT THE AUTHOR

D R. JOSHUA WEST IS A pastor, evangelist, and author. He currently serves as the lead pastor and teaching elder of Truth Bible Church in Hollywood, Maryland. He also speaks at conferences, crusades, and churches all over the world. The goal and focus of his ministry is biblical preaching and teaching with a high view of God and the Scripture that is centered around the Gospel of Jesus Christ. He partners in life and ministry with his wife and best friend, Kiara. They live in Lexington Park, Maryland, with their son, Jameson.

CONNECT WITH JOSHUA WEST:

www.joshuawest.net

www.facebook.com/pastorjoshuawest

ENDNOTES

CHAPTER 2

1 John MacArthur, *Romans 1-16 MacArthur New Testament Commentary Two Volume Set* (Chicago: Moody Publishers, 1994).

2 David Martyn Lloyd-Jones, *Romans: An Exposition of Chapter I: the Gospel of God* (Edinburgh: Banner of Truth Trust, 1985).

3 John Piper, "How the Supremacy of Christ Creates Radical Christian Sacrifice," YouTube Video, April 17, 2008, 1:04:55, https://www.desiringgod.org/messages/how-the-supremacy-of-christ-creates-radical-christian-sacrifice.

4 Lloyd-Jones, ibid.

5 John MacArthur, "When God Abandons a Nation," Grace to You, August 20, 2006, https://www.gty.org/library/sermons-library/80-314/when-god-abandons-a-nation.

CHAPTER 4

6 "Romans 2 Bible Commentary," Christianity.com, accessed August 22, 2025, https://www.christianity.com/bible/commentary/matthew-henry-complete/romans/2.

7 R.C. Sproul, "God's Judgment Defended," November 27, 2005, https://learn.ligonier.org/sermons/gods-judgment-defended.

8 MacArthur, ibid, 81.

9 C. H. Spurgeon, *Spurgeon's Sermons: Volume 2* (Peabody: Hendrickson Publishers, 2011), 124.

10 Spurgeon, Spurgeon's *Sermons: Volume 4* (Peabody: Hendrickson Publishers, 2011), 321.

CHAPTER 5

11 Spurgeon, *All of Grace* (Chicago: Moody Publishers, 2010), 73.

CHAPTER 7

12 A. W. Tozer, *The Best of A. W. Tozer Book Two*, compiled by Warren Wiersbe, (Chicago: Moody Publishers, 2007).

13 MacArthur, ibid, 255.

CHAPTER 8

14 MacArthur, ibid, 239.

CHAPTER 11

15 Jason Meyer, *Don't Lose Heart: Gospel Hope for the Discouraged Soul* (Grand Rapids: Baker Publishing Group, 2019).

CHAPTER 12

16 Thomas Brooks, *Complete Works of Thomas Brooks: Vol. III*, compiled by Alexander B. Grosart (Norderstedt: Hansebooks GmbH, 2021), 211.

CHAPTER 13

17 MacArthur, *Romans 1-8 MacArthur New Testament Commentary* (Chicago: Moody Publishers, 1991), 347.

18 Warren Wiersbe, *Wiersbe Bible Commentary, Vol. 5* (Colorado Springs: David C. Cook, 2007), 293.

19 Lloyd-Jones, *Romans: An Exposition of Chapter I: the Gospel of God* (Edinburgh: Banner of Truth Trust, 1985).

CHAPTER 15

20 Charles Hodge, *Commentary on the Epistle to the Romans* (Grand Rapids: William B. Eerdmans Publishing Company, 1993), 226.

21 Spurgeon, *The Complete Works of C. H. Spurgeon, Volume 32: Sermons 1877-1937* (Salisbury: Delmarva Publications, Inc., 2015).

CHAPTER 18

22 Richard Wurmbrand, *Tortured for Christ* (Living Sacrifice Book Company, 1998).

23 Unknown, "He Paid a Debt He Did Not Know," Hymnary.org https://hymnary.org/hymn/SNP21979/21, 1979.

24 John Owen, *Mortification of Sin* (Reformed Church Publications, 2015), 17.

CHAPTER 20

25 Spurgeon, *The Complete Works of C. H. Spurgeon, Volume 35: Sermons 2062-2120* (Salisbury: Delmarva Publications, Inc., 2015), 873.

26 MacArthur, *Romans 1-8 MacArthur New Testament Commentary* (Chicago: Moody Publishers, 1991), 502).

BIBLIOGRAPHY

Brooks, Thomas. *Complete Works of Thomas Brooks: Vol. III*. Compiled by Alexander B. Grosart. Norderstedt: Hansebooks GmbH, 2021.

Hodge, Charles. *Commentary on the Epistle to the Romans*. Grand Rapids: William B. Eerdmans Publishing Company, 1993. https://www.desiringgod.org/messages/how-the-supremacy-of-christ-creates-radical-christian-sacrifice.

Lloyd-Jones, David Martin. *Romans: An Exposition of Chapter I: the Gospel of God*. Edinburgh: Banner of Truth Trust, 1985.

Lloyd-Jones, David Martin. *Romans: An Exposition of Chapter I: the Gospel of God*. Edinburgh: Banner of Truth Trust, 1985.

MacArthur, John. "When God Abandons a Nation." Grace to You. August 20, 2006. https://www.gty.org/library/sermons-library/80-314/when-god-abandons-a-nation.

MacArthur, John. *Romans 1-16 MacArthur New Testament Commentary Two Volume Set*. Chicago: Moody Publishers, 1994.

MacArthur, John. *Romans 1-8 MacArthur New Testament Commentary*. Chicago: Moody Publishers, 1991.

Meyer, Jason. *Don't Lose Heart: Gospel Hope for the Discouraged Soul*. Grand Rapids: Baker Publishing Group, 2019.

Owen, John. *Mortification of Sin*. Reformed Church Publications, 2015.

Piper, John. "How the Supremacy of Christ Creates Radical Christian Sacrifice." YouTube Video. April 17, 2008, 1:04:55.

"Romans 2 Bible Commentary." Christianity.com. Accessed August 22, 2025. https://www.christianity.com/bible/commentary/matthew-henry-complete/romans/2.

Sproul, R.C. "God's Judgment Defended." November 27, 2005. https://learn.ligonier.org/sermons/gods-judgment-defended.

Spurgeon, C. H. *All of Grace*. Chicago: Moody Publishers, 2010.

Spurgeon, C. H. *Spurgeon's Sermons: Volume 2*. Peabody: Hendrickson Publishers, 2011.

Spurgeon, C. H. *Spurgeon's Sermons: Volume 4*. Peabody: Hendrickson Publishers, 2011.

Spurgeon, C. H. *The Complete Works of C. H. Spurgeon, Volume 32: Sermons 1877-1937*. Salisbury: Delmarva Publications, Inc., 2015.

Spurgeon, C. H. *The Complete Works of C. H. Spurgeon, Volume 35: Sermons 2062-2120*. Salisbury: Delmarva Publications, Inc., 2015.

Tozer, A. W. *The Best of A. W. Tozer Book Two*. Compiled by Warren Wiersbe. Chicago: Moody Publishers, 2007.

Unknown, "He Paid a Debt He Did Not Know." Hymnary.org. https://hymnary.org/hymn/SNP21979/21, 1979.

Wiersbe, Warren. *Wiersbe Bible Commentary, Vol. 5*. Colorado Springs: David C. Cook, 2007.

Wurmbrand, Richard. *Tortured for Christ*. Living Sacrifice Book Company, 1998.

This book is published in association with World Challenge.

Transforming lives through the message and mission of Jesus Christ.

For more information about
WORLD CHALLENGE
and
Unashamed of the Gospel
please visit:

www.worldchallenge.org

World
Challenge
PUBLISHING

Ambassador International's mission is to magnify the Lord Jesus Christ and promote His Gospel through the written word.

We believe through the publication of Christian literature, Jesus Christ and His Word will be exalted, believers will be strengthened in their walk with Him, and the lost will be directed to Jesus Christ as the only way of salvation.

For more information about
AMBASSADOR INTERNATIONAL
please visit:

www.ambassador-international.com
@AmbassadorIntl
www.facebook.com/AmbassadorIntl

AMBASSADOR INTERNATIONAL
GREENVILLE, SOUTH CAROLINA & BELFAST, NORTHERN IRELAND

www.ambassador-international.com
Magnifying Jesus while promoting His gospel through the written word.

Thank you for reading this book!

You make it possible for us to fulfill our mission, and we are grateful for your partnership.

To help further our mission, please consider leaving us a review on your social media, favorite retailer's website, Goodreads or Bookbub, or our website, and check out some of our other books!

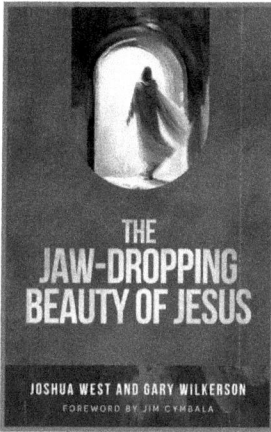

Most of us know Who Jesus is and would admit that He was a good and kind Teacher while here on earth. But He is so much more. Through an in-depth study into the book of Hebrews, Joshua West and Gary Wilkerson take apart each verse, drawing the reader to a closer look at the Man Who lived here on earth for a short time and then became our Sacrifice to save us from our sins and live with us eternally in Heaven with Him. If you are searching for something more from God, dive into this study and drink in the jaw-dropping beauty of our Jesus.

Scripture gives us a guide for navigating our greatest trials. In the first volume of this devotional series, Gary Wilkerson, pastor and president of World Challenge, examines the first twelve psalms and how each is a unique invitation to authentic prayer. Our heavenly Father desires a deep, genuine relationship with each one of us, but that can happen only if we are completely transparent with God about our doubts, struggles, and sorrows.

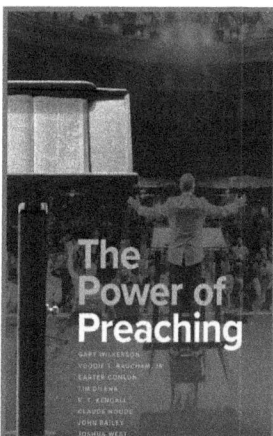

In our churches today, we have allowed ourselves to hold to a low view of God instead of seeing Him as Who He really is. And in today's world of seeking the most likes and followers, many Christian pastors and leaders are finding themselves preaching what people want to hear instead of what God wants to say. In *The Power of Preaching*, eight experienced men of God, who have stayed true to the preaching of God's Word, offer guidance on how to avoid appealing to the masses and instead encourage the reader to let God's Word speak for itself.

www.ingramcontent.com/pod-product-compliance
Lightning Source LLC
Chambersburg PA
CBHW070018100426
42740CB00013B/2540

9 7 8 1 6 4 9 6 0 7 3 5 5